Ethical Issues in College Writing

STUDIES IN COMPOSITION AND RHETORIC

Vol. 1

PETER LANG
New York • Washington, D.C./Baltimore • Boston • Bern
Frankfurt am Main • Berlin • Brussels • Vienna • Canterbury

Ethical Issues IN College Writing

EDITED BY
Fredric G. Gale, Phillip Sipiora,
and James L. Kinneavy

PETER LANG
New York • Washington, D.C./Baltimore • Boston • Bern
Frankfurt am Main • Berlin • Brussels • Vienna • Canterbury

LIBRARY OF CONGRESS CATALOGING-IN-PUBLICATION DATA

Ethical issues in college writing /
edited by Fredric G. Gale, Phillip Sipiora, and James L. Kinneavy.
p. cm. — (Studies in composition and rhetoric; vol. 1)
Includes bibliographical references and index.
1. English language—Rhetoric—Study and teaching—Theory, etc.
2. Report writing—Study and teaching (Higher)—Theory, etc. 3. Rhetoric—Moral and ethical aspects—Study and teaching. 4. College teaching—
Moral and ethical aspects. I. Gale, Fredric G. II. Sipiora, Phillip.
III. Kinneavy, James L. IV. Series.
PE1404.E84   808'.042'0711—DC21   97-17932
ISBN 0-8204-3072-2
ISSN 1080-5397

DIE DEUTSCHE BIBLIOTHEK-CIP-EINHEITSAUFNAHME

Ethical issues in college writing / ed. by Fredric G. Gale, Phillip Sipiora,
and James L. Kinneavy. –New York; Washington, D.C./Baltimore; Boston; Bern;
Frankfurt am Main; Berlin; Brussels; Vienna; Canterbury: Lang.
(Studies in composition and rhetoric; Vol. 1)
ISBN 0-8204-3072-2

Cover design by Lisa Dillon

© 1999 Peter Lang Publishing, Inc., New York

All rights reserved.
Reprint or reproduction, even partially, in all forms such as microfilm,
xerography, microfiche, microcard, and offset strictly prohibited.

Table of Contents

Acknowledgment   vii

Memorial Preface   viii

Foreword	The Ethics of Ethics *David Bleich*	ix
Chapter 1	Ethics and Rhetoric: Forging a Moral Language for the English Classroom *James L. Kinneavy*	1
Chapter 2	Legal Rights and Responsibilities in the Writing Classroom *Fredric G. Gale*	21
Chapter 3	Ethics and Ideology in the English Classroom *Phillip Sipiora*	39
Chapter 4	Doing English *W. Ross Winterowd*	63
Chapter 5	Ethics, *Ethos*, Habitation *James Comas*	75
Chapter 6	Encountering the Other: Postcolonial Theory and Composition Scholarship *Gary A. Olson*	91
Chapter 7	*Ethos* and Ethics: Ancient Concepts and Contemporary Writing *Rosalind J. Gabin*	107

Chapter 8	Ethics, Rhetorical Action, and a Neoliberal Arts *Kathleen Ethel Welch*	137
Chapter 9	The Hermeneutics of Suspicion and Other Doubting Games: Reclaiming Belief in the Writing of Reading and the Reading of Writing *C. Jan Swearingen*	155
Chapter 10	*Ethos*, Ethical Argument, and *Ad Hominem* in Contemporary Theory *James S. Baumlin* *George H. Jensen* *Lance Massey*	183
Chapter 11	A Rhizomatic Ethics of Interpretation *David L. Erben and Kelli Erben*	221
Notes on Contributors		237
Index		241

Acknowledgement

We would like to thank Michael G. Sullivan and Maureen D. Ivusic of the University of South Florida for their efforts and editorial skills in bringing this manuscript from the dark of night to the light of day. They have been consummate professionals in painstakingly preparing a manuscript that came to them in many forms. Any remaining errors are those of the editors.

Frederic G. Gale
Phillip Sipiora
James L. Kinneavy

In Memoriam
James L. Kinneavy

James L. Kinneavy was the author of *A Study of Three Contemporary Theories of Lyric Poetry* (1956), *A Theory of Discourse* (1971), *Greek Rhetorical Origins of Christian Faith: An Inquiry* (1987), and six other books in addition to over fifty articles and chapters in books dealing with literary criticism, rhetorical history and criticism, and the teaching of composition.

For more than fifty years, Professor Kinneavy played a major role in the resurgence of rhetoric and the development of composition theory, not only as a consequence of his voluminous and penetrating writing, but also through his teaching, directing of dissertations, organizing professional workshops, and lecturing across the country for more than half a century. It is no exaggeration to say that he is one of the seminal influences in late twentieth-century rhetoric and composition. In speaking of influential teachers, Georges Gusdorf once said, "The great educator is he who spreads around himself the meaning of the honor of language as a concern for integrity in the relations with others and oneself." This description epitomizes the life of James L. Kinneavy.

Professor Kinneavy's essay in this volume, "Ethics and Rhetoric: Forging a Moral Language for the English Classroom," probes the relationship of ethics to the English classroom. This essay is a crystallization of his work-in-progress on the formation of a common moral code that might be accepted by both religious and non-religious individuals and could be taught in the public school system. Such a moral code, according to Kinneavy, must necessarily be undogmatic, an ethical system untethered by inherited sectarian dogma. Kinneavy was working on this book, *A Moral Code for Use in Public Schools and Colleges*, until his untimely death at the age of 79 on August 10, 1999, following a brief illness. As he approached the end of his life, James L. Kinneavy continued to lecture, write, and remain actively involved in the profession he so loved. Professor Kinneavy's life work was the inspiration for this volume.

Phillip Sipiora
Fredric G. Gale

Foreword

The Ethics of Ethics

David Bleich

This book is about how faculty members in English and in writing, after a long drink of identity politics and social construction, are broaching a subject that reconsiders individual subjectivity in the context of the social and political awareness painfully established in our curricula. Sometimes the essays will imply that ethics is a new accent given as a substitute for the existing ones; but that is not the case. The subject of ethics is broached in this volume as an addition-for-today to the discussions about writing that have gone on for generations. I offer this caution only because of my fear of academic habits: when a new accent appears, too many people treat it as "the answer."

I direct readers immediately to James Comas's citation of the academic "stock market" (first formulated by Northrop Frye, with different elements):

> ... the key terms of composition studies boom and crash in an imaginary stock exchange; 'social constructionism,' for example, has reached its peak and has begun to taper off; 'hypertext' and 'webbed' classrooms may be in for a slight flutter; but the 'political' stocks are still bearish. . . . .while 'ethics' appears to be a good short-term investment it is not yet clear whether its performance is likely to continue into the long-term. Perhaps . . . ethics will [experience an] . . . unprecedented explosion in growth; or perhaps . . . we are witnessing . . . only an 'irrational exuberance.' (76–77)

Neither Frye nor we think our interests vary with the same unpredictable movements as the stock market; nor do most of us think the term "capital" is more than a cute metaphor, which Comas also discusses in regard to cultural, political, and professional value. Comas's use of this figure in his approach to the work of Kenneth Burke sounds the change from 1957 to 1997. The West's victory in the cold war has given market and capital vocabulary (thinking, discourse, or rhetoric, for those who prefer other terms) a different authority. There is less irony in this metaphor now: it seems more literally true. Academic life is an arbitrary market; stocks of ideas go up and down as people "buy into" them; the only cause is getting "rich" for some and a job for others, in both cases winning the competition for being "in" or "*au courant.*" To have values—to hold principles and convictions—is coming to seem a luxury just as having capital is a luxury. These conditions were less in evidence when Frye wrote. Comas turns to Burke: to one who, when New Critics wrote with solemn certainty, wrote with celebration and interest, and not in pursuit of utter certainty.

Burke wrote about motives, performance, and took some pleasure in confounding taken-for-granted pairs of concepts like act and scene. His writings could not add up to a dogma; as a result, he now has students rather than disciples.[1] Comas looks to Burke to learn how to cope with uncertainty, and perhaps to do this coping without leaning on the national obsessions with capital, without following fads, without assuming the overwhelming mercantile mentality that is reaching outlandish proportions even in academic life.

Comas may also be saying that we finally are going to stop thinking of ourselves as either writing teachers or English teachers alone. We ought finally to resist disciplinary boundaries and, regardless, light out for territory that is already occupied. Comas and the other contributors to this volume say that the interest in ethics is a call for self-evaluation and for engaging the subject in ways that honor the tradition of writing represented by Burke whose metaphorical inventiveness is part of the substance of his communication with us, as Comas cites: have we become accustomed to dwelling with what Burke will call "the Scramble, the Wrangle of the Market Place, the flurries and flare-ups of the Human Barnyard, the Give and Take, the wavering like of pressure and counterpressure, the Logomachy, the onus of ownership, the Wars of Nerves, the War"?

Comas's turn to Burke, not an argument in a traditional sense, is a gesture of appeal to authorize the feeling that Burke expressed or shared in his uses of language, his rhetorics of commitment and purpose. Perhaps Comas rejects the idea that expressions of feeling and commitment are "investments," a term most academics now use to describe what ought to be called principle, devotion, loyalty, or belief.

Jan Swearingen makes belief her point of entry into this reconsideration[2] of how to introduce ethics into the subject of writing, language use, and rhetoric. Her discussion of belief and leaps of faith tries to teach us that our own vocabularies are helping to do us in. From one standpoint, it may appear as if she is advocating religious values. If you are religious, her perspective would welcome you; but that is not, I think, the main movement of her essay, which is, rather, this:

> There are Western academic paradigms such as dialogues and hermeneutics that have emphasized interactional and collective models of mind, discourse, self, and meaning. These, however, have often held a minority position in relation to the practices of skepticism, and programmatic doubt, and hyperindividualism that since Descartes have dominated Western academia and its values. (157)

In this grouping, I take special note of Swearingen's relating of doubt to individualism. To put the matter in more experiential terms, the habits of doubt are to her part of the social style of combat and argumentation. If you doubt others, you tend to argue with others; if you have an open mind, with the attempt to believe, you will exchange thoughts with others. The approach of "belief" as Swearingen is advocating it, is an interpersonal posture not characteristic of the academy. If the teaching of writing and language use is the issue, and if scholars of this subject show the habits of individualism *themselves,* how will it be possible to teach the subject of writing any differently? If these scholars *only say* that the subject is dialogue, interaction, and cooperative enterprise, but don't enact these values, how can they be taught? Swearingen explicitly relates "belief" to "conviction and reasoned action" (159). This is an appeal for the change of our states of mind rather than for a kind of belief that merely accepts blind faith or superstitious belief. One practical result of this state of mind is the authorization of emotional contents and genres, a project that, undoubtedly, Burke's work was approaching but did not reach.

At this juncture Swearingen discusses something perhaps only one or two other contributors mention—the question of "women's ways of knowing" (160–61). Swearingen's emphasis on belief alludes to the feminist project, whose set of values other contributors approach through abstraction and, in some cases, euphemism. She presents a commentary (a reading?) on Christa Wolf's novel *Cassandra* in which the heroine's perspective is an alternative to the "Hellenic understandings of language and religion" (162). Swearingen also urges us toward viewing the feminist perspective as bringing values to academic life that do not dissociate thought from experience, spirit from body. By removing the censorship of this strand of thought in classical Greek civilization, Swearingen promotes an inclusivist attitude that changes the mix of what we take the "classical" to be. On this basis, she aims to "surmount the hermeneutics of suspicion, and supplement its rigorous questions with prudent interpretive conjectures that begin to ring true."

It is perhaps of interest to consider why Swearingen relates "belief" to the matter of ethics. Her sources suggest that this is not a plea for tolerance, but a plea for pragmatism. The classical population of figures is varied, but has been read too selectively and narrowly. The academic style is too nervous and fearful, driven by self-interest and suspicion of others rather than by eagerness to discover and social purpose. Swearingen's essay urges us to find the grounds to celebrate more, to believe not in new dogmas but in the connectedness of "other" knowledge to our own needs.

That Swearingen's perspective is needed is shown in Fredric Gale's essay, which provides a clear example that "suspicion" at this point in history is more than just an academic posture, that it has begun to be part of the classroom feeling. Gale engages the question of how writing pedagogy has moved steadily toward the solicitation of candid autoethnography while society has urged values of self-protection and keeping one's own counsel—literally: depending more on one's lawyer. As a result, writing teachers have "exposed" themselves to lawsuits in a variety of ways described by Gale. One should bear in mind the economic factor mentioned by Comas in this connection. Because college has begun to cost so much, problems raised by students have a "cost factor" in that the teachers' responsibilities have been linked by the public to the students' satisfaction: the "product" delivered by schools through teachers must be good or the "providers" may be liable.

Gale warns us that "the law . . . has an independent design that does not necessarily track the majority or consensus view of what is just or even what is moral" (21). This means, practically, that the law can be appropriated to serve the interests of those in power, who are now sophistic in the sense of believing that "the truth of a case could never be known." As a result, the it's-my-word-against-yours presumption acquires more authority. In the classroom this is especially dangerous, since slanders and lies can finally prevail in actions against teachers, who do not have something like teacher-student confidentiality to protect them.[3] Contrary to the view of some that "power-relations" in the classroom favor the teacher, Gale's discussion shows that the reverse is true more and more. Students become pawns of university administrators and Boards of Trustees who are more and more anxious about tuition dollars and who may be willing to sacrifice employees (faculty members) if necessary to this cause.

As a result, Gale shows, any teacher's willingness to help students who seem to be in trouble ought to be tempered with the reminder that sometimes, the helper "exposes" him- or herself to liability if the help doesn't work out just right—something that happens more often than not when teachers consider how and why students are motivated. Writing teachers "hear" the cries for help more than other teachers. The subject matter itself admits such writing into the classroom, but some elements in society warn us that this is prying or otherwise inappropriate for "learning" how to write. I can't help wondering about who should be hearing Jan Swearingen's advocacy. Probably, we teachers are willing to take it seriously, but will administrators and Boards of Trustees hear her justification for this more accommodating posture as scholars and teachers?

Similarly, will our society hear a justification for collaboration through ethos given by Rosalind Gabin's essay? Her basis for conceiving ethics is the authority (*ethos*) developed in classrooms when collaborative and collective activities are what people do in class:

> A collaborative writing classroom can foster an education in human relations as well as in composition when it stresses not only the writing process but also the social process in which students engage as they participate in the maturation of each other's ideas and language. (124–25)

Gabin's discussion suggests that working within a collaborative pedagogical paradigm necessarily includes attention to individual ethics alongside attention to the implication of individuals in the collective needs of others. But this attitude has been increasingly contested by establishmentarian forces, such as the Trustees of the University of Texas in their action against the writing course approved by its English department, and which operates under the foregoing assumptions.

Gabin wants students to be "mindful of *ethos* as a component of their language exchanges" (129). Her discussion suggests that what we are now saying is "ethical" is rooted in the idea of deriving individual authority from the togetherness of people with whom we are working. Because writing involves the exchange of language, her vision is that ethics in the traditional sense—consideration of others—is also the basis of *ethos*, of individual authority, of ethics in the revised sense proposed by contributors to this volume: authority in writing and the use of language for individuals is developed by a collective action of mutual consideration of the membership of individuals in different groups as well as in the classroom group.

James Kinneavy's essay and Kathleen Ethel Welch's endorsement of its perspective remind us of certain traditional groups represented by the values of respect for life, family, property, and truth. Kinneavy characterizes these values as "the four cornerstones of most ethical systems" (8). A distinctive feature of Kinneavy's discussion is that he identifies these values as being part of the "Judeo-Christian" tradition. While I, for one, may want to contest this category itself, the fact that Kinneavy is willing to identify his sense of *our own* values is an essential step in overtaking the collectivist approach to ethics suggested by Gabin and other contributors. The issue in this volume is not whether there are such "cornerstones," but how, once the discussion has been opened and admitted to our classrooms, once ethical feelings become part of the pedagogical picture, we will be able to find what is "universal," and what, even, the idea of universality is.

Welch suggests that people in all disciplines need vigorous training in rhetoric as persuasion and communication. This view suggests a path toward universal values, a basis, a foundation for the combination of ethics and rhetoric. Like Kinneavy, her taste in approaching the living classroom contexts is to look for the manifestations of the universal, which she represents as the need for "persuasion and communication." Welch places this need opposite to "expository writing," which, while a discredited foundation for the teaching of writing among some, is "still the monarch of academic literacy." Welch proposes to substitute "persuasion and communication" for expository writing as a foundational value for the teaching of writing and as a basis for relating rhetoric to ethics.

A similarly universalist value is given by Gary Olson: ethics is the "encounter with the Other." Spelled with a capital "o," "Other" has become a term used by dominant elements in society to describe subordinate groups. The genre *Other* derives from classical psychoanalysis's attention to "self-object" differentiation in infants, and then from "object relations" psychology that moved beyond an exclusive attention to the self. Gradually, the harsher term "object" as referring to people became "other." The Other may be understood as "those who are not-me," and can be singular, plural, or abstract. I cite this derivation to emphasize the political use of "Other" as referring to the subordinate "not-me" groups. The ethical task entailed by using this term is to accept equivalence of others as social and political figures.

In this way, Olson makes use of an unmarked status for his own perspective, a status Kinneavy also tried to overcome through his explicit identification of the morality he outlines. Although Olson highlights "postcolonial theory," he sees the "trend in composition scholarship to interrogate how gender, race, ethnicity, and power relationships manifest themselves in discursive practices" to be "a move toward the ethical, toward understanding the encounter with the Other" (100).

If Welch and Olson assume "self"-centered perspectives from which ethical recognition of the Other is sought, David and Kelli Erben make a special point of viewing writing and ethics as part of uncentered systems: "Writing is an ethical project, and hermeneutics must become productive, instead of being merely reproductive, reappropriating and re-cognitive. To talk about the ethical project of writing means that the functions of textuality and ethics do not stand in a relation external to each other" (233).

Citing Deleuze's rhizome figure, they continue, "the rhizome is non-centered, non-hierarchical and a-signifying. The book-rhizome takes the multiple as a substantive: but then multiplicity is liberated from the grips of the One—whether subject or object" (233–34).

The Erbens' formulation quietly moves away from the governance of the self-other concept and toward a collectivist sense of self and ethical values (the multiple as substantive). With regard to writing, this means that texts—novels as well as students' essays—are already authored by their society. This idea was brought out by Toni Morrison in 1988 in her reading of Melville's chapter on the whiteness of the whale as a representation in this novel of society's unconscious recognition of its struggle with an unmarked white identity. Morrison's essay, like Barbara Christian's "The Race for Theory," might be taken, by some, as voices of "Others." But following the Erbens' formulations, that would be a mistake and, perhaps, unethical. Morrison's critique of literature and Christian's critique of theory are also both "authored by society." "Their" whiteness or the status of theory as a genre of writing[4] would continue to presuppose a hierarchy of language uses in which "we" use the privileged forms. It is just this kind of self-examination that Swearingen is working toward in her essay.

Essays in this volume are struggling with this transition toward an ethical style of speaking and writing that preserves the habits of speaking about real people in living situations, without rendering these people as "Other" and without feeling obliged to declare artificial solidarities with them. This is perhaps one way to consider Baumlin, Jensen, and Massey's essay. Their return to Burke seems also to be a plea for including our affective experiences as we respond and write as scholars and teachers. In addition, they seem to be moving toward recognizing and even admitting a language space for hostile thoughts as they wonder why the *ad hominem* can't be part of our discussions.

> ... there are benefits to becoming more conscious of what we have been doing all along: once we have acknowledged that *ad hominem* arguments are typically present, ... then we can begin to discuss what it means to "kill off" another or one's self. ... If we are, as writers, stereotyping an opponent (or, as readers, type-casting an author), we can discuss the implications of these largely unconscious, though highly rhetorical strategies. (204–05)

This is definitely an ethical project, as it highlights the self-awareness originally sought by psychoanalysis as it was practiced before it was academicized into a "text-only" entity by poststructuralists. At least three of the contributors to this volume find in Burke an early source for viewing psychoanalysis as a valuable contributor to literary and language use pedagogy, and as a source germane to our academic ethical project of maintaining the exchange of language through feeling, commitment, awareness of one another and of collective loyalties. Burke may be said to be engaged in a project to review psychoanalysis as a pedagogical enterprise, whatever else it does as a therapy. To make the unconscious conscious is not very far from the kind of teaching we hope to achieve.

It would be a new item in academic writing if the at-the-person argument had a well-integrated place on the menu of scholarship, criticism, and pedagogy. Baumlin, Jensen, and Massey's essay does warn in its citation of vocabulary examples ("killing off" an author) of the dangers. We need not look far to see that military usages are frequent in academic discussions: "attack," "deploy," "drew blood," to name a few. Harold Bloom's use of agonistic development is tacitly an endorsement of the extreme and highly academic use of the Oedipus story. He raised "influence" to the status of a mystical preternatural force working on writers. The ethical perspective pursued in this volume tries to teach us to include the personal and the judgmental, but to develop a new vocabulary that greatly lessens the combativeness of these traditional tropes.

Phillip Sipiora's essay cites a brief but important example of how things may change if an ethical perspective were weighted at least equally with competitive individualism. He describes how an accomplished student-writer picked an important issue, did well with it, but excluded reference to any of his own convictions, beliefs, or principles. As a result Sipiora judges the essay a "failure" with regard to "radical exploration" (54). This example implies that a writer's active inclusion of ethical considerations converts his or her skills into arts or rhetorical energies. It implies an infusion of human concern that other contributors, such as Swearingen, described in different terms (belief) amount to similar values. An individual's including a sense of personal implication in writing converts skills into living social contributions.

However, one wonders, in reading Ross Winterowd's essay, what hope there is for reaching a way of functioning that is both ethical and politically responsible. "Doing" English is his ideal; a similar ideal was derived from speech-act theory: the recognition that language is already "doing" something. Winterowd includes this view of language in his utopian vision, as his essay suggests repeatedly that, yes, language and writing are already doing a great deal. But his real question is the most difficult and challenging posed in this volume: who is really helped by the work we do? How are those who really need help benefiting from what we say in our classrooms and what we are saying in this volume? What is the point of *talking about* ethics when the ethical path toward those in need is blocked by boundaries that we have helped to create?

> The University of Southern California is an island fortress of learning, culture, propriety, prosperity, and entrepreneurial spirit in a sea of poverty, crime, grime, and hopelessness. As my colleagues write their literary papers . . . the world just outside the well-patrolled perimeters of the University seethes with anger and frustration; children learn early that their only possible hustle . . . is peddling dope or doing burglaries. The balm of literature, the healing properties of poetry, the ennobling effect of great novels never seeps out of the university, to cross its boundaries into the community which, the English-department creed would hold, so desperately needs what the texts discussed by the term papers in the journals can bring to humanity. (70–71)

In this paragraph, Winterowd enacts the reason people are thinking of ethics. Academic discussions of identity politics have not crossed the boundary Winterowd mentions; Marxian readings have not crossed the boundary; white feminist efforts have moved slowly. In saying this, I do not want to claim that academics have acquired the smugness of the rich, though, in many cases I know about, this is true. It works differently, I think: we teachers of language use and writing are paid by institutions who create and maintain the boundaries. We can function ethically only when the populations on the other side of the boundaries enter our classrooms, something that is happening more and more in many universities.

I don't know if I agree with calling Winterowd's vision "utopian." I probably don't agree that those on the other side of the boundary will be helped by reading "great books." Neither will they be helped by coming to class only to tell their stories. But neither will they or we be helped by a commitment to a new academic mode such as the "ethical combined with the political" as I have already endorsed regardless. In a variety of ways, the truth of the matter is that what we say in these collections, in our journals, in our books and treatises, no matter how ethically oriented and politically enlightened, will not help the problem posed by Winterowd.

The kinds of things that help, the kinds of things that answer the ethical question posed when we let ourselves think about ethics are those things that emerge from a commitment to teaching, to students lives, to the very risks that Fred Gale warns us about. Some teaching experiences have entered and can continue to enter the scholarly literature; they have reached younger generations of teachers. But a key term in the discussions of ethics in teaching writing and language use has not been mentioned in this volume—the role of teaching in maintaining our livelihoods. We are paid to teach, but we are honored for writing. We have been fooled by this "hustle," as Winterowd might also observe. I find it hard to say how even the best-selling academic authors "help" in an *ethical* way. What I do know to provide ethical help is the contact I have with living students; I see small changes in people's lives, changes that are hardly worth reporting. Yet these are the changes that finally matter. These changes don't enter our collections of essays; they don't enter our academic treatises; they don't enter the standards for promotion and tenure; they don't help get us better working conditions. In the relationship between each of us contributors and our employers, they don't matter.

This is the challenge I pose to those of us who want to take the interest in ethics seriously. How do we communicate the fulfilling, satisfying, helpful relationships we have with our students to those who run universities and expect "results" from our teaching? How do we achieve local and public recognition of the lives that change and grow because they passed through our classrooms? How does the ethical relationship we have with colleagues make a difference in our circumstances of work? How do *any* interpersonal achievements enter into our formal work situations? The truly ethical aspects of our jobs have not entered the academic discussion—relationships with students, supervisors, colleagues, recommenders, and so on. Moreover, with few exceptions, some cited by contributors to this volume, the ethical character of students' interactions with one another is also not part of the academic literature.

I do not doubt that the "doing" of English in academic life is the teaching of it and what is related to it. To do anything in the academy is to teach it and not to talk *about* it. Teaching, in turn, is interpersonal action that can and does change individuals and institutions. The matter of ethics as a new item to consider is welcome. As this volume puts ethics on the menu, the next volume might follow by presenting, reporting, evaluating, disseminating what happens in ethical and other ways when the people involved in teaching and learning are "doing" the subject together.

Notes

1. However, see Christine Iwanicki, *The Materiality of Language*, unpublished dissertation, Indiana University, 1994, for a detailed discussion of Burke's struggles as a thinker.

2. I make a note of my eschewing the term "conversation" in my own writing. Oakeshott's term, remanufactured by Rorty, wants to informalize the serious, disciplined work of thinking through social problems in academic settings. In no sense is "mankind" having a "conversation"; rather, a few privileged and predominantly white men are writing away, most of the time posturing to one another, with only the smallest concern for what is really happening in society and the rest of the world, a point made by Winterowd and to which I'll return.

3. Those concerned about this problem might read, in addition to the sources cited by Gale, the recent short book by Jane Gallop, *Feminist Accused of Sexual Harassment*, Durham: Duke University Press, 1997.

4. Ralph Cohen identified "theory" during its "peak" periods of academic interest as itself a genre of writing, thus starting the project of marking theory as no longer "above" other kinds of writing and thinking.

Chapter 1

Ethics and Rhetoric: Forging a Moral Language for the English Classroom

James L. Kinneavy

Interrelationships between ethics and rhetoric go back to the dawn of both. A famous anthropologist, speaking of the duty to abstain from lying and the duty to keep one's promises, says, "Within certain limits these two duties seem to be universally recognized" (Westermarck, *Origin* II, 72). In other words, the rebuke of ethics to rhetoric is a universal moral principle.

Many of us in rhetoric have been explicitly concerned with the dangers of the techniques of our own discipline. A book published seven years ago won an award at a recent Conference on College Composition and Communication. It is called *Rhetoric and Irony* and its subtitle is *Western Literacy and Western Lies*, and it chronicles a serious strain of immorality in both our rhetorical and our literary tradition.

By circumstances rather than by design, my studies of this issue have gone through four separate stages, but the chronological evolution took on a curious conceptual development. Consequently I would like to devote some time to each of the following four stages: (1) the need for a social, rather than an individual, ethic and the language to talk about it; (2) the major dimensions of such a social ethic; (3) the anthropological basis for a such a meta-ethics; (4) the motivation behind such an ethic for students at various levels and the pedagogical methodologies for teaching such an ethic.

A Social Ethic and Ethical Language

I have been a teacher for fifty-eight years, with stints in elementary school, high school, and undergraduate and graduate college teaching; and I have asked my students at all of these levels to write about moral and political issues. But until about eight or nine years ago, I had not given particular attention to the disparity between their abilities to carry out such assignments and their abilities to analyze or write about issues in their own fields or in literature, which I frequently taught. In 1983 at The University of Texas we organized an English course for upper-division students, a course which required the students to write about issues in their fields. It became a course required of all students in all undergraduate major programs. This course, which was implemented in 1983–84 for the first time required 158 classes and handled 3,762 students in four different areas: sciences and technology, humanities, fine arts, and business. I taught the course for several years with quite a range of majors, and it was in these courses that I first became aware of this disparity. Students did not have the language and conceptual skills to write about moral issues in their own chosen major fields. In fact they did not even have the language or the concepts to talk about such issues.

I spoke about this matter to several of the people who taught ethics in the philosophy department and asked them if there had been any recent studies in the abilities of people to speak about ethical issues. I found out that only one in ten undergraduate students ever takes a course in ethics in the college programs at The University of Texas at Austin. And, of course, only those students who had gone to private religious schools have had ethics courses at the high school or elementary levels. There is, of course, ethical instruction given in churches, for the 60% of Americans who say they attend church regularly (*U. S. News and World Report*, April 4, 1994, p. 50). I was also referred to some experts who had indeed done some analyses of the language abilities of Americans to speak or write about moral issues.

Reading these authorities constituted the first stage of my investigation, which culminated in my speech at Le Salle University in Philadelphia in 1987. Since then I have added some other authorities. The common denominator to all of these studies is an effort to establish or partly reestablish a social ethic and the language to communicate about it, rather than an individual ethic, which many of these authorities feel is the dominating ethic and language about ethics today in Europe and America.

Two major figures in the movement started from different positions, but reached much the same conclusions. Alasdair MacIntyre, a significant figure in this movement, has written seven books on ethics and morality, the most prominent being *After Virtue: A Study in*

Moral Theory, 1981 (2nd ed., 1984) and *Whose Justice? Which Rationality?* (1988). He has also written many articles about ethics. He summarizes his position early in *After Virtue*:

> The hypothesis which I wish to advance is that in the actual world which we inhabit the language of morality is in . . . [a] state of grave disorder. What we possess, if this view is true, are the fragments of a conceptual scheme, parts which now lack those contexts from which their significance derived. We possess indeed simulacra of morality, we continue to use many of the key expressions. But we have—very largely, if not entirely—lost our comprehension, both theoretical and practical, of morality. (2)

He admits that most of us feel that we would be aware of such a situation, if it were true. As he says,

> If a catastrophe sufficient to throw the language and practice of morality into grave disorder had occurred, surely we should all know about it. It would indeed be one of the central facts of our history. (3)

In fact, half of his book is an attempt to prove—I believe successfully—that such a catastrophe has come about without our realizing it.

The morality and the language which we have lost was grounded on a philosophical view of human nature, derived from the Greeks, which had been grafted onto Judaism, Christianity, and Islam. The Greek view and that of the three religions were compatible because they both viewed human nature as having a purpose (a *telos*) and a notion that achieving that purpose brought about happiness to human beings. The two concepts also had a view of the roles of a human being in society and of the harmony of these roles with the fulfillment of human nature. All four views were social ethics, and they dominated Western civilization's moral theory from the fourth or fifth century BCE until the seventeenth century. MacIntyre calls this the classic view of morality.

Since the seventeenth century, according to MacIntyre, this view has been gradually supplanted by an opposing view of morality, which he calls emotivism. Another term might be libertarianism, implying complete individual choice in any situation. It is a very common view in contemporary Western culture that each individual decides for him- or herself what is morally good. There is no universal principle, and there is no teleological view of human nature which determines what a human being is supposed to aim at. It is not a rational view which can be shared with others because each person is an isolated entity out for him- or herself. With such a view of morality permeating important areas of society, all choices are selfishly determined and social agreements are built upon competitive interests. Such a moral system, in effect, cannot logically entail a rational public policy except as an arena of competition.

MacIntyre believes that Nietzsche best epitomizes this view of morality. At the present time, it possibly is best represented by some postmodernists, such as Jean-Francois Lyotard. Such people are variously called radical individualists, libertarians, anarchists, or emotivists.

The title of William Sullivan's book, *Reconstructing Public Philosophy*, indicates that his initial concern was more political than moral. However, there is an interesting symmetry to his methodology, when compared with MacIntyre's. While MacIntyre set out to establish a social ethic and move away from the individual, he inevitably ended considering the place of the individual in the polis. In other words, he "politicized" the individual morality. Sullivan, looking at the problems with the modern state, found it lacking in morality. In other words, he moralized the political situation. As he says, speaking of three liberal thinkers, Fred Hirsch, Daniel Bell, and Robert Heilbroner, they "make out a strong case that liberal capitalist affluence finds itself entangled, indeed, nearly immobilized, by its own contradictions" (12-13). And all three turn to morality or something like a religious tradition to curb the inherently uncontrollable appetites of a liberal capitalism, even though such a tradition is not a component of such a theory, indeed is incompatible with it (163-170).

Sullivan is one of the co-authors with Robert Bellah and others who, in a celebrated anthology, *Habits of the Heart*, made a further plea for a sense of community and for a social ethic in public issues.

Another very vocal group, the Communitarians, headed by Amitai Etzioni, The Responsive Community, William Galston of Maryland, and Mary Ann Glendon of Harvard, have added their voices to those of people like MacIntyre, Sullivan, and Bellah. They insist on the importance of the community and oppose radical individualist positions in morality, economics, and politics. Many of these thinkers decry the overemphasis on rights and entitlements and the neglect of the accompanying duties and responsibilities which rights of others entail. Terry Eagleton, in a speech at The University of Texas, called all of these people Communitarians.

Communitarianism is not, however, a novel phenomenon. A good deal of MacIntyre's two books mentioned above, as well as his *A Short History of Ethics*, document the fact that the interweaving of the individual and the social life has been a constant concern of ethical systems since their beginning. Sullivan's analyses also have long historical antecedents. Stephen Toulmin, who has written on the academic history of the divorce of ethical and social concerns from the development of the individual disciplines, scientific and humanistic, also has joined the voices of the Communitarians by insisting that the separate disciplines have a long list of IOUs to society for their neglect of such issues in the past three hundred years (Toulmin 116).

From a historical perspective, MacIntyre lines up a fairly impressive list of moral systems which have practiced social ethics: he includes Greek moral philosophy, Judaism, Christianity, Islamism, Marxism, utilitarianism, Kantianism. I believe that authors like Cicero, whose *De Officiis* is based on natural and social fitness, should be included. I also believe that the "other" philosophers, such as Heidegger and Sartre and Camus, should be added. So should Buddhism and Hinduism and Confucianism. And of course, so should the modern Communitarians. And so should philosophers of fairness and justice, like Dworkin and Rawls.

This group is a fairly impressive assemblage. Thus, at least, under the umbrella of a social ethic, many quite diverse groups can be gathered. This umbrella provides the common language and axioms which we can use in teaching. Given this umbrella, people of many quite varied groups can still engage in dialogue with one another, such as Marxists and Christians, Muslims and Jews, and agnostic utilitarians with all four of these groups.

The first stage of my research thus came to an important conclusion: there are many different moral systems across the world which share a social ethic and which opposed the radical individualism of Nietzsche and post-modernism. Indeed, many of the students in the classes at my secular university share this social ethic.

The Major Dimensions of a Social Ethic

This conclusion represented my thinking at about the middle of 1992, with a few extrapolations. Then, by a curious circumstance of fate, I was pushed into a new dimension of this inquiry. On October 16, 1991, an ex-merchant Marine, George Jo Hennard, drove a truck into Luby's Restaurant in Killeen, Texas, and killed 25 people and wounded 23 more in a terrible tragedy. About nine months later, I was asked if I could speak to a group of high school and elementary teachers at a memorial conference to be held on the anniversary of the tragedy. I was asked to speak about the educational implications of the tragedy.

At first I hesitated, but then I accepted, although I did not really yet know exactly what I would end up talking about.

I first decided to refresh my mind with the details of the incident and to read what journalists had written about it at the time and after. I checked on microfiche what the *Houston Post* had written about it in the 32 stories or columns which it ran on the tragedy over a period of about a month following the massacre. These stories confirmed a persistent perspective which I remembered from the Austin coverage during the same time period. Was this reaction larger than the state of Texas I wondered? So I checked the *New York Times* index and read the 13 accounts and reactions which this prestigious newspaper had in the week following the incident. The same emphases were repeated. Would they change when the story crossed the ocean? I checked *The London Times* and found a clear approximation of the same reactions and emphases. Through the database Lexis-Nexis, I read over 500 coverages of the event from a good number of countries of the world, though not from some. Reuters, a wire-service based in Germany, ran 16 stories on the tragedy in the first 37 hours after it happened; Agence France Presse ran 8 stories in the same period.

What was interesting about these 500 coverages from many countries, many cultures, and several languages was that the same pattern of reactions recurred throughout, This pattern gave me my educational theme for the talk in Killeen, and the same pattern introduced a second dimension to my search for a common ethic and language for classroom use.

What was this general pattern of the local, national, and international reactions to the drama in Killeen? I would say that there were four major recurring features in the vast majority of the nearly 500 treatments of the tragedy. These four features were a sense of shock at the brutal murders, an expression of sympathy for the victims and the families of the victims, a surprise at the destruction of property involved in this particular massacre, and a meticulous concern for truth and accuracy in reporting the details of the drama, both in the news stories and in columns and editorials. There were other concerns that came up now and then: the Congress was at that time considering a law about gun control, and this was brought in, even in other countries; the psychological background of Hennard was also an issue in some items. But these four features dominated all reports. Now these four features may seem fairly obvious, but I think that they are more important than they appear on the surface. Let me explain each in a little detail.

Shock at Murder

The aspect of the tragedy which captured most of the headlines and the leads in the news stories and the theses in the editorials and columns was the shock at the number, the ruthlessness, and the senseless nature of the murders. This sense of shock is true of both the news stories and the editorials and columns. The headline for the story in the French newspaper *Le Monde* on October 18, that year, was typical: "A 'mad gunman' kills twenty-two persons in Texas." There was universal concern for the immediate victims, the twenty-five killed and the killer and the twenty-three wounded. This concern was not rooted in any evident ideology, either religious or political.

Concern for Family

This was the first emphasis, the headline interest for the first story. But in the ensuing week a second motif took over: the concern for the families as well as the victims. The following headline from an October 18 story in the *Houston Post* typifies the local, national, and even international coverage: "Shootings leave families, friends trying to cope with grief, questions."

Concern for Property

A third, though minor, concern runs through the same stories, and was usually given prominence in photos accompanying the stories: the destruction and devastation of the cafeteria in which the shootings took place. And the reopening of the cafeteria, about a year ago, occasioned a spate of articles from across this country and Canada to wire services for the Pacific Press, Reuter's of Germany, and Agence France Presse for French readers. As I say, however, this was a minor motif.

Concern for Truth

A fourth feature remains to be singled out. When I first began looking at a large number of stories, especially outside of Texas, I wondered whether there would be wild distortions and stereotypes. I found that my fears were groundless. Generally, there was a professional restraint, even in headlines. Facts were generally accurate; names were correct: estimates were cautious; generalizations were circumspect, prudent, and accompanied with justifying facts. This concern for truth is as evident in the news stories as in the many editorial treatments of gun control issues, the most frequent editorial concern here and abroad, especially since the U. S. Congress was considering a gun control law at that time. An article on gun sales in Texas and Killeen in *The London Times* was typical. One exception was a story from *Le Monde*, the French daily. After the first headline, "A 'mad gunman' kills twenty-two in Texas," a second headline, in considerably larger print, read: "A Cowboy syndrome." But this stereotype was not exploited in the article, which did not even mention "cowboys," but which first presented the facts of the story and then spent three-fourths of the space on gun control and the crime bill then before the House of Representatives.

I believe that these four features have major educational implications: a universal respect for life and shock at murder, a global sympathy for families, a worldwide concern for property destruction, and an ubiquitous solicitude for truth. These four characteristics dominate the many treatments of the Killeen tragedy. I think that it is more than coincidental that these same four concerns are the four cornerstones of most ethical systems, whether religious, philosophical, or just practiced without elaborate theoretical undergirding.

Let me illustrate this common moral system by comparing it to another, with which most readers are already familiar—the Judeo-Christian moral edifice. This structure is most explicitly defined in the Ten Commandments of the Bible, The religious dimension of this system is expressed in the first three commandments which outline man's relations with the deity. I will return to these three shortly. But, first let us look at the remaining seven. Three of them relate to the family (I will use the Oxford translation, approved by both Catholic and Protestant groups): Honor your father and your mother, You shall not commit adultery, You shall not covet your neighbor's wife. One commandment relates to life; You shall not commit murder. One relates to truth: You shall not give false evidence against your neighbor. And two relate to property: You shall not steal, You shall not set your heart on your neighbor's house, his land, his slave, his slave-girl, his ox, his ass, or on anything that belongs to him.

These four concerns, respect for life, family, truth, and property, are also the basis for many other moral edifices. Buddhism, for example, parallels these four concerns in the first four of its five precepts, which admonish the Buddhist "to abstain from taking life (including animal life), stealing, wrong sexual relations, abuse of speech (such as lying and malicious gossip), and the consumption of alcohol or drugs (*Funk and Wagnall's New Encyclopedia* 4:323). This fundamental social ethic is paralleled in Hinduism in the Hindu respect for all living beings and the common duties that all classes must observe. Unlike Judeo-Christianity, there is not a religious foundation at the base of either of these ethical systems. Thus the Killeen tragedy gave some specific axioms to the social ethical system which MacIntyre, Sullivan, Bellah, Etzioni and other Communitarians felt the need of. These authorities, however, had not spelled out the specifics of such a system.

In the fall of 1993, a year after I had given my talk to Killeen, the World Parliament of Religions met in Chicago, with representatives of nearly all of the world religions. They wrestled over a document which eventually was signed by a majority of the representatives present at the meeting—150 signatures of representatives from 15 major world religions, both of the East and of the West. The document was entitled "A Global Ethic: The Declaration of the Parliament of World Religions" and was published in 1993. There are four principles at the basis of this global ethic:

1. Commitment to a culture of non-violence and respect for life.
2. Commitment to a culture of solidarity and a just economic order.
3. Commitment to a culture of tolerance and a life of truthfulness.
4. Commitment to a culture of equal rights and partnership between men and women. (Küng, Table of Contents).

These four principles are another version of the respect for life, property, truth, and family, which I have examined earlier. I was quite delighted to see that the World Parliament of Religions had taken a stand quite closely aligned to the four principles which I had seen in the Killeen tragedy and in my anthropological studies, as I will attempt to show in the next section.

The Anthropological Basis for a Social Ethic

At the end of the first section, I summarized a fair number of religious and philosophical systems of ethics which embrace a social ethic. Some critics of talks which I have given on these matters have raised the issue of a more general look at civilizations and cultures. Does an anthropological view of ethics in many different cultures lend any support to the sort of social ethic represented by these religious and philosophical systems? Or, on the contrary, does anthropological evidence support a more individualized, diversified, and subjective view of morality?

The third stage of my study attempts a partial answer to that question. And I am still working on this, so this stage of my report has to be taken as a progress report of an unfinished project. I have read several histories of morality and ethics, including one by MacIntyre, but his and most of the others tend to focus on philosophical issues and distinctions with little attention to anthropological data. Two studies, however, are in marked distinction to the others. Edward Westermarck, a Swedish-speaking Finn, who wrote his major works in English, published a two-volume work, *The Origin and Development of the Moral Ideas* and another book called *Ethical Relativity*. His last work was entitled *Christianity and Morals*, and an earlier one was on *The Goodness of Gods*. He has four other books on marriage, its history and its future. He also has a two-volume work on *Ritual and Belief in Morocco* and another book on *Early Beliefs and Their Social Influence*. His work shows a life-long interest in ethical issues and in their embodiment in particular cultures. He spent the better part of four decades doing field research, particularly in Morocco.

In meta-ethics, Westermarck is usually listed as both an ethical relativist—as one might suspect from the title of his book on the subject—and an ethical subjectivist. He is also considered an excellent field researcher and a superb summarizer of other anthropologists' studies. In fact, the bibliography *for The Origin and Development of the Moral Ideas* is eighty pages long.

An ethical relativist and an ethical subjectivist would not seem, at first blush, to be a support for something like a social ethic with rather common dimensions of respect for life, property, family integrity, and truth. But Westermarck is a special kind of relativist and subjectivist, and he has managed to reduce ethical issues to relatively few major concerns. Let us first look at the second of these matters—the dimensions of an ethical theory.

Westermarck insists on limiting his investigation into the "major modes of conduct with which the moral consciousness is concerned." He focuses on six groups:

> The first group includes such acts, forbearances, and omissions as directly concern the interests of other men, their life or bodily integrity, their freedom, honour, property, and so forth. The second includes such acts, forbearances, and omissions as chiefly concerns a man's own welfare, such as suicide, temperance, asceticism. The third group, which partly coincides with,

but partly differs from, both the first and the second, refers to the sexual relations of men. The fourth includes their conduct towards the lower animals; the fifth, their conduct towards dead persons; the sixth their conduct towards beings, real or imaginary, that they regard as supernatural. (I, 328)

Now if one ignores the conduct towards lower animals and towards supernatural beings, one is left with the same major concerns which preoccupied us in the previous section: respect for life, for property, for family integrity, and for truth. He devotes eleven chapters to homicide, suicide, bodily injuries and cannibalism (I, 327-526, II, 229-64, 553-81). He devotes two chapters to property (II, 1-71). He devotes six chapters to family and sexual issues (I, 597—669, II, 364-552). By far the vast majority of Westermarck's energies is devoted to these four issues.

Secondly as I remarked above, Westermarck is a curious sort of relativist. Consider, in this regard, his statements on the concern for these four issues in the different civilizations which he investigated, either by primary or secondary sources. At the beginning of eleven chapters devoted to murder and bodily injuries, he says:

> It is commonly maintained that the most sacred duty which we owe our fellow-creatures is to respect their lives. I venture to believe that this holds good not only among civilized nations, but among the lower races as well; and that, if a savage recognizes that he has any moral obligations at all to his neighbors, he considers the taking of their lives to be a greater wrong than any other kind of injury inflicted upon them. (I, 328)

He does give a few quite rare exceptions of tribes-seven all told—in which homicide does not seem to have been considered wrong (I, 328-9).

About property, he begins with this statement:

> Hence the universal condemnation of what we call theft or robbery proves that the right of property exists among all races known to us. (II,1)

He devotes two chapters to truth and good faith. At the beginning of his second chapter on the issue he says:

> Men have a natural disposition to believe what they are told. This disposition is particularly obvious in young children; it is acquired wisdom and experience only that constitutes incredulity . . .
> But men are not only ready to believe what they are told they also like to know the truth. Curiosity, or the love of truth, is coeval with the first operations of the intellect; it seems to be an ultimate fact in the human frame. (II,109-110)

His statements with regard to the family are also most interesting. His major field of expertise in anthropology has to do with the family. About the family he says,

> In the human race the family consisting of father, mother, and offspring is probably a universal institution, whether founded on a monogamous, polygamous, or polyandrous marriage. (I, 190)

> Besides parental, conjugal, and filial attachment we find among all existing races of men altruism of the fraternal type, binding together children of the same parents, relatives more remotely allied, and, generally, members of the same social unit. (II, 194-95)

Marriage (II, 399), prohibitions against incest (II, 364-66) and against adultery (II, 447-50) are fairly universal. Seven exceptions are given for adultery (II, 447, fn. 1). Rape and conjugal infidelity are less universally condemned.

Now for a theorist who calls himself an ethical relativist, these are rather remarkable statements. He states rather categorically that respect for life, for property, for family integrity, and for truth are concerns that we find almost universally. The number of exceptions is statistically almost insignificant.

The point which concerns me is that such near universality does give us the major axioms for a language of morality. Beginning with these, we can go into differences and hopefully in most cases discuss them. Thus, a basic respect for the life of the other has not precluded taking a life in self-defense in nearly all civilizations. The accommodation of the principle to the situation can be made without sacrificing the principle; in this case, it would seem that there is a choice between respecting one's own life and that of the attacker, With regard to polygamy, the definition of the family differs when one compares the Islamic and, for example, the Judaic-Christian notions. In both cases, however, the respect for life and for family integrity are still upheld.

I am still working on this anthropological base for the language of morality. Westermarck, after all, published *Ethical Relativity* in 1932, and *The Origin and Development of Moral Ideas* came out, in the second edition, in 1917. Consequently, I have tried to update Westermarck and anthropological views since that time.

Westermarck still commands respect today. In 1982 three books appeared, assessing his contributions to anthropology and ethics. One was an anthology with thirteen experts in either anthropology or ethics taking a retrospective view of his work in this century. All thirteen still consider him a major figure.

Claude Levi-Strauss, writing in 1945, a few years after Westermarck's death, considered him a giant. He lauded Westermarck's concept of what Levi-Strauss called a "permanent humanity" in all civilizations (in Stroup, 180). He also spoke of the "monumental character" and prodigious erudition" of Westermarck's work (190). J. L. Mackie, writing in 1967 in *The Encyclopedia of Philosophy,* concludes his article on Westermarck with this statement:

> Nevertheless, some contemporary moral philosophers believe that Westermarck's views on ethics are substantially correct and have made an important contribution to the development and defense of views of this kind. (VIII, 286)

Speaking of subsequent developments in comparative anthropology, by, for example, Ruth Benedict, Melville J. Herkovits, Clyde Kluckhohn, and by himself, Abraham Edel said, in 1982, that these people had added a morally explicit evaluative component to the descriptive, causal, and classificatory dimensions of Westermarck (in Stroup, 85 ff.) A few pages later he added,

> The anthropological revelation of differences [emphasized by Westermarck] had produced multiple reactions. Prominent among them had been a renewed search for the moral unity of mankind. But this search was successful only to a limited extent . . . it helped us understand common grounds for morality. (92)

This is my understanding and use of Westermarck. None of these assessments, however, questioned the anthropological data and the descriptive conclusions which Westermarck had drawn from them.

The Ethical and Pedagogical Ramifications of a Common Social Ethical Language

Given the importance of establishing a modern moral language for a social ethics, the point made by MacIntyre, Bellah, Sullivan, Etzioni, Toulmin and others, which I addressed in the first section of this chapter; given further the underlying moral axioms which can undergird such a language and its relative neutrality which I attempted to show in the second part of the chapter; and given the fairly universal character which these axioms have, as is illustrated by comparative anthropology, what can be done with this framework of a language in the public schools and in public debate about these matters?

As I see, from trying to implement this position in the classroom for the past five or six years, there are four major problems in motivating students to consider using such an approach in their papers. The first is to convince the students of the necessity or usefulness of a moral language. The second is to teach them how to adjust a metalanguage such as this one to their own particular moral codes; this problem is interwoven with the pedagogical problem of the neutrality of the teacher and of his or her respect for the individual moral codes of the students. Fourthly, I would like to illustrate this methodology by applying it to literature, both classical and contemporary.

Convincing Students of the Usefulness of a General Moral Language

Judging by my own classes over the past several years, MacIntyre is right about at least one major issue. Generally, students have only the fragments of a moral language to communicate about moral issues, even with each other, at a degree of fluency parallel with their abilities to discuss other academic issues. As MacIntyre says, this deficiency is in part due to the loss of such a language in society at large. But part of this inadequacy is the lack of academic training in these matters at both the pre-college and the college level.

Many of the students recognize this inadequacy when faced with writing about such issues, and many welcome the possibility of learning such a language. This is a positive motivation. But frequently the talk of a moral language strikes students as negative, restrictive, and confining. This is also reflective of our current society's largely libertarian and individualistic views of the nature of moral decisions. A recent poll by *U. S. News and World Report* reported that 70% of Americans believe that "Each individual must determine what is right or wrong" and 48% agree that there is no one set of values that is right (April 4, 1994, p. 51). Now, neither MacIntyre, nor Bellah, nor Sullivan, nor Etzioni, nor I would disagree with the notion that moral judgments are matters of individual free choice. But if the statement "Each individual must determine what is right or wrong" means that moral choices are completely a-social, then all of these people would dissent from this inference. How can one integrate individual free choice with a social ethic?

One way is to approach a moral code precisely from the point of view of the libertarian. Start with an individual's rights. If I assert that I have right to life, then those in my surrounding society cannot take away that life. In other words, any right has a corresponding social duty. If you have a right to property, then neither I nor anyone else in your society can steal. If you have a right to family integrity, then I cannot rape or commit adultery. In other words, my rights are your responsibilities, your rights are my responsibilities. Etzioni especially, among the Communitarians, has emphasized this reciprocity of rights and duties, arguing that too many individual radicalists emphasize their rights without taking into consideration the corresponding duties which they impose on society.

In fact, any assertion of an individual right does impose a social burden on society. The four principles of respect for life, for property, for family integrity, and for truth are the assertion of four basic rights of individuals. A moral code can thus be read as an affirmation of basic rights. There is also the insistence that not only I but my neighbors have such rights. My rights impose moral burdens on my neighbors, and their rights impose moral burdens on me. This is the compromise that we arrive at: individual rights for everyone are decreed, and the social corollaries of social duties follow. To achieve my moral rights, I agree to respect the rights of others, There is a moral social contract which parallels the legal social contract, a notion which has been a feature of legal theory from Cicero, through Christian and Protestant theologians, and in international law with Grotius, through major French, English, and German thinkers in the eighteenth century, on down to our own day.

Such a view presents a moral code as a means to an end, individual happiness and rights. This perspective is called a teleological view of morality. It does not view the moral code as a law dictated by an outside authority; such an ethic is called a deontological system. Students generally view ethics deontologically, rather than teleologically. A teleological presentation of a moral code is consequently much more appealing to them. This way of presenting a moral code is the usual manner in which utilitarian views of ethics are characterized.

This does not mean that such a a teleological system cannot be compatible in its major dimensions with a deontological system. Thus this general social ethical language with its four basic axioms is certainly compatible with the Ten Commandments of the Bible, usually looked upon as a deontological code. However, it is perfectly possible to consider the Ten Commandments as a Bill of Rights, embodying the rights to life, family integrity, property, and truth—considering only the moral dimensions of the code, the last seven commandments.

The teleological view of a moral code, in addition to giving a positive turn to the presentation of a moral code, also provides a useful response to extreme libertarians, anarchists, and individualists, the opponents of a social ethic. A radical individualist, who would claim the right to do anything he wanted to do, would effectively deny freedom to the rights of those in his environment: if he can kill, his neighbors are deprived of the right to life; if he can steal, his neighbors are deprived of their rights to property; if he can commit adultery, his neighbors are deprived of their rights to family integrity; if he can lie, they are deprived of their rights to the truth. Such a radical individualist, in effect, deprives neighbors of all of their rights. He asserts freedom for himself, while denying it to others. This reciprocity of rights and duties is often not grasped by libertarians or anarchists.

The Adjustment by the Student of the General Code to an Individual Ethic

The compatibility of the general code with individual codes, whether deontological or teleological, bridges the discussion to the second part of this section, the use of the general code in conjunction with the particular moral code of individual students. As I pointed out earlier, the moral code of Judaism and Christianity embedded in the last seven of the Ten Commandments is compatible with the general code which I have outlined. Thus a teacher can use the general code and Jewish and Christian students can resonate with their Biblical code. This system allows a deontological motivation supplied by a particular student to provide the inspiration and support in specific case under consideration. This holds true not only for Judaic and Christian students; it also holds true for all of the other groups who espouse social ethics—and their number is legion. It also holds true, if Westermarcks's scholarship is at all valid, of most of the civilizations of mankind.

Such a general language of morality is particularly useful with the teacher in a class whose students have different moral codes. It allows the teacher to speak to each group with the same language. And individual students can write papers which respect both the common language and the language of their particular code. But the common language also bridges another barrier—students talking to one another.

If students find difficulties talking to one another because of differences in their moral codes, for example, an Islamic student with a different view of family integrity talking to a Christian student, then the two students can be asked to articulate these differences and try to work out their difficulties under the terms of the common language. The same can be said of two students whose ideas about abortion differ, owing to different religious backgrounds. If we can agree to have them talk to one another in the common language of respect for human life, then maybe some problems can be solved. In this case, the discussion will probably boil down to a definition of "human life."

Thus the common language based on respect for the rights of all to life, family integrity, property, and truth enables the teacher to take a neutral stand in a class while allowing students with many different compatible moral codes to work out their own problems, and it also enables students with different moral codes to talk to one another. The one group that is excluded from this consensus is the radical individualist or extreme libertarian or anarchist.

In my use of this system in class, I encourage students with different moral codes which are compatible with this general system to go into specifics in their own papers, using their own moral code to work out their own moral solutions to issues. But if they are addressing more heterogeneous groups, I tell them that they have to consider the make-up of these audiences.

The procedure usually consists in the articulation of a student's particular moral code and then the deductive application of its principles to the particular case in hand. I and the other readers of the paper pay careful to the articulation and to the logic of the application.

The same methodology applies to those who happen to profess a libertarian position in morality. I ask the student to see what would happen in a world in which, for instance, anyone who could get away with it, could steal. It is clear, as MacIntyre and many others have pointed out, that this leads to anarchy, and in an anarchy, the physically strongest prevails. Might becomes right.

How would this general system work in particular situations? Let me apply this four-fold social ethic to some specific cases. As a teacher of literature, I have used, in both high school and college, drama, fiction and poetry which bring these four issues to the foreground. Both *Hamlet* and *Macbeth* are common high school fare. I usually paid attention to the aesthetic structures of plot construction, juxtaposition and development of character, the rhythm of the poetry, and so on. But any treatment of *Hamlet* has to face up to the tragedy of Hamlet and the tragedy of this play is built around the four ethical issues of life, family, property, and truth. Hamlet's father has been murdered, and this one murder motivates the entire play. Further, Hamlet's father has been murdered by a member of the family, his uncle, in a conspiracy with Hamlet's own mother. The family motif is very important in the play. So is the issue of theft because the murder of Claudius has been perpetrated in order to enable Hamlet's uncle and Gertrude, his mother, to take over the kingdom. The truth of Gertrude and Hamlet's uncle is at stake, and the play revolves around Hamlet's uncovering their lies. The four cornerstones of the moral system which we saw in the Killeen tragedy are here the heart of the drama. And one does not have to be doctrinaire to talk about the murders, the destruction of the family, the theft of a kingdom and the truth and falsity of some of the major characters. *Macbeth* is in many ways similar to *Hamlet*. It is based on the murder by Macbeth and Lady Macbeth of Duncan, king of Scotland, and, as in *Hamlet*, this murder is the motivating force behind the play. Two major families are involved, that of the murderers, Macbeth and Lady Macbeth, and the family of the victim, Duncan (and his kinsman MacDuff), who eventually avenges Duncan's murder by killing Macbeth. Theft is involved because, to achieve his ambition to steal the throne, Macbeth must murder. The truth of several of the major characters is again an issue, including the truth of the witches' prediction of the slayer of Macbeth and Macbeth's misinterpretation of this.

Let us move to two great Greek epics, often taught, at least in myth form, at the high school level, and to several great Greek dramas to examine these same major moral issues. The *Iliad* is the story of the abduction of Helen, the wife of Menelaus, king of Sparta, by Paris of Troy, and the attempts of the Greek chieftains to enable Menelaus to rescue Helen and reunite her with Menelaus. Killings are involved in the war, especially the killing of Achilles by Paris, and the eventual killing of Paris. One of the men involved in the Trojan war, and the author of the stratagem by which the Greeks defeated the Trojans, was Odysseus and the second great Greek epic is the story of his attempts to return home and reunite himself with his wife Penelope and his son Telemachus. The story involves, on the one hand, Odysseus' adventures as he tries heroically to return to his family, and on the other hand, Penelope's efforts to fend off attempts by others to break up the family and take over Ithaca. Again, murder, family, theft, and truth are the cornerstones of the story, which cannot be taught without talking about these themes and their interweavings with plot, character, setting, and the poetry of the language.

The great Greek dramas illustrate the same point. Possibly the greatest tragedy of all literature, *Oedipus*, by Sophocles, is the tragic story of a man who unknowingly killed his own father and eventually married his own mother. In this play, murder and family are intricately interwoven. When Oedipus discovers what he has done to his own family, he puts out his own eyes. Antigone is one of the daughters of the incestuous relationship between Oedipus and his mother Jocasta and accompanies her father in his travels after his tragic discovery until his death in *Oedipus at Colonus*. The play *Antigone*, sometimes taught at the high school level, continues the story of the family of Oedipus. The two brothers of Antigone, the sons of Oedipus and Jocasta, killed each other in battle, and Creon, the king of Thebes will not allow Antigone to bury her brother, Polynices. Her opposition to the unjust law is the theme of the play. Eventually, after burying her brother, she is shut up in a subterranean cave, where she and her lover, the son of the king, both kill themselves. Again, killing and family are interwoven almost as intricately as in *Oedipus* and *Oedipus at Colonus*. Indeed, all great literature seems to involve interrelations among these moral cornerstones of respect for life, for family, for property, and truth. In fact, there are moral, social and political issues in all disciplines, and I believe that the teachers in those disciplines ought to point out these issues to students studying these different fields. This critical discussion cannot wait until college, since most students do not go on to college. Yet even in college, many disciplines are taught as if there were not issues of this nature involved.

There is a moral system and a common language in which to discuss these matters, as I have attempted to show in this chapter. We can teach students at all ages and in all disciplines a respect for life, for family, for property, and for truth. We can teach students in a nondoctrinaire way that respects their own personal opinions without imposing a given ideology on them.

Works Cited

MacIntyre, Alasdair. *Whose Justice? Which Rationality?* Notre Dame, IN: Notre Dame UP, 1988.

———. *After Virtue: A Study in Moral Theory.* Notre Dame, IN: Notre Dame UP, 1981.

———. *A Short History of Ethics.* New York: Macmillan, 1966.

Mackie, J. L. "Westermarck, Edward Alexander." *The Encyclopedia of Philosophy.* Vol 8. Paul Edwards, ed.-in-chief. New York: Macmillan Publishing Company, 1967: 284–86.

Steneck, Nicholas H., ed. *Science and Society: Past, Present, and Future.* Ann Arbor: U of Michigan P, 1975.

Stroup, Timothy, ed. *Edward Westermarck: Essays On His Life and Works.* Helsinki: Philosophical Society of Finland, 1982.

Sullivan, William M. *Reconstructing Public Philosophy.* Berkeley: U of California P, 1982.

Sullivan, William M., Robert Bellah, et. al. *Habits of the Heart: Individualism and Commitment in American Life.* Berkeley: U of California P, 1985.

Swearingen, C. Jan. *Rhetoric and Irony: Western Literacy and Western Lies.* New York: Oxford UP, 1991.

Toulmin, Stephen. "The Twin Moralities of Science." Steneck. 111–24.

Westermarck, Edward. *Ethical Relativity.* Westport, CT: Greenwood Press, 1970.

———. *Christianity and Morals.* Freeport, NY: Books for Libraries Press, 1969.

———. *The Origin and the Development of the Moral Ideas.* 2 Vols. London: Macmillan, 1906–08.

Chapter 2

Legal Rights and Responsibilities in the Writing Classroom

Fredric G. Gale

The Compact Oxford English Dictionary defines ethics as "The rules of conduct recognized in certain associations or departments of life" (528). Usually when a student of mine begins a paper with a dictionary definition I leap to the contingent conclusion, based on experience, that the student failed to find anything interesting to say about the topic word defined and therefore used the dictionary definition to put off, perhaps forever, confronting the topic. My chapter is not guilty of this sin: I do it here not because I want to write *from* the definitional cue provided by the dictionary but *in opposition to it*. The definition seems to correspond closely to what we consider to be professional ethics, the conduct expected of a teacher or other professional doing his or her work. I am going to write in opposition to that definition because I want to demonstrate how writing teachers may respond to students' writing in ways that are sensible, responsible and ethical in their own minds and in the minds of their colleagues and still subject themselves and even their school to civil or criminal liability.

Why does this seemingly unjust state of affairs exist? The answer is that the law is not simply a codification of the moral conventions of a society; it has an independent design that does not necessarily track the majority or consensus view of what is just or even what is moral. For example, the Eighteenth Amendment to the Constitution made the consumption of alcoholic beverages illegal and brought about the most widespread subversion of the law in our history. It was unpopular but it was the law for a decade. Conversely, although the biblical commandment not to covet thy neighbor's wife may be considered the moral imperative, coveting and acts well beyond coveting are not currently illegal.

To understand this moral alienation of the law, we need to understand something of our history. Our modern legal system owes much more to the sophists than to Plato and Aristotle, the philosophers to whom we give the most honor. The reason for the relatively greater influence of the sophists in the history of Anglo-American jurisprudence is that rhetoric and law developed together, and it was the sophists, not Plato or Aristotle, who first recognized the importance of rhetoric to the delivery of practical justice. The sophists saw, as Plato did not, that the truth of a case could never be known and that the more probable truth must prevail. In a modern democratic society, Plato's conception of truth is of little help. Although a trial may take the form of a dialectic, the participants have little concern for an abstract truth: each side simply wants to win.

Hardly anyone doubts that the Greek idea of justice is implicit in the modern Anglo-American judicial system, so when we begin to talk about the responsibility of teachers to themselves—not to be confused with their responsibility to their students—we must be aware of the unavailability of any absolutes of truth and justice. The relative importance of the "appearance" of things and events in contradistinction to their abstract "reality" was the central concern of the sophists as it is of the legal machinery of today. This view of the world, typified by the philosophy of Protagoras, leads to an ethics of relativism and to legal realism, the view that the interpretation of laws is a pragmatic, situational concern deeply involved with social practices and economic interests. The sophistic dialogue mainly turned on the opposition between the terms *physis* and *nomos*, between nature, on one hand, and custom or social convention, on the other. Because of their heritage of Protagorean relativism, the Greeks tended to think that all customs were equally valid, and therefore equally arbitrary. Thus, the struggle was between arbitrary conventions and the *real* state of things. There was also a third view, voiced by the younger sophists, that no natural law exists in human society; and if there is no universal conduct, then all laws, including so-called natural laws, are also arbitrary and must either be accepted or rejected as such.

This view merges into the social compact theory of laws, the view closest to the modern sociological view, that of *nomoi* as a social contract. Historically, the weight of opinion seems to have turned at some point in the latter half of the fourth century in favor of the practical necessity of social constraints, perhaps as the only possible response to a weakened belief in the power or even the existence of the ancient gods. Thus, Lycophron is represented in Aristotle's *Politics* as having argued in support of the right of the state to concern itself with morals. Aristotle writes,

> The political society becomes a mere alliance . . . and law becomes a compact, and as Lycophron said, a guarantor of men's rights against one another, not a means of making the citizens good and just. (1280b10)

It is important to note that the laws of men, although recognized as necessary to the state, have at this historical point been reduced to the negative role of protecting the citizens from each other and are not admitted to the greater role of codifying ethics that was the place of the divinely-inspired laws. This shift in the role of laws—from statement of the moral code to carefully worked-out set of rules for maintaining relationships—is one of the more important trends we can find in the sophistic works, for it surely foreshadows the limited role of human laws in modern value determinations.

The Opposition of Morality and Justice

It is interesting that the Greeks were thinking about this limitation on the theoretical purpose of laws very early; limitations were examined by Hippodamus before the middle of the fifth century BCE. Protagoras wrestled with the question of how *nomos* equates to *dikaion* (morality) and to *dike* (justice)—a question still problematic today. Socrates represents Protagoras as saying that according to the social compact, the application of the laws might lead to an unjust decision in an individual case, but the citizen must still accept it in consideration of the benefits of citizenship. The conflict between those who see the law as equating to justice and those who see it merely as a barrier against individual harm is with us still. It remains an integral part of the very current debate between the formalists/idealists and pragmatists/antifoundationalists in legal theory who argue either that the law is a transcendent force for good or it is a temporary expedient in a relativistic society.[1]

With that background, I will discuss some of the responsibilities and some of the problems and difficulties that lie in wait for writing teachers not from a moral or ethical perspective but from a legal one.

I am going to discuss both the justice that intervenes to provide parity between individuals and the justice that constrains the relations between the individual and the state. I will consider new developments with respect to two areas of law that writing teachers are likely to encounter in practicing their profession: the obligation to intervene or refrain from intervening in the life of another, and the right of privacy. My purpose is to briefly suggest how teachers may protect themselves and their students against being visited by punishing lawsuits without crippling their efforts to teach and without consulting a team of lawyers every few minutes.

The Law and the Impulse to Do Good

Good people generally try to do good, that is, to behave ethically, and this applies especially, it seems, to teachers. Evidence of this impulse to do the right thing for students is amply provided in Richard Miller's article, "Fault Lines in the Contact Zone." Miller refers to Scott Lankford's paper, "Queers, Bums, and Magic," delivered at a CCCC panel in 1992, in which Lankford discusses an essay written by a student in one of his writing classes at Foothill College in California. The student described a trip he and some of his friends made to San Francisco to study "queers and bums." Miller reports that

> The narrative follows the students into a dark alleyway where they discover, as they relieve themselves drunkenly against the wall, that they have been urinating on a homeless person. In a frenzy, the students begin to kick the homeless person, stopping after '30 seconds of non-stop blows to the body,' at which point the writer says he 'thought the guy was dead.' Terrified, the students make a run for their car and eventually escape the city. (392)

Lankford received a variety of responses from his aroused audience, a preponderance of which, according to Miller, were that the student should "be removed from the classroom and turned over either to a professional counselor or to the police. Such a response, audience members argued repeatedly, would be automatic if the student had described suicidal tendencies, involvement in a rape, or having been the victim of incest" (392). Miller remarks that one member of the audience, substantiating the point, mentioned Marc LeClerc, saying that the Canadian gunman had revealed his hatred of women to many of his college professors prior to his murderous rampage. Of course both the alleged crime of the student and LeClerc's reported murderous rampage are extreme cases, hence most of us are unlikely to face these circumstances. Also, as Miller points out, the story by the California student may be fictional, and, indeed, Lankford responded to it as if it were fictional, thus avoiding confrontation but perhaps not legal responsibility.

What I find appalling about Miller's discussion is the assumption of most of the audience, without having met the student or read his essay, and without any knowledge of what the law requires and allows, that they could "send" him anywhere they chose. As I will show later, the obligation to prevent injury or death by reporting presumed facts in a student's paper to authorities may be limited by the prohibitions on invasions of privacy. This sort of conflict between rights and duties abounds in American law, for example, between free speech and hate speech, or between the right of privacy and the right of the public to know certain private matters. What places the Lankford case in the list of things that teachers need to be concerned about, besides teaching, is that sometimes (as I will later show in another California case) students actually mean what they say.

Perhaps surprisingly to some, ordinarily one has no duty to assist a helpless person or one in danger (*Plutner v. Silver Association*), and no person is required to assist a stranger, even though he or she may be able to do so without the slightest danger to himself or herself (*Lloyd v. S.S. Kresge*). The courts have on occasion recognized a moral obligation to assist the ill or helpless but no legal obligation, and the courts have recognized a legal obligation only when the relation of the parties justifies it (*L. S. Ayres & Co. v. Hicks; Carey v. Davis*). The courts in most jurisdictions have repeatedly said that a person not responsible for the perilous situation of another is generally under no duty to rescue (*Thomas v. Williams*) except when some special relation exists that creates an unusual obligation apart from the situation, such as the relation of doctor or nurse to patient. One may, of course, rescue in one way or another (the term *rescue* is not limited to such heroic acts as jumping overboard to save a drowning person) without any legal obligation. However, one does so at his or her peril, because the courts have also repeatedly said that if one actively or inactively pursues a course of action that may result in injury, then one may be liable for the injury. For example, sending a customer away who is so intoxicated that he is liable to injury results in liability for that injury (*Adams v. Chicago Great Western R.R.; Louisville etc. R.R. v. Ellis*).[2] The almost universally accepted (with exceptions) Good Samaritan Rule provides that one who undertakes to act, even gratuitously, is required to exercise due care (*Blessing v. U.S.*).

Consistent with this, the law imposes no liability upon those who stand idly by and fail even to try to rescue a stranger who is in danger (*Miller v. Canal Corp.*). The national law digest of choice for most lawyers and judges, *American Jurisprudence*, lays out the well-settled law in matters of this type: "Those duties which are dictated merely by good morals, or by humane considerations, are not within the domain of the law" (57 *AmJur* 2d 98). The law requires that the savior and victim must have come in contact and the victim must have been injured thereby (57 *AmJur* 2d 99).[3] For example, railroads have been held responsible for helping a person injured by a train even though the railroad was innocent of causing the harm in the first place. A teacher understanding this must be aware that offering assistance to a student who appears to the teacher to be in peril or offering assistance to someone that the teacher thinks is imperiled by a student is not without risk to the teacher.

A citizen has the right to inform police of criminal activity (*U.S. v. Bufalino*) but apparently has no automatic duty to do so (*People v. Iannacone*).[4] In Lankford's case, it is not as clear to the law as it was to many of his listeners that he had the right and duty to inform the police. Nor does one have the legal obligation to do anything else. "As a general principle, and in the absence of statute or special relationship or circumstances, an individual has no duty to protect another from a criminal assault or willful act of violence of a third person" (57 *AmJur* 2d 104).[5] But, as in all legal principles, there are exceptions. Whether or not a duty exists depends upon "a weighing of the relationship of the parties, the nature of the risk, and the public interest in the proposed solution" *(Romero v. National Rifle Association).*[6] Even in a position of trust, as baby-sitter, a person was held not liable for an attack by a child on another child *(Campbell v. Haiges)*. On the other hand, in an Arizona case and in a California case the court held that a special relationship giving rise to a duty to warn a potential victim exists between a school and a student (*Jesik v. Maricopa Community College; Peterson v. San Francisco Community College District*). In jurisdictions that recognize the tort liability of public schools and institutions of higher learning, the underlying legal principle seems to be that ordinarily the school is not liable for the acts or omissions of students except where school personnel were negligent and such negligence was the proximate cause of injury to other students. So where injuries are inflicted by a student with "known assaultive propensities," the school (and perhaps the teacher) may be liable to the injured student (*Ferraro v. Board of Education*). The opposite result was obtained in another recent case where a student was struck without warning because the school had no prior notice of the attacking student's "assaultive proclivities" (*May v. Board of Education*). These are civil cases. What of possible criminal liability for failing to be a good samaritan? The general rule is that such omissions to act are not punishable, but certain specific failures to take action may result in criminal liability, for example, between parents and small children, husband and wife, employers and employees (Moore 57). Apparently the exception to the rule flows out of the close relationship between the parties in which trust and responsibility are implied. Naturally, professionals are also liable for neglect of duty to patients, clients, and so on.[7] As usual, there is another exception: If one voluntarily assumes the care of another, he or she must follow it through. But there is no duty under criminal law to rescue a stranger in distress in the absence of a statute imposing such a duty (Freeman 1458). Vermont has such a statute, and it imposes the duty to give "reasonable assistance" to one in grave danger if there is no risk to the rescuer. Except in states having statutes similar to the Vermont law, a physician seeing someone lying ill or injured by the side of the road as the physician drives by is legally (although not morally) better off not stopping. The good doctor who stops may be sued for negligence, but the bad doctor who drives on cannot be touched.

This state of affairs may be in the process of change, according to a number of legal scholars. In a recent symposium, Samuel Freeman, citing European laws that impose criminal liability for failure to rescue, argues for such statutes in the United States because "some cases of failure to rescue those in distress are sufficiently wrong [in moral terms] to warrant retribution." Freeman goes on to say that because "the law recognizes no civil liability [in these cases] is not an argument against the criminalization of such omissions" (1460). Similarly, Mary Kate Kearney, arguing for the imposition of civil liability for failure to act in child abuse cases, explains that injuries to and the deaths of abused children are adequate warning. She notes that children who die from abuse have been beaten over a long period of time (406). Susan Collier, writing in the *Pacific Law Journal*, agrees: "Abuse is not simply the product of one isolated event; it represents a pattern of violence" (191). In Kearney's view, an adult "who knows or should know of ongoing child abuse should have an affirmative duty to take reasonable steps to protect the child" (407).[8] We should note that these are not legal decisions by judges I am citing but law review articles by legal scholars. However, legal journals do have an influence on cases—they are often cited by counsel and by judges—and they may signal a change that is coming, perhaps belatedly, in this area of the law. While one's moral sense should be delighted by this foreshadowed trend toward a broadening of the exceptions to the Good Samaritan Rule, or even its complete overturning, one's sense of self preservation should at the same time be alerted; wherever in the history of the law some lawyers have succeeded in broadening the application of the law, they and other lawyers have quickly used the new rule to sue.

We should not take too much comfort from the fact that some of the journal articles cited are about child abuse, for the term *child* has been very broadly interpreted at times. How old, then, might a "child" be in the law? In *Farwell v. Keaton* the court held that a sixteen-year-old had a duty to seek medical attention for his injured friend of the same age. Could an eighteen-year-old, a freshman in a writing class, also be a child for this purpose? Perhaps, if the child were living at home under a parent's presumed care, and the injured child were suing a teacher on the theory that the teacher had the kind of "special relationship" of care that Kearney suggests creates a duty to act. That the teacher may in law—if not in fact—have this kind of special relationship may be inferred from another California case. *In Tarasoff v. Regents of the University of California* the court held a campus psychologist liable for the death of Tarasoff, a student, because her boyfriend, Poddar, revealed to the psychologist his intention to kill her. The court reasoned that a "special relationship" existed because "the relationship gave the therapist the opportunity to detect the danger to the victim" (Kearney 419). That line of reasoning should probably strike fear into the hearts of many teachers who are accustomed to receiving confidences from their students. More worrisome still is Kearney's assertion—for which she offers ample argumentative support—that "an examination of the bases for the duty, however, reveals that the duty *arises in spite of, not because of* the special relationship . . . between Poddar and his therapist" (419; emphasis added). Kearney infers that applying to the campus police the same criteria as the court applied to the therapist "the court easily could have concluded that the campus police fit within the special relationship exception and owed Tarasoff a duty of protection" (421). I infer that it would not be difficult to fit many teachers within the same exception to the Good Samaritan Rule and hold them responsible for the acts of students confiding in them, particularly, I believe, if the teacher made a practice of listening to these confidences.

The Right to Privacy

The right to privacy is the right to be free from (1) the unwarranted appropriation or exploitation of one's personality, (2) the publicizing of one's private affairs with which the public has no legitimate concern, or (3) the wrongful intrusion into one's private activities, in such manner as to outrage or cause mental suffering, shame, or humiliation to a person of ordinary sensibilities (*Jacksonville State Bank v. Bamwell; Smith v. National Broadcasting Co.*). The concern in this area of the law is not liberalism run amok; the right to privacy is as basic a right as freedom of speech, against which the right of privacy must be balanced. Such prominent legal scholars as Zelman Cowen and Louis Brandeis have argued for the importance of preserving this right against the creeping encroachment of the press, the government, and others. In the 1977 *Tagore Lectures* Cowen warned that

> The right to privacy goes far beyond a claim to be protected from the unjustifiable intrusions of the press and the other media. A rapidly developing technology, which makes it easily possible to exercise surveillance over the activities and conduct of individuals by the use and exploration of a variety of devices, has become a matter of increasing and anxious concern. (9)

Half a century earlier, in the celebrated *Olmstead* case, Brandeis, in dissent, argued prophetically: "Discovery and invention have made it possible for the Government by means more effective than stretching upon the rack to obtain disclosure in court of what is whispered in the closet" (478). These dire predictions have little to do with teachers, directed as they are to the Big Brother tendencies of even Republican forms of government, but, as I said earlier, the writings of legal scholars often indicate trends in the law. When judges become concerned that the balance between privacy and free speech and freedom of the press is being tipped too far from individual rights in the direction of societal rights, decisions begin to appear that reverse the direction of the trend. Teachers, therefore, although they do no wiretapping or infrared surveillance, need to be concerned and to react in specific ways that I will discuss a little later.

This "Right to privacy" should be understood, along with actions for defamation,[9] as the contrary of free speech and freedom of the press protected (not guaranteed) by the First Amendment to the Constitution: "Congress shall make no law . . . abridging the freedom of speech or of the press." As Cowen notes, "Those words [in the First Amendment] have been considered many times by American courts in the present context and the tenor of judicial interpretation has not been harmonious" (27). Perhaps the problem causing this lack of predictable consistency is that, as R. Wacks suggests, we need to narrow the focus of our concern with psychological privacy and come to grips in this Information Age with the right to maintain privacy of information:

> Instead of pursuing the false god of "privacy," attention should be paid to identifying what specific interests of the individual we think the law ought to protect. . . . At the core of the preoccupation with the "right to privacy," is the protection against the misuse of personal, sensitive information. (10)

Terry Thomas term "personal information" as "information relating to our family life, personal relationships and that which we consider private. It would include health and sexual matters, and anything which has no direct significance for the community at large" (14). This definition, of which the American and English cases generally approve, blankets many of the papers submitted by student writers to their teachers, particularly but not exclusively in their first and second year writing courses.

Of course, teachers do not go out of their way to publicize the personal disclosures of their students, but there are some things that we as writing teachers do that may constitute publication amounting to an actionable offense. One thing I do with many of my colleagues is talk about student papers, sometimes quoting or paraphrasing from them, sometimes reading from them, sometimes asking a colleague to read the paper and informally comment on it. Our interest in these papers is not prurient or unhealthy but purely professional. Nevertheless, the teacher may be guilty of "publicizing one's private affairs" or of "misuse of personal, sensitive information." Another thing I do that I know many other writing teachers do is have students read their papers in class. Often students are happy to read aloud to the class, but occasionally a student asked to read an A paper to the class demurs. Of course, I never push students to read aloud when that happens, but I have on occasion read aloud a paper with some very personal revelations without disclosing the name of the writer. I think, based on my recent research into the law of privacy, that I will discontinue this practice (unless I can obtain the written consent of the student before class) because of the risk that one or more students will correctly guess the name of the student writer. Third, I sometimes ask students to form groups of three or four in class and read and comment on the papers within the group or even exchange their papers with another group. I have occasionally had students ask to be excused from having their papers read by other students because of the confidential matters disclosed in them.

It seems likely that in England the disclosure by a teacher of personal information about a student acquired by reading the student's paper submitted as a required assignment would be liable for damages in a suit for "breach of confidence." The English Law Commission defines this kind of action as "a civil remedy affording protection against the disclosure or use of information which is not publicly known and which has been *entrusted to a person in circumstances imposing an obligation not to disclose or use that information*" (10; emphasis added). This sounds, not too surprisingly, like the language used to impose a "special relationship" in Good Samaritan cases. In my opinion it requires no stretch to cover the student-teacher relationship. American law is similar but perhaps not so clear-cut. According to a California court, the right to privacy is not so much one of right to total secrecy as it is the "right to define one's circle of intimacy" (*Kinsey v. Macur*). Another court offers this additional distinction between invasion of privacy and defamation: the gist of the cause of action in privacy cases is not injury to one's public reputation as in defamation cases, but injury to emotions and consequent mental suffering (*Jensen v. Times Mirror Co.*). Generally speaking, the presence of malice is not required as an element—as it would be in a defamation case—nor is the absence of malice a defense.

The requirement of public disclosure means disclosure to many as opposed to one or a very few others (*Corcoran v. Southwestern Bell Telephone Co.*). In the Corcoran case the court held that a teacher, whose score on a certification test was erroneously mailed to another teacher, was not entitled to recover for invasion of privacy. However, there is no magic formula or quantified body count that determines how many people must be involved before the public disclosure requirement is satisfied, and the means of disclosure can be any whatsoever, including by word of mouth (*Cummings v. Walsh Construction Co.*). Going back to the practice of reading students' papers to colleagues or discussing papers with them, on the authority of the

Corcoran case one might assume that discussing a paper with one colleague or allowing one colleague to read it would be safe. I think that the practice can never be safe, because one can never be sure that one's colleague will not discuss the paper with others or that the student's name will not come up in the discussion. Clearly, republication in an article of excerpts from students' work, even if not a copyright violation, would certainly be such publication as would meet the test for a cause of action. Perhaps it is not necessary to mention this, as I assume that none of us would be so foolish as to publish any portion of a student's writing without the written consent of the student. It seems pretty clear to me that telling or even asking a student to read a paper aloud in class can be considered a publication that meets the test for slow death by litigation. Most students would not dream of withdrawing their oral consent to read to the class, but it only takes one recantation and litigious parents to produce a memorable result, hence my insistence on written consent. The same risks probably apply to student conferencing, where the student's paper might be read by only two other students. One cannot be sure that one of the other student readers will not go back to the dorm and regale other students with details from the potentially embarrassing paper. But what of the student's consent when he or she compliantly handed over the paper to be read by other students? I would not recommend that anyone rely on this; as attorney for the embarrassed student I would argue in court that the teacher's authority in the classroom overrode the student's implicit objection, and I would probably win that skirmish.

How far, then, should we go—or perhaps I should say, where must we stop—to keep from invading the privacy of our students? Powerful writing, as all writing teachers know, often comes out of personal experience, especially in the case of high school and first-year college students. Student writers, we have found, begin to find their voices in many writing classes by writing about themselves, their families, and their friends, including boyfriends and girlfriends. But, as Edward Jenkinson points out,

> That kind of writing has prompted some critics of education to charge teachers with invasions of student and family privacy. Some critics are scrutinizing textbooks and student assignments, searching for what they deem objectionable, including invasions of privacy. Nothing escapes their attention. (9)

We should note that what Jenkinson is talking about is not publication of students' writing that invades their privacy, even writing that invades their privacy, but writing assignments that could possibly invade their privacy. Is Jenkinson's concern farfetched? Not at all. For example, there are Mel and Norma Gabler of Longview, Texas who (according to Jenkinson) have been reviewing textbooks for three decades. As the founders of Educational Research Analysts, they try to scrutinize every book submitted for adoption by the school system in the state of Texas. Jenkinson reports that "they review textbooks line by line, searching for material that does not coincide with their points of view. One of those points of view is that students in Texas need to be carefully guarded against invasion of their right to privacy. Jenkinson offers many examples of the Gablers' vigilance, such as this, from their list of objections to a book published in 1983:

> "Skills to Practice," page 433.
> The text: "Write a personal profile of yourself. Describe your goals and how you plan to reach them."
> Objection: Invasion of Privacy. (20)

I do not offer this example of the alertness and care of those in opposition to personal writing assignments because I think that writing assignments as such pose a real threat to teachers. I frankly doubt that the mere giving of a writing assignment that asks students to discuss their goals or to give a "personal profile" of themselves is itself actionable. On the other hand, such an assignment does open the door for the kind of disclosures in the handling of which teachers must exercise great care.

There is one other kind of disclosure that teachers might occasionally encounter, so I will discuss it, briefly. This is a report about a student to some office or person within the school, perhaps a progress report or something similar. Ronald Eades, writing in the *Journal of Law and Education*, cautions that teachers and counselors must make reports and statements about students "only as required or permitted by the job," in which case they are probably "privileged," that is, exempt from legal action (115). But when are teachers' statements about students actually "required or permitted" and who decides these things?

Conclusion

Although there are many ways to fall afoul of the law and lawyers, I have addressed only those legal issues that are especially significant for teachers of writing. My omission of others should not be understood as advocating a carefree attitude towards sexual harassment, copyright laws, censorship and the many other pitfalls that the law has placed in the path of all of us who teach and many of us who don't. Moreover, and here I must sound like the lawyer I once was, my brief discussion does not and could not possibly cover every one of the problems and outcomes that may occur in our society under the complicated, ambiguous and comprehensive legal system of America in the 1990's. Teachers should not take for granted that they know and understand the law in all its varieties because they have read this or any other effort to simplify that which cannot be simplified.

Readers may note that I have asked more questions than I have answered. Some teachers might be critical of a student paper that does this, although coming from a lawyer it should be excusable. To earn that excuse I would like to close with some advice that falls short of practicing law without a license but is nevertheless helpful. I shall do so by addressing first Miller's advice to us as teachers not to "give free rein to one's self-righteous indignation" and not to "exile students to the penitentiaries or the psychiatric wards" (408). Part of this is good advice: teachers had better not in this especially litigious time in our history give free rein to indignation or any other emotion. On the other hand, to assume, as Miller seems to, that we can choose whether to send potential perpetrators to the asylum, send them to prison (as if we actually had the power to send them someplace), or invite them to our offices for tea, cookies, and a chat, is probably being too optimistic. I would emend Miller's well meaning advice with this: know the law and stay within it or you may find yourself supplementing your day job as a teacher with a night job at a fast food outlet, trying over the span of twenty years to pay off a punishing judgment.

Does this mean everyone bent on a career in teaching ought first to attend a law school and then practice trial law for ten or fifteen years? I hope not; it seems to me we have more than enough lawyers already. What I can suggest as a positive measure is for teachers to find out whether their school has legal guidelines for dealing with potential problems of the sort I have discussed. If not, then teachers ought to make it their business to get something in writing from the school, and, for good measure, I would suggest pushing for training sessions and workshops led by the school's legal representatives so that, whatever happens, teachers can at least show that they have done exactly what experts have advised them to do. Be wary, therefore, but do not cower: the law is essentially fair, and goodwill is always rewarded with a just outcome—well, nearly always.

Notes

1. For more on this binary opposition, see Gale 46–54 and 61–64.
2. See also *Carey v. Davis*.
3. See also *Thomas v. Willia*.
4. Note that one can report criminal activity but that one should not report mere suspicions as criminal activity without running the risk of defamation of character or invasion of privacy. Moreover, merely saying that one would like to kill another or even that one intends to kill another is not criminal activity.
5. See also *St. Louis-San Francisco R.R. v Mills*.
6. See also 57A AmJur 2d 104.
7. See also Macaulay 493–94.
8. See also D'Amato.
9. Defamation is similar to invasion of privacy but differs from it in that an action for defamation requires that the publication must be of information that is both derogatory and untrue.

Works Cited

Aristotle. *Politics*. Trans. Ernest Barker. Oxford: Oxford UP, 1946.

Collier, Susan A. "Reporting Child Abuse." *Pacific Law Journal* 15 (1983): 189–215.

Cowen, Zelman. *Cowen's Individual Liberty and the Law*. Dobbs Ferry, NY: Oceana Publications, 1977.

D'Amato, Anthony. "The Bad Samaritan Paradigm." *Northwestern U.L.R.* 70 (1975): 798–812.

Eades, Ronald. "The School Counselor or Psychologist and Problems of Defamation." *Journal of Law and Education* 15 (Winter 1986): 115.

Freeman, Samuel. "Criminal Liability and the Duty to Aid the Distressed." *U. Penn L.R.* 142 (May 1994): 1455–92.

Gale, Fredric G. *Political Literacy: Rhetoric, Ideology, and the Possibility of Justice*. Albany, NY: SUNY Press, 1994.

Jenkinson, Edward. *Student Privacy in the Classroom*. Bloomington, IN: Phi Delta Kappa Educational Foundation, 1990.

Kearney, Mary Kate. "Breaking the Silence: Tort Liability for Failing to Protect Children from Abuse." *Buffalo L.R. 42.2* (Spring 1994): 405–62.

Lankford, Scott. "'Queers, Bums, and Magic': How Would You Grade a Gay-Bashing?" Paper presented at CCCC, Cincinnati, March 19, 1992.

Law Commission. *Breach of Confidence*. Report No. 110. London: Command 8388, HMSO, 1981.

Macaulay, Lord. *Works of Lord Macaulay*. Vol. 1.7. London: Longmans, Green & Co., 1897.

Miller, Richard. "Fault Lines in the Contact Zone." *College English* 56 (April 1994): 389–408.

Moore, Michael S. *Act and Crime: The Philosophy of Action and Its Implications for Criminal Law*. New York: Oxford UP, 1993.

Thomas, Terry. *Privacy and Social Services*. Brookfield, VT: Ashgate Publishing, 1995.

Wacks, R. *Personal Information*. Oxford: Clarendon Press, 1989.

Table of Cases

Adams v. Chicago Great Western R.R., 135 N.W. 21

Blessing v. U.S., 447 F. Supp. 1160

Campbell v. Haiges, 504 N.E. 2d 200

Carey v. Davis, 180 N.W. 889

Corcoran v. Southwestern Bell Telephone Co., 572 S.W. 2d 212

Cummings v. Walsh Construction Co., 561 F. Supp. 872

Farwell v. Keaton, 240 N.W. 2d 217

Ferraro v. Board of Education, 212 N.Y.S. 2d 615

Jacksonville State Bank v. Bamwell, 481 So. 2d 863

Jensen v. Times Mirror Co., 634 F. Supp. 304

Jesik v. Maricopa Cty. Comm. College Dist., 611 P. 2d 547

Kinsey v. Macur, 107 Cal. App. 3d 265

Lloyd v. S.S. Kresge, 270 N.W. 2d 423

Louisville etc. R.R. v. Ellis, 30 S.W. 979

L.S. Ayres & Co. v. Hicks, 40 N.E. 2d 334

Miller v. Canal Corp., 632 P. 2d 987

Olmstead v. U.S., 277 U.S. 438

People v. Iannacone, 447 N.Y.S. 2d 996

Peterson v. San Francisco Community District, 685 P. 2d 1193

Plutner v. Silver Association, 61 N.Y.S. 2d 594

Robertson v. Allied Foundry & Mach. Co., 447 So. 2d 720

Romero v. National Rifle Assoc. 749 F. 2d 77

St. Louis-San Francisco R.R. v. Mills, 271 U.S. 344

Smith v. National Broadcasting Co., 292 P. 2d 600

Tarasoff v. Regents of the University of California, 551 P. 2d 334

Thomas v. Williams, 124 S.E. 2d 409

Traudt v. Chicago, 240 N.E. 2d 188

Tubbs v. Argus, 225 N.E. 2d 841

U.S. v. Bufalino, 518 F. Supp. 1190

Chapter 3

Ethics and Ideology in the English Classroom

Phillip Sipiora

> Ethos anthropoi daimon.
> Character for man is destiny.
> —Heracleitus

> We always eventually find, *at the edge of the text*, the language of ideology, momentarily hidden, but eloquent by its very absence.
> —Pierre Macherey

The role of ethics in the humanities in general, and in the English writing classroom in particular, has only recently begun to reassert itself as relevant to contemporary education as it was to classical *paideia*. Yet English writing instructors clearly have not embraced the notion that the "pursuit of virtue" (Werner Jaeger's phrase) is integral to humanistic education. Indeed, the recurring question over the role of ethics in the classroom is often constructed interrogatively: Can one teach ethically?[1] How might one teach ethically? Perhaps at least some of us have lost the thirst for making in the English classroom the formal judgments of right and wrong that so inspired the ancients. In speaking of the widespread neglect in making ethical judgments, Barbara Herrnstein Smith has remarked, "It is a curious feature of literary studies in America that one of the most venerable, central, theoretically significant, and pragmatically inescapable set of problems relating to literature has not been a subject of serious inquiry for the past fifty years" (17). This charge is surely relevant to the historical teaching of writing.

The term "ethics," deriving from the Greek word *ethos* meaning "character" and carrying a multiplicity of nuances and complications,[2] has been a master word in Western humanism for a long time, certainly at least back to the golden age of Greece and probably much further than that.³ Ethics, as a normative concept, plays a central role in Plato's philosophical system, Aristotle's metaphysics and rhetorical order, and Isocrates' influential program of "cultural philosophy." However, ethics also played a significant role in literary education, or "grammar" in ancient Greece. Indeed, students in the gymnasium and ephebia were encouraged to engage systematically in the inference of morality as a strategic result of their literary study. Dionysius tells us that the first three stages of grammatical study were directed toward evaluation—the finest flower of the grammarian's art. But literary analysis clearly was not restricted to aesthetic judgment; it also meant discerning morality. It also signified that students searched for heroic examples of "human perfection"—the ideal of *arete* or virtue, which, according to Jaeger, "is the central ideal of all Greek culture" (169). The poets, especially Homer, and Mediterrean and Afroasian students sought a substantively articulated ethical code. An acquaintance with the poets was regarded as a fundamental characteristic of the educated person, an explicit sign of "culture."

There is no question about the critical significance of ethics in ancient education, particularly in the corpus of Aristotle,[4] and especially in his emphasis on the "good" in political education, and in the interdependence of private morality and public good. In the *Nicomachean Ethics*, Aristotle's major treatise on ethics, he distinguishes between excellences of the intellect (*dianoetikas*) and excellences of character (*ethikas*). Book Two explores how one obtains "moral virtue," which is "the product of habit (*ethos*) and has indeed derived its name . . . from that word" (II.i.1). Aristotle's emphasis on the relationship among virtue, character, and habit invokes the importance of practice (which has special relevance to the contemporary English classroom): "The virtues on the other hand we acquire by first having actually practiced them, just as we do the arts. . . . [W]e become just by doing just acts" (II.i.4). The practice of establishing (and critiquing) ethical positions is a transactional activity: "It is by taking part in transactions with our fellow-men that some of us become just and others unjust" (II.i.7). According to Aristotle, the conjunction of practical wisdom and ethics facilitates human ends as well as means: "Prudence as well as Moral Virtue determines the complete performance of man's proper function: Virtue ensures the rightness of the end we aim at, Prudence ensures the rightness of the means we adopt to gain that end" (VI.xii.6).[5] This conjunction of ethics and practical wisdom (prudence) is a critical issue in the contemporary writing classroom.[6]

In the English classroom, "ethics" usually signifies the articulation or criticism of patterns, norms, or codes of conduct: the taking of a stand for or against something on the presumptive ground that it is either good or undesirable.[7] Ethics as a formal activity also involves the apprising and, sometimes, revising of behavioral codes. Exploratory discourse, for example, often investigates the proposing of differing ethical standards, new patterns of conduct, and various other recommendations. Students often challenge established codes or rules, written and unwritten, by defying them, a commonplace practice in many writing classrooms. This activity is often called critical writing because it exposes received opinion to rigorous scrutiny, subjecting this writing to the transactions of which Aristotle speaks. In this age of "fragmentation," the ethical debate has often moved from the articulation of uncontested "right" principles and conclusions to moral dilemmas. And nowhere is the debate more contested than in the ideological arena, which necessarily carries explicit ethical implications. Indeed, no ideological position can be taken without acknowledging underlying ethical dimensions, and this would include an understanding of how ethics and ideology are energized in the classroom. One such understanding involves the relationship between the timely and the reasonable.

Paul Tillich, a twentieth-century theologian, has written extensively on the relationship between *kairos* and *logos*, which might loosely be defined as timeliness and reason. Tillich has articulated a calculus of ethics that is based on the conjunction of the timeless or absolute with the immediacy of contextual experience. More specifically, he suggests that values are represented by *logos* and the occasions of the circumstantial or contingent are represented by *kairos*.[8] Ethical judgments, according to Tillich, are never static but are always dynamic. The concept of ethics necessarily invokes the meeting of inherited, "timeless" systems of values with the situational context of the immediate circumstances. That is, *logos* must confront *kairos*; transcendent values are inert until catalyzed by the exigencies of the circumstantial. The implications of Tillich's marriage of *logos* and *kairos* are significant for the writing classroom. Such implications include the emergence of ethical stances based on the interaction between "old" values and "new" circumstances. Ethical judgments in the writing classroom, or any other classroom, should be the culmination of the confrontation between *kairos* and *logos*.[9]

The English classroom, whether oriented toward reading or writing or both, is one logical setting for thrashing out ethical issues and the examination of ethical implications according to Tillich's model of *kairos* and *logos*. Our students need this kind of intellectual stimulus and there are ways in which, for example, a course in advanced writing might appropriate the dimensions of ethics suggested by Tillich in bringing ethical theory down to the level of the ordinary language and pragmatic situations that students continually address. It is critical for students to perceive the connections between the ethical activities of the classroom and issues of ontology.[10]

Complications of Ideology

"Ideology," like "ethics," has become a master word in the official discourse of the human sciences, as evidenced by its ubiquitous presence in the titles of panel presentations at regional and national meetings in the humanities, as well numerous scholarly essays over the past dozen years.[11] Indeed, there has been a plethora of recent books and articles which focus on one aspect or another of ideology. There are good reasons for examining ideology in the writing classroom, as John Schilb points out:

> [C]omposition studies isn't exempt from ideology itself. If we should embrace the invitation to analyze the composition of ideologies, we should also ponder the ideologies of composition. This latter imperative seems pressing for at least two reasons. First, as the profession is increasingly institutionalized through graduate programs as well as undergraduate curricula, its impact on the lives of students broadens. Second, as more composition scholars adopt the kind of scientific discourse often associated with professionalism, the chance of obscuring ideology behind merely 'empiricist' language increases. (22)

Yet the investigation of ideology in composition studies or elsewhere begs an obvious question. What has ideology come to mean? Has the ubiquity of the term devalued its currency to the point where the term is without any specialized meaning? (And was "ideology" ever without complications?) Twenty-five years ago Clifford Geertz observed that the term carries negative connotations in American academic circles, a form of "radical intellectual depravity" (197). This is still often the case, although the term carries different connotations in language studies: "In discourse theory, for example, the reference to ideology has little to do with overtly held political doctrine or even a coherent system of beliefs. Instead, it is used to refer to systems of meaning, to the sum of ways in which we work and live, and to the symbolic ways we represent our existence to ourselves" (Clifford 121).

Numerous literary critics and philosophers have called attention to the problematics of the concept of ideology.[12] In speaking of the myth of cultural ideology, Roland Barthes points out how the metastasis of cultural attitudes delimits its power of critique: "Bourgeois ideology can therefore spread over everything and in so doing lose its name without risk. . . . It is therefore by penetrating the intermediate classes that the bourgeois ideology can most surely lose its name" (139–40). Commenting on linguistic reference, particularly ideological ascription, Paul de Man observes that "it would be unfortunate to confuse the materiality of the signifier with the materiality of what it signifies," and he proceeds to define ideology as "the confusion of linguistic with natural reality, of reference with phenomenalism" (*Resistance* 11). Richard Rorty has remarked, "There is a large and depressing literature about the equivocity of the term 'ideology'" (229). David McLellan notes that ideology is a slippery concept, as it touches upon one's essential predispositions and beliefs: "Ideology is the most elusive concept in the whole of the social science. For it asks about the basis and validity of our most fundamental ideas" (1). Terry Eagleton defines ideology as the "ideas and beliefs which help to legitimate the interests of a ruling group or class specifically by distortion and dissimulation" (30). He goes on to characterize ideology as "false or deceptive beliefs not from the interests of a dominant class but from the material structure of society as a whole" (30). John Thompson calls attention to the strategic relationship between ideology and language: "The analysis of ideology *is*, in a fundamental respect, the study of language in the social world, since it is primarily within language that meaning is mobilized in the interests of particular individuals and groups" (73). Wayne Booth asserts the inseparable connection between ideology, value, and all discourse: "[I]deology cannot be conceived as something to be avoided at all costs; it is inescapable in every moment of human speech. We speak with our ideology—our collection of languages, of words-laden-with-values" (57). For Mikhail Bakhtin, language systems as a whole represent the ideological: "Languages are philosophies—not abstract but concrete social philosophies, penetrated by a system of values inseparable from living practice and class struggle" (471). And for Louis Gates, no system of critical interpretation is without an ideological foundation: "No critical theory . . . escapes the specificity of value and ideology" (15). It is this pursuit of the locus (and focus) of power and authority that has caught the attention of the advanced writing classroom.

Ideology, as it is sometimes presented, implies a stability that is highly questionable, particularly in writing situations where students represent ideological positions that have not been vigorously interrogated. As Gayatri Spivak has observed, "Received dogma is another name for ideology. Ideology in the critical sense does not signal an avowed doctrine. It is rather the loosely articulated sets of historically determined and determining notions, presuppositions, and practices, each implying the other by real (but where does one stop to get a grip on reality?) or forced logic, which goes by the name of common sense or self-evident truth or natural behavior in a certain situation" (*IOW* 97). One cannot speak of writing or reading without a working notion of ideology as a more expansive concept than individual consciousness or will, yet reading and writing courses are taught all the time on the assumption that teachers and students can interpret and create texts without considering ideological or ethical assumptions and implications.

Spivak's reading of ideology raises yet another side of the issue. What is *not* ideological at a time in which it is often taken for granted that most human intellectual activities (particularly roles played out in higher education) reflect assumptions, mores, and social, cultural, political, and economic activities that constitute ideological frames of experience? Can there still be opposition to explicit attention to ideology within the academy? There would seem to be declining support for the view that English studies should focus primarily or exclusively on the nature of the aesthetic.[13] It is obvious that the guiding organization of English studies, the Modern Language Association, has in recent years presided over a dwindling number of sessions devoted to aesthetics. Regional associations and organizations seem to be following the same pattern. Ideology is the sub-stratum of what are called the human sciences in Europe and the humanities in America.[14] I would like to reflect upon that statement, exploring the subject of ideology in the teaching of writing, particularly advanced writing. The central issue—ideological presence in English studies—is important because if English studies as a disciplinary activity is to have any meaning, now and in the next decade, "our" ideological formulations have to be questioned, as collective doctrine(s) and individual manifestations. And I am not suggesting, as do some, that "ideology" reflected in American colleges and universities is fundamentally monolithic, but rather that "ideologies" in their full pluralistic possibilities and oppositions be brought out of the closet, where they have been forced to hide because of academic formalities and niceties fostered by traditions and circumstances.[15]

To advocate that one read or write with ideological sensitivity is not to suggest that one is capable of working "outside" of the issue(s) under investigation. As Ducrot implies in his theory of argumentation, "[O]ne cannot draw a clear line of separation between descriptive and argumentative levels of language: there is no neutral descriptive content; every description (designation) is already a moment of some argumentative scheme; descriptive predicates themselves are ultimately reified-naturalized argumentative gestures" (qtd in Zizek, 11). If students, as readers and writers of texts, are made to believe in and perpetuate what might be called institutional perspectives or "received dogma" in the classroom, principally in literary texts in literature courses and professional and student writing in composition courses, then the work of the teacher and student can go on quite comfortably, as long as there is no serious and intensive questioning of the texts that are read and written. This is not to say that some teachers of writing do not attempt to recognize the ideological implications of what we and our students say and write; clearly many do. Yet the major problem lies not exclusively in our failure to recognize our blindness to ideology, but also in failing to name those ideologies that circumscribe us: "Whether we know it or not, all of us have an ideology, even those who claim openly that they do not. We all value something—property, friends, the law, freedom, authority and so forth. We all have prejudices, even those who claim to be free of them" (Macridis and Hulliung 1). Recognizing and openly talking about ideologies is not easy; it requires personal commitment and courage. Students need tenacity to voice their beliefs as they come to grips with ideological positions, especially their own unexamined attitudes and frames of reference. Students must be encouraged to write papers as private as well as public individuals. Advanced writing should emphasize the importance of bringing both ethics and ideology into consciousness, and awareness is a critical issue. It is imperative that we develop a pedagogy that integrates both the verbal text(s) and the social text(s) and dissolves distinctions between the private and the public. Understanding the dimensions, contradictions, and implications of our ideologies, as much as this is possible, is strategic to the teaching/learning of writing, and I would like to propose some general elements of an ideologically-conscious approach to advanced writing, especially the issue of forestructure.

In generating their texts, students necessarily bring their pasts with them, the "previously acquired and culturally interpretative scheme" in the ideological unconscious, as codified by Frederic Jameson, and the concept of "forestructure" as codified in the hermeneutics of Heidegger. We cannot forget that language is traversed by the formations and systems of representations that define a particular society's cultural and ideological assumptions. Whatever the characteristics of a student's background, part of the pedagogical calculus is an awareness of the limitations and possibilities of discourse, written and spoken. In the words of Paul Ricoeur, there must be a "hermeneutics of suspicion"; in the lexicon of Paul de Man and his co-rhetorico-critics, readers must confront the *aporia* present in all discourse. Students must become "critical rhetoricians," aware of the power and potential of their language as well as sensitive to effects produced through the language of others. The stakes are high, as Derrida has warned: "In our techno-scientifico-militaro-diplomatic incompetence, we [that is, language specialists] may consider ourselves as competent as others to deal with a phenomenon whose essential feature is that of being *fabulously textual*, through and through." ("No Apocalypse" 23). Because language is our primary weapon, or at least should be, in ameliorating conflict, students must engage and challenge inside *and* outside ideologies. One utilitarian benefit of post-structuralist reading and writing is that this approach problematizes or "opinionizes" much professional and student writing, and *doxa* has its place in the writing classroom. Once students begin the act of critical reading, they begin to accept questioning, omissions, incompletions, and contradictions—according to circumstances—in the texts they write as well as read. And for those writing classes that use no text other than student writing in a process-oriented, workshop atmosphere, this methodology may motivate students to investigate their fellow students' writing in a way fundamentally different from traditional approaches directed toward the production of consensually determined, "epistemic" texts.

A common criticism of this type of teaching writing asserts that it is subversive and undermines authority. Yet this kind of subversion, I would argue, is profitable. It is insurgent because beliefs are questioned, particularly the received opinions held by all students, and is that not what a humanistic education is designed to accomplish—allowing free individuals to exercise their minds to their fullest potential? Neither ideology nor ethics are minor issues here. To read and write, fully conscious of the limitations and possibilities of language, forces students to rethink their cultural, social, political, and ethical beliefs as they reform them under more contingent and open conditions. Reading *is* writing, as Derrida insists, because both activities are analytical as well as evaluative. Reading and writing are lifetime processes, rather than hastily completed projects at the end of a term. As Robert Scholes points out, "Learning to read books—or pictures, or films—is not just a matter of acquiring information from texts, it is a matter of learning to read and write the texts of our lives" (qtd. in Gillespie and Singleton 451). The process of the kind of critical reading and writing I am talking about might easily be integrated into common points of departure in writing classes. Instructors often ask students to write "about a problem," which at many colleges and universities involves literary problems in second-semester courses and disciplinary problems in advanced or writing-across-the-curriculum courses. The *investigation* of problems, rather than the "solving" of them, is precisely what this methodology emphasizes, and a crucial first step in the process of investigation is the recognition of the importance of ideology.

Applied Ethics and Ideology

Most colleges and universities in America now require at least one writing course beyond the freshman year. This course is generally conducted without specific subject matter; indeed, the "content" of the course is usually an examination of the various components of the process of composition, process and invention having generally informed classroom procedures over the past ten years or so. Students are often encouraged to write about topics in the area of their majors.

I would suggest that advanced writing students (and perhaps first-year students too) be required to write more than one essay (in fact, several essays), emphasizing the articulation, as far as it is possible, of the unconscious and unquestioned ideological formulations undergirding their thinking and writing, with an emphasis on an explicit discussion of the ethical and ideological grounds of these processes (with attention to explicit and implicit implications of the subject matter). For many students, this writing will be the only opportunity in which they examine formally contemporary political issues, many of which will directly affect their lives. Most students, I hope, are concerned about such issues as AIDS (more than one hundred *million* persons will be infected by the year 2000, according to the World

Health Organization), and environmental problems (we risk losing much of the rest of the world's fragile rain forests, the source of so many medical advances). Moreover, drug testing, nuclear armament, a reconstituted Europe, political and economic change in Hong Kong, America's relationship with China, Latin America, the Middle East, and the many other important geo-political issues that confront us today might profitably be addressed in the writing classroom. Each of these explicitly ideological topics carries ethical assumptions and implications. One cannot write persuasively about AIDS or any other "ideological" topic without at least implying a moral stance. Yet unless a student is a government, political science, sociology, or history major, there is often little opportunity to approach these issues in a logical and systematic manner, or to attempt to persuade fellow students, much less themselves, of the efficacy and morality of a particular position.

The kind of advanced writing course I am talking about would first, and this issue is perhaps the most decisive of all, encourage students to self-reflexively examine their values, or "ethics." We should teach values and one such value is the importance of continually challenging and rethinking our values. Those forestructures housing our values are in a constant state of change and we must be sensitive to subtle shifts in attitudes and beliefs. In the writing classroom there should be an emphasis on value theory and pragmatics, yet no composition textbook, to my knowledge, considers value theory and use in an organized, systematic manner. Students should be encouraged to articulate and defend the grounds of their value-based propositions and conclusions, and encouraged to recognize contradictions (perhaps unresolveable) between their internal value systems and those of others in any given investigation. As Heidegger says, there is no discourse act that is value-free.

Traditional (and some non-traditional) writing teachers routinely ask their students for thesis statements, a writing strategy graphically emphasized in freshman writing. Why not ask our students to provide an explicit statement of teleology in their writing—what ends or purposes do they a hope to achieve and in which ways are their teleologies ethically determined and ideologically grounded? Many writing teachers expect students to follow accepted, formal prescriptions of grammatics, syntactics, and pragmatics. Why not ask students to consider (and acknowledge) the guiding deontological principles which undergird their writing? Which rules, coded and uncoded, determine their values—those dynamic beliefs and doctrines that reflect their thinking and stimulate their writing? I believe that student writing which self-reflexively considers its guiding principles and ends is ideologically and ethically more informed and informing, a richer mode of writing than traditional classroom compositions.

There is no question that it is sometimes difficult for students (and instructors) to confront the ideological assumptions of others, much less their own. Yet this kind of transactional confrontation has an inherent ethical component. The very act of "positioning" carries ethical and ideological overtures. In speaking of literary interpretation, J. Hillis Miller has argued that the act of reading is necessarily ethical: "In what I call 'the ethical moment' there is a claim made on the author writing the book, on the narrator telling a story within the fiction of the novel, on the characters within the decisive moments of their lives, and on the reader, teacher, or critic responding to the work" (8). The claim to which Miller refers is a dual responsibility between author and reader to make choices in the process of interpretation. This act is necessarily ethical because it involves the reader in assuming responsibility for taking interpretive positions. One cannot read without accepting (and rejecting) premises, assumptions, corollaries, conclusions, and so forth. Miller's position is echoed in the work of Jean-François Lyotard, who argues in *The Differend* that disputes are adjudicated through phrases, the basic currency of discourse. The protocols for linking phrases are called genres: "Genres of discourse determine stakes, they submit phrases from different regimens to a single finality: the question, the example, the argument, the narration, the exclamation are in forensic rhetoric the heterogeneous means of persuading. It does not follow that differends between phrases should be eliminated. Taking any one of these phrases, another genre of discourse can inscribe into it another finality" (29). The careful choosing of genres becomes an ethical act precisely because it calls for the assumption of responsibility in making choices. Lyotard insists that one "ought to link on like this in order to get to that" (116). For Lyotard, the linking of phrases is clearly an ethical obligation.

What Miller and Lyotard suggest about the act of reading also applies to the act of writing. Levinas, Lyotard, and Miller, like Aristotle, locate ethics in commitments to acts. Our students make many choices, ethical as well as ideological, every time they write, and they bear a responsibility to be aware of the ideological dimensions of the decisions they make. Escape from the ideological bonding of their positions is not possible. As Spivak says, "One cannot of course 'choose' to step out of ideology. The most responsible 'choice' seems to be to know it as best one can, recognize it as best one can, and, through one's necessarily inadequate interpretation, to work to change it, to acknowledge the challenge" ("Politics" 351). Students must be aware not only of their value positions, but also, as much as it is possible, of those of their readers, as Wayne Booth has remarked: "[A]ny ethical criticism we try to develop in a systematic way must take into account the ethics of the reader as well as an ethics of what is written" (79).

Most academic (and professional) writing is recursive, yet writers at all levels often do not begin to critically examine the ethical positions or ideological bases (and implications of their positions) of others or themselves until they begin to articulate them (which, of course, changes them as them as part of the process of articulation). As ideological positions and their implications move from the unconscious to the conscious, from the implicit to the explicit, students quite knowingly make choices (Miller's ethical moment), promoting a more rigorous understanding of themselves and their writing. Miller insists that "the ethical moment in reading leads to an act. It enters into the social, institutional, political realms" (4). So, too, does the art and act of writing.

I regularly teach an advanced writing course entitled, "Writing about Social, Political, and Ethical issues," which is specifically intended to motivate students to write and talk about ideological assumptions. This particular course probably fails more often than it succeeds, most likely because I am unable to elicit sincere, critically rigorous responses from students—that is, responses in and about *their* writing and that of others that is critical in the ways suggested above. Perhaps the writing classroom, or at least mine, is too concerned with respecting the sensitivities of others, for there is obviously a personal investment in the decision to ignore ideology. In peer review, or whatever other term describes student discussion of student writing, there is often a silent agreement that if you leave my writing alone, I'll leave yours alone, and we can cite inoffensive mechanical or stylistic weaknesses, conveniently ignoring issues which are naturally contentious, or, worse yet, be forced to confront our own unexamined opinions. The writing process is too often an unnatural act.

The Writer and the "Other"

A critical dimension of this unnatural act is the relationship of the writer (or self) to the "other." It is a complicated, tense relationship, with positions and forces of authority and power shifting according to changes in circumstances. Mikhail Bakhtin reminds us that our discourse never remains ours once disseminated: "Language is not a neutral medium that passes freely and easily into the private property of the speaker's intentions; it is populated—overpopulated—with the intentions of others. Expropriating it, forcing it to submit to one's own intentions and accents, is a difficult and complicated process" (294). Emmanuel Levinas locates ethics in the relationship between the self and the other (his term is *alterite*, alterity: things, elements, otherness): "For me, the term ethics always signifies the fact of the encounter, of the relation of myself with the Other: a scission of Being in the encounter—without coincidence!" (qtd. in Critchley 17). The agitator in the ethical transaction is the manner in which the other sparks self-recognition in the self: "For the ethical relationship which subtends discourse is not a species of consciousness whose ray emanates from the I; it puts the I in question. This putting in question emanates from the other" (*Totality* 195). One dimension of the "putting in question" movement is the generation of positive resistance, a force which is necessary for productive dialogue. For Levinas, positive resistance is a discernibly ethical act: "The 'resistance' of the other does not do violence to me, does not act negatively; it has a positive structure: ethical" (*Totality* 197). According to John Wild's reading of Levinas, a response to the resistance of the other, to the "questioning glance," is necessary for effective, ethical discourse that translates into social action: "[I]f communication and community is to be achieved, a real response, a responsible answer must be given. This means that I must be ready to put my world into words, and to offer it to the other. There can be no free interchange without something to give. Responsible communication depends on an initial act of generosity, a giving of my world to him with all its dubious assumptions and arbitrary features" (14). It is the phenomenological dimension of the discourse with the other that renders behavior, especially language acts, as ethical: a "world into words."[16] In the philosophy of Merleau-Ponty, one must practice the "explication of perceptual relations," as they are revealed in the subject's "opening to the world."[17]

Maurice Blanchot, like Levinas and Merleau-Ponty, examines the phenomenology of the other (Blanchot's approach is fictive rather than conceptual), writing about the relationship between the self and the other (with specific human reference). In *The Writing of the Disaster*, Blanchot observes the dynamic of the "receding other" as one attempts to embrace the conceptualization of him or her: "In the relation of *myself to the Other*, the Other exceeds my grasp. The Other:

the Separate, the Most-High which escapes my power—the powerless, therefore; the stranger, dispossessed" (19). We can never come to know the other in any sort of comprehensive way, of course, but engaging the other can increase our understanding of the complexities of our readers so that we can write in a self-conscious, ethical gesture that is not naive. Such a moment has been summed up eloquently by Simon Critchley: "[T]he paradigmatic ethical moment is that of being pre-reflectively addressed by the other person in a way that calls me into question and obliges me to be responsible. This is the concrete context for ethics" (48). An awareness of ideological contexts very much involve the ways in which students perceive themselves, and this awareness is a critical first step in promoting self-conscious, self-critical discourse. As Lester Faigley remarks, "No matter how well we teach our students, we cannot confer power as an essential quality of their makeup. We can, however, teach our students to analyze cultural definitions of the self, to understand how historically these definitions are created in discourse, and to recognize how definitions of the self are involved in the configuration of relations of power" ("Judging Writing" 411). One critical dimension of the cultural definition of the self is the (self) recognition that the self is composed of many "selves." Michel de Certeau has articulated (and exemplified) the multiple roles that one might play according to given cultural situations. Wlad Godzich summarizes de Certeau's establishment of situational context: "There results an internal division of the subject between the kind of self that one needs to be in certain situations, generally linked to one's means of livelihood, and the kind of self that one is in other settings. The individual no longer feels his or her self to be a whole, but rather a series of diverse zones, subject to differing constraints, frequently of an irreconcilable sort" (ix).

Should not teachers of expository writing promote the engagement and challenge of these various selves, as they reflect both inside and outside ideologies? It is critical that students see the ideological context of their writing as larger than their personal histories. As Spivak argues, "It is difficult to speak of a politics of interpretation without a working notion of ideology as larger than the concepts of individual consciousness and will" ("Politics" 347). We are reminded that each analytical situation is circumstantial and no understanding of ideology, personal and "otherly," is capable of sustaining comprehensive critique without simultaneously suggesting new avenues of interrogation. Indeed, students should be encouraged to recognize the inherent limitations of reading and writing, as Edward Said suggests: "The critical consciousness is awareness of the differences between situations, awareness too of the fact that no system or theory exhausts the situation out of which it emerges or to which it is transported. And, above all, critical consciousness is awareness of the resistance to theory, reactions to it elicited by those concrete experiences or interpretations with which it is in conflict" (242). Advanced writing should necessarily be argumentative and persuasive. This position is not radical pedagogy. Most teachers of expository writing encourage some combination of these kinds of discourse. Yet I doubt that these forms of writing still dominate most advanced writing syllabi. I suspect that much student writing continues to focus on informative essays that address topics of disciplinary or personal interest written for a non-specialist reader. Over the past decade, the metaphor of community has been a powerful informing principle for the teaching of writing. Yet, as Greg Myers has argued, the result all too often is an ideology that encourages cohesion and discourages open disagreement.[18] I also suspect that many writing classes do not emphasize exploratory writing, at least in the most rigorous sense of the term. I am not speaking of a sanitized, soft question-posing kind of writing that generates very little rigorous inquiry. I refer to a kind of ideological thinking/writing that the *OED* refers to as "Relating to, or occupied with ideas, especially of a visionary kind; dealing with ideals as opposed to facts; ideal, speculative, idealistic." Ideological writing is performative in calling attention to the ethical assumptions and implications of the subject at hand.

This kind of composition represents a rigorous *dialectical* writing that begins the process of exploration with a critical investigation of the author's assumptions as well as examining oppositional grounds, perspectives, and forms of discourse. This method of inquiry acknowledges the dimension (and force) of those linguistic elements that are absent yet reveal themselves in the trace of their presence.[19] Derrida has referred to this concept of writing as *gram* or *differance*, a gesture in which "[t]he play of differences supposes, in effect, syntheses and referrals which forbid at any moment, or in any sense, that a simple element be *present* in and of itself, referring only to itself. Whether in the order of spoken or written discourse, no element can function as a sign without referring to another element which itself is not simply present" (*Positions* 26). These elements are, of course, the Derridean concepts of differences and traces (of traces), components of rigorous thinking and writing that inform the ethical and ideological dimensions of any discourse activity. For this kind of exchange to take place productively, there must be a radical embrace of resistant thinking/writing. Students should be encouraged to explore the forces of *multiple* positions in tension with one another, thus moving away from monologism and towards dialogism. Bakhtin has been particularly articulate in challenging notions of the atomic self, disengaged and separate from outside influences.

Writing Without Ethics

Let me offer a brief example of what this activity might entail, of what is often produced as irresponsible discourse. In a recent, advanced writing class, I asked my students to explore a local issue that has generated considerable controversy. A student, who was probably the best "natural" writer in the class, wrote an essay investigating the water problem in Florida's Pinellas county, the densest county in the state with millions of residents. His essay was unassertive. He demurely pointed out interwoven conflicts among pro-growth advocates, environmentalists calling for restricted growth, and the complicated technical problem of the destruction of the aquifer that serves most of South Florida. His essay was successful in so far as it was stylistically fluid, mechanically sound, and generally informative. His uninformed classmates and I learned something about the basic state of the water supply, purported causes, adversaries, and so forth. However, on the grounds of radical exploration—a confrontation of ethical and ideological stances—the essay was a dismal failure. This "A" student did not examine the basis of his own position; he was obviously on the side of the environmentalists and assumed, undoubtedly correctly, that everyone in the class agreed. After all, who could be against clean drinking water? The implication was clear that growth advocates and industrial polluters were mutually culpable in harming the environment. The ideological beliefs and attitudes informing his position, as well as his undergirding moral justifications, were blandly asserted rather than vigorously demonstrated.

The essay was fundamentally descriptive and, therefore, unacceptable as far as the goals of the course were concerned—to encourage rigorous exploratory writing. I was dissatisfied with the student's inability to articulate the beliefs, doctrines, and desires that constitute the substructures of his position (and those of others), as well as his failure to speculate, using more than clichés, on the rationales for oppositional perspectives. I don't believe that this academic exercise encouraged him to hone his critical skills, which must be one of the goals of any writing course. His ethical stance and ideology—as well that of the "other" and "others"—remained static and unexamined, thus the goal of ethics as *ethos* (mode of character) was not fulfilled. In his essay he did not "live" his ideological attitudes and moral beliefs.[20] This example demonstrates a dangerous situation if advanced writing claims any pretense to teaching rigorous thinking. In order to do this, unconscious ideologies must be brought to some level of consciousness and he clearly failed to do so. My student neither explained nor asked how his position was constructed out of ethical and ideological influences, and he never articulated why the reasoning of his adversaries was unconvincing. The loci and conditions of his stance never emerged. *Logos* never met *kairos* and the self never confronted the other.

Notes

1. Virginia Anderson offers a detailed discussion of how ethical obligations and ideological exigencies come together in the contemporary writing classroom. In particular, she addresses the issue of confrontation and how it relates to ethical obligations.

2. Heidegger interprets *ethos* as "abode" or "dwelling place," suggesting that the meaning of ethics is where one experiences daily activities, the "being" of one's life. For further discussion, see Bernasconi (122–24), Critchley (15–16), and Comas (in this collection) (79ff).

3. This is the position taken by Martin Bernal in his controversial explanation of humanistic influences preceding the Greeks (*Black Athena*).

4. For Aristotle there is one controlling practical science, the way of human goodness or happiness. A human being is a political animal (*zoon politike*), according to Aristotle, and lives in communities for the pursuit of a good life, which necessarily involves social action. The science of politics is instrumental in determining the way of life in which happiness consists and, by implication, in promoting the form of government and social institutions that secure this kind of life. As Aristotle, says, "The good of man must be the end of the science of politics" (I.ii.7–8).

5. Book Six of the *Nichomachean Ethics*, which analyzes the intellectual virtues, contains a detailed discussion of the importance and interconnections between virtue and practical wisdom.

6. Timothy Crusius refers to prudence as "ethics in action," underscoring the moral dimension of prudential thinking and action.

7. As James Kinneavy points outs in his essay in this collection, it is crucial that writing classrooms have a language of morality in which ethical positions may be presented, particularly if students in the class employ varying ethical codes. Writers generally draw their ethical positions from a teleological system (moral codes are identified as a means to an end) or a deontological paradigm (moral codes are determined by written and unwritten norms or rules of conduct; for example, the Ten Commandments). Oftentimes, ethical positions are compatible with both teleological and deontological systems. One benefit of introducing students to formal moral systems is that it gives them an opportunity to systematize (and question) those ethical positions as they surface from the unconscious to the conscious.

8. In 1941, at the height of Tillich's influence, W. H. Auden published a poem, "*Kairos* and *Logos*," which calls attention to the circumstantial in determining critical moments in value judgments:

The apple tree that cannot measure time
Might taste the apple yet not be condemned
They to enjoy it must renounce the world . . . .

Auden's poem and Tillich's theory reflect a strategic dimension of determining theological values with an important implication for the writing classroom: rejection of unified explanations of absolute or relative value(s).

9   In *Just Gaming*, Lyotard argues that justice is best served when ethical decisions are made on an individual basis (*kairos*), rather than under the rubric of absolute justice (*logos*). In summarizing Lyotard's position on the ethical subject, Lester Faigley states: "Instead of starting with preestablished criteria and then applying those criteria to a particular case, Lyotard holds out for an indeterminate notion of justice that acknowledges the singularity of the particular event. Thus Lyotard's notion of justice is one compatible with the Sophistic doctrine of *kairos*" (*Fragments* 236). This position is close to Levinas' emphasis on the concrete particularity of the other person, on the notion of individuals determined by the exigencies of circumstances, rather than according to universal laws.

10 Robert Bernasconi recounts the following story about Heidegger that underscores the connection between ethics and ontology. Soon after the publication of *Being and Time* (1946), Heidegger was asked by a student when he was going to write a treatise on ethics. Although Heidegger never did write a treatise on ethics, he responded to this question many years later in his "Letter on Humanism," in which he quotes Beaufret as saying that he has for a long time been trying "to determine the relationship between the relation on ontology to a possible ethics." Heidegger then refers to his own position—the very questioning of supplementing ontology with an ethics "no longer has any basis in this sphere [of the truth of being]" (qtd. in Bernasconi 122-23). In other words, Heidegger did write a treatise on ethics—*Being and Time*. Heidegger's conjunction of ethics echoes Tillich's concern for a pragmatic, ontological ethics and reinforces the ethical implications of the writing classroom.

11 It was not until 1990 that the Conference for College Composition and Communication designated "Ideology" as a formal category for presentation submissions.

12 Paul de Man's posthumous work, *Aesthetic Ideology*, offers a systematic and provocative rethinking of ideology, particularly in its relationship to aesthetics and rhetoric.

13 It would be naive to deny the historical (including contemporary) importance of aesthetics in the humanities, yet it is my presumption that the *delectare* justification for literary studies is less pronounced today than the critical examination of literary persuasion. It seems to me that a major concern is not only "what ideology" but "whose ideology."

14 A more extensive discussion of this topic would expand on differences between "humanistic" education in America and elsewhere, particularly Europe, as Stuart Hall has pointed out, ideology embraces a pragmatics that is generally absent from American education.

15 Ideology, like, feminism, would seem to be one of those polysemous terms that cannot be expressed in the singular. It may be more useful to speak of competing ideologies within larger ideological frameworks.

16 For an extended reading of Levinas and the "ethics of exteriority," see Peter Baker.

17 Kinneavy points out the relevance to expressive discourse of Merleau-Ponty's emphasis on the subject and its relationship to the "outer" world as a multi-disciplinary movement: "Merleau-Ponty maintained that this emphasis on the consideration of the subject and the consideration of the 'other' through intersubjectivity is characteristic not only of philosophy (in phenomenology and existentialism), but has parallel movements in language, religion, sociology, and other disciplines" (*Theory* 397).

18 There has been much probing discussion of the "openness" of classroom writing scenes and their ideological implications. In addition to Myers, see Spellmeyer, Villanueva, and Walters.

19 Geoffrey Chase has observed that discourses are also marked by the absence of ideological features, which in turn may not promote the intended political purposes of the writer: "[It is the] inclusion *and/or* absence of particular cultural values, processes, and dynamics that give any discourse on composition a particular expression, one that may or may not serve emancipatory interests" (23).

20 Phenomenology and performance theory have much to offer for the writing classroom, particularly in the works of Husserl, Cassirer, Barthes, Merleau-Ponty, and Levinas.

Works Cited

Anderson, Virginia. "Confrontational Teaching and Rhetorical Practice." *College Composition and Communication* 48 (1997): 197–214.

Aristotle. *Nichomachean Ethics.* Trans. H. Rackham. Ed. G. P. Goold. 1926. Cambridge: Harvard UP, 1982.

Baker, Peter. *Deconstruction and the Ethical Turn.* Gainesville: U of Florida P, 1995.

Bakhtin, Mikhail. *The Dialogic Imagination.* Trans. C. Emerson and M. Holquist. Austin: U of Texas P, 1981.

Barthes, Roland. *Mythologies.* Trans. Annette Lavers. New York: Hill and Wang, 1972.

Bernal, Martin. *Black Athena: The Afroasiatic Roots of Classic Civilization.* New Brunswick, NJ: Rutgers UP, 1987.

Bernasconi, Robert. "Deconstruction and the Possibility of Ethics." John Sallis 122–39.

Blanchot, Maurice. *The Writing of the Disaster.* Trans. Ann Smock. Lincoln: U of Nebraska P, 1986.

Bolter, Jay David. *Writing Space: The Computer, Hypertext, and the History of Writing.* Norwood, NJ: Erlbaum, 1991.

Booth, Wayne. "Freedom of Interpretation: Bakhtin and the Challenge of Feminist Criticism." Mitchell 51–82.

Charney, Davida. "The Impact of Hypertext on Processes of Reading and Writing." Hilligross and Self. 238–63.

Chase, Geoffrey. "Accommodation, Resistance and the Politics of Student Writing." *College Composition and Communication* 39 (1988): 13–22.

Clifford, John. "Ideology into Discourse: A Historical Perspective." *Journal of Advanced Composition* 7 (1987): 121–30.

Clifford, John, and John Schilb, eds. *Writing Theory and Critical Theory.* New York: MLA, 1994.

Critchley, Simon. *The Ethics of Deconstruction.* Oxford: Blackwell, 1992.

Crusius, Timothy W. *A Teacher's Introduction to Philosophical Hermeneutics.* Urbana: NCTE, 1991.

De Certeau, Michel. *Heterologies: Discourse on the Other.* Trans. Brian Massumi. Minneapolis: U of Minnesota P, 1986.

De Man, Paul. *Aesthetic Ideology*. Ed. Andrzej Warminski. Minneapolis: U of Minnesota P, 1996.

———. *The Resistance to Theory*. Minneapolis: U of Minnesota P, 1986.

Derrida, Jacques. "No Apocalypse, Not Now (full speed ahead, seven missles, seven missives)," *Diacritics* (1984). 20–32.

———. *Positions*. Trans. Alan Bass. Chicago: U of Chicago P, 1981.

Ducrot, Oswald. *Le dire et le dit*. Paris: Editions de Minuit, 1986.

Eagleton, Terry. *Ideology: An Introduction*. London: Verso, 1991.

Faigley, Lester. *Fragments of Rationality: Postmodernism and the Subject of Composition*. Pittsburgh: U of Pittsburgh P, 1992.

———. "Judging Writing, Judging Selves." *College Composition and Communication* 40 (1989): 395–412.

Gates, Henry Louis, Jr., "Writing, Race, and the Difference It Makes." *"Race," Writing, and Difference*, Ed. Henry Louis Gates, Jr. Chicago: U of Chicago P, 1986.

Geertz, Clifford. *The Interpretation of Cultures*. New York: Basic Books, 1973.

Gillespie, Sheena, and Robert Singleton. *Across Cultures*. 3rd ed. Boston: Alyn and Bacon, 1996.

Godzich, Wlad. Introduction. *Heterologies: Discourse on the Other*. By Michel de Certeau. Minneapolis: U of Minnesota P, 1986. vii–xxi.

Hampshire, Stuart. *Innocence and Experience*. Cambridge: Harvard UP, 1989.

Haraway, Donna. *Simians, Cyborgs, and Women*: The Reinvention of Nature. New York: Routledge, 1991.

Heim, Michael. *Electric Writing: A Philosophical Study of Word Processing*. New Haven: Yale UP, 1987.

Hilligross, Susan S. and Cynthia L. Selfe. *Literacy and Computers: The Complications of Teaching and Learning With Technology*. New York: LA, 1992.

Jaeger, Werner. *Paideia: The Ideals of Greek Culture*. Trans. Gilbert Highet. 2nd ed. 3 vols. 1944. New York: Oxford UP, 1971. Vol 3.

Kinneavy, James L. *A Theory of Discourse*. New York: W. W. Norton, 1980.

Landow, George. *Hypertext: The Convergence of Contemporary Critical Theory and Technology*. Baltimore: Johns Hopkins UP, 1992.

Lanham, Richard. *The Electronic Word: Democracy, Technology, and the Arts*. Chicago: U of Chicago P, 1993.

Levinas, Emmanuel. *Totality and Infinity: An Essay on Exteriority.* Trans. Alphonso Lingis. Pittsburgh: Duquesne UP, 1969.

Lyotard, Jean-François. *The Differend: Phrases in Dispute.* Trans. Georges Van Den Abbeele. Minneapolis: U of Minnesota P, 1988.

Lyotard, Jean-François, and Jean-Loup Thebaud. *Just Gaming.* Trans. Wlad Godzich. Minneapolis: U of Minnesota P, 1985.

Macridis, Roy C., and Mark L. Hulliung. *Contemporary Political Ideologies: Movements and Regimes,* 6th ed. New York: HarperCollins, 1996.

McLellan, David. *Ideology.* 2nd ed. Minneapolis: U of Minnesota P, 1995.

Merleau-Ponty, Maurice. *The Phenomenology of Perception.* Trans. Colin Smith. New York: Humanities P, 1962.

Miller, J. Hillis. *The Ethics of Reading.* New York: Columbia UP, 1987.

Mitchell, W. J. T., ed. *The Politics of Interpretation.* Chicago: U of Chicago P, 1982.

Myers, Greg. "Reality, Consensus, and Reform in the Rhetoric of Composition Teaching." *College English* 48 (1986): 154-74.

Poster, Mark. *The Mode of Information: Poststructuralism and Social Context.* Chicago: U of Chicago P, 1990.

Pringle, David L. "*Breaking the Sentence: Hypertext, Poststructuralism, and the Fragmentation of Grammar.*" Diss. U of South Florida. 1995.

Rorty, Richard. "*Feminism, Ideology, and Deconstruction: A Pragmatist View.*" Slavoj Zizek 227-34.

Said, Edward W. *The World, The Text, and The Critic.* Cambridge: Harvard UP, 1983.

Sallis, John, ed. *Deconstruction and Philosophy: The Texts of Jacques Derrida.* Chicago: U of Chicago P, 1987.

Schilb, John. "Ideology and Composition Scholarship.*" Journal of Advanced Composition* 8 (1989): 22-29.

Smith, Barbara Herrnstein. *Contingencies of Value: Alternative Perspectives for Critical Theory.* Cambridge: Harvard UP, 1988.

Spellmeyer, Kurt. "On Conventions and Collaboration: The Open Road and the Iron Cage." Clifford and Schilb. 73-95.

Spivak, Gayatri Chakravorty. *In Other Worlds: Essays in Cultural Politics.* New York: Methuen, 1987.

———. "Politics of Interpretation." Mitchell. 347-66.

Thompson, John B. *Studies in the Theory of Ideology.* Berkeley: U of California P, 1984.

Tuman, Myron C. *Literacy Online: The Promise (and Perils) of Reading and Writing with Computers.* Pittsburgh: U of Pittsburgh P, 1992.

Ulmer, Gregory. "Gramamtology (in the stacks of) Hypermedia, A Simulation: Or, When Does a Pile Become a Heap?" Tuman 139-58.

Villanueva, Victor Jr. "'Rhetoric Is Politics,' Said the Ancient. 'How Much So,' I Wonder." Clifford and Schilb. 327-34.

Vitanza, Victor, J. *CyberReader.* Boston: Allyn and Bacon, 1996.

Walters, Frank D. "Writing Teachers Writing and the Politics of Dissent." *College English* 57 (1995): 822-39.

Wild, John. Introduction. *Totality and Infinity: An Essay on Exteriority.* By Emmanuel Levinas. Pittsburgh: Duquesne UP, 1969. 11-20.

Zizek, Slavoj, ed. *Mapping Ideology.* London: Verso, 1994.

Chapter 4

Doing English

W. Ross Winterowd

The greatest ethical question in the field called English is this: What should we as professionals be *doing*?

Of course, anyone who has been around as long as I have can chart the phases in our evolution from the New Criticism through myth criticism to structuralism and beyond that to post-structuralism and the present era of division among deconstructionists, cultural critics, and new historians (with, of course, mostly indistinct boundaries and a good deal of overlap). In other words, English has always been in an exciting state of flux. However, through it all, from Ransom's 1938 manifesto, *The World's Body*, to the 1992 MLA manifesto *Redrawing the Boundaries*—members of the profession have been preoccupied with ontology and ontogeny, with thinking and writing about the nature of literature and its development. There's another way to state the point—actually a better way: scholars in English have, by and large, been preoccupied with questions of being to the virtual exclusion of doing.

In *The English Department*, at this moment in press, I argue that the field is no longer evolving. We are in a state of chaos preliminary to a revolution, and there is no clearer symptom of that chaos than the MLA volume *Profession 1996*, a collection of essays that assess the crisis and suggest remedies. I want to mention one of the pieces in this annual now, for it goes, though inadvertently, I think, right to the heart of the problem I'm talking about. In "Literary Study in the Transnational University," J. Hillis Miller asks, "What possible role can literary study have in the new technological transnational university?" "How can literary study survive?" is the question that Miller is really asking:

> In the new research university rapidly coming into being it will be extremely difficult to justify what we do in the old way, that is, as the production of new knowledge, the *Wissenschaft* appropriate in the humanities, as new knowledge about living things is appropriate in biology. New knowledge about *Beowulf,* Shakespeare, Racine, Hugo, or even Emerson, William Carlos Williams, and Toni Morrison is not useful in the same way new knowledge about genes is when it leads to the making of a marketable medicine . . .
> *The product of value we make in the humanities is discourse of a particular kind: new readings, new ideas.* (12; emphasis mine)

Reacting to the very real crisis in "English," Miller simply calls for more of the same—more papers to be published in the journals that line the walls of the English department conference room. However, as we shall see, *Profession 1996* also contains another view, one that buoys up my spirits and, I hope, indicates a change in the professional organization that wields such power, and such a change will entail realigning theories of imagination and invention.

From the Enlightenment until very recently, the doctrine of imagination and the doctrine of invention, coexisting in the English department as an institution, created both schizophrenia and a class hierarchy. All that transpired in the realm of imagination was valued; all that transpired in the realm of invention was devalued. Thus, teaching, writing about, and creating "imaginative" literature (i.e., poems, stories, and dramas) had transcendent value, while teaching, writing about, and creating "inventive" texts (themes, biographies, essays, histories) was devalued.

In his "Defense," Shelley provides what amounts to a standard explanation of what I call "imagination" and "invention." There are three entities in Reality: raw experience, the perceiving mind, and the shaping power of poetry or, to use a synonym, imagination, which Shelley opposes to reason thus: "Reason is the enumeration of quantities already known; imagination is the perception of the value of those quantities, both separately and as a whole" (277). Thus, Reason is amoral, and Imagination is moral. "Reason respects the differences, and imagination the similitudes of things. Reason is to imagination as the instrument is to the agent; as the body is to the spirit; as the shadow to the substance" (277).

Now before I proceed, I must underscore this point: *the imaginative-inventive dichotomy was, like most rigid binaries, false.* However, the results were very real.

Magnificent works, products of invention or, in Shelley's term, of reason, such as *The Snow Leopard, Pilgrim at Tinker Creek,* Dianne

Middlebrook's biography of Anne Sexton and David Lewis's equally magnificent biography of W. E. B. DuBois, *In Cold Blood*, Loren Eiseley's essays—these and other "inventive" works have been, at best, on the periphery of the canon. In fact, the canon as we have known it would have puzzled and appalled Samuel Johnson. In other words, the imagination-invention false dichotomy split and hierarchized the canon.

That same false dichotomy also resulted in the disaster of "composition." Whereas in creative writing, students produce pseudo-literature, valued because it is presumably the product of the imagination, in composition, students produce pseudo-non-literature, scorned because it is the product of invention. I borrow my terms, of course, from Robert Scholes, who says, "The literature/composition opposition must not only be deconstructed in critical writing, it must be broken down in our institutional practice as well" (7).

Do I need to say more? Composition is the fuel that drives graduate programs. Slevin has estimated that 70 percent of all postsecondary English classes are composition. Divorced from the rhetorical tradition, to which it rightfully belongs (just as cardiology belongs to the field of medicine and cliometrics now belongs to history), composition was stripped of theory, concepts, and history, and it was pursued as if it were outside the realm in which ethics operates. In fact, I avoid the bare term "composition" and speak instead of "composition-rhetoric," that term reminding us that the theory, history, and practice of composition are as integral a part of the humanistic tradition as is the study of literature.

My point, of course, is that both the devaluing of texts that, for whatever reason, are not viewed as "imaginative" and the ghettoization of composition have resulted from the same historical forces. The 1990 MLA convention program was the one hundred and sixth formal statement of the marginalization of composition-rhetoric and literary nonfiction. Of the 699 sessions listed, sixty-four were indexed under "literary criticism and theory," but none of these seemed directly to concern the "other" literature. Eleven sessions were indexed under "Nonfictional Prose," and six appeared under "Rhetoric and Rhetorical Theory." None appeared under "composition" theory, teaching, or other.

The status and practice of teaching in English has also puzzled me. Let me begin with an anecdote. One of my colleagues at USC argued that a justification for our graduate program was precisely this: we were preparing our students to teach literature. I responded thus: "We are teaching our graduate students about literature, but nothing about teaching literature, except the ability that comes by the way. A group of actors sitting around reading their scripts are not rehearsing the play." As Jasper Neel says in an unpublished paper, "No one finds it odd that only four of the MLA's 111 subgroups have 'teaching' in their titles even though the vast majority of the MLA's 32,000 members earn their professional incomes exclusively from teaching." The status of teaching in "English" has been paradoxical. On the one hand, we glorify the idea of teaching, but eschew pragmatic questions about pedagogy, questions about how to make our teaching more effective. On the basis of my own experience, I can assure you that the official code for promotion at USC puts heavy emphasis on teaching, but I can also assure you that when the department meets to consider tenure for an assistant professor, teaching weighs very little, and traditional literary scholarship tips the scales. A friend of mine, up for tenure at Cal State-LA, tells me that for promotion the department demands ten papers published in refereed journals, and that in a university with teaching as its primary goal!

One more shot at the point: Survey the journals in our field, as I did recently. Look through *American Literature, Chaucer Newsletter, Critical Inquiry, Kansas Quarterly, Kentucky Review, Notes and Queries, PMLA, Renaissance Quarterly, William and Mary Quarterly* . . . and I could go on and on with this list. You will find, as I did, that pedagogy, teaching literature, is not a fit subject for scholarly papers—except in such marginal, and largely ignored, journals as *Research in the Teaching of English* and *College English* (which, unfortunately, is becoming more and more like *PMLA*).

There is one notable exception. The theme of the January 1997 issue of *PMLA* is teaching—but the editor of the special edition hedges the organization's bet. In her introduction, Biddy Martin worries

> about the fate of reading practices that the term *literature* invites, permits, or requires, the fate of reading that suspends the demand for immediate intelligibility, works at the boundaries of meaning, and yields to the effects of language and imagination. (7)

In other words, Martin is both defensive and nostalgic, defending the tradition of *ars gratia artis* and longing for the good old days when literature for its own sake didn't need defending.

What I'm getting at is this: until very recently, English either banned or devalued any scholarship or activity that was "applied." I think that tacitly most of us agreed with Northrop Frye's conception:

> In literature, questions of fact or truth are subordinated to the primary literary aim of producing a structure of words for its own sake, and the sign-values of symbols are subordinated to their importance as a structure of interconnected motifs. Wherever we have an autonomous verbal structure of this kind, we have literature. Wherever this autonomous structure is lacking, we have language, words used instrumentally to help human consciousness do or understand something else. (74)

(Parenthetically, in response, I must say that I agree with Frank Lentricchia, who poignantly says, "For Frye actual history can be nothing but a theater of dehumanization, a place of bondage and torture" (26).)

Well, so far, although I've given readers nothing but gloom and doom, let me assure them that from this point forward, my basically sunny nature and my sanguinity about the future will prevail. I think the best is yet to be—primarily because our profession is refocusing its attention, from problems of being to problems of doing. In effect, the rest of what I have to say is a rebuttal to Miller's prescription.

I would like to limn a view of what I think "English" can become, an "English" in which literature would once again be *belles lettres* (with an updated and expanded definition of that term); in which writing would be simply writing, without the disastrous schism "creative" and "composition"; in which outreach to the community and to society at large would be valued as highly as literary scholarship of the traditional "term paper" variety; in which pedagogy would be viewed as a legitimate subject for research, as one of the most important problematics in the field.

The revision of "English" that I am about to outline is not, after all, so radical. I refer once again to *Profession 1996*, the annual statement issued by the MLA, which concludes with a report by the Commission on Professional Service.[1] One sentence captures the spirit of the report and should hearten everyone whose professional life is identified with English: "[Intellectual work] should contribute to the knowledge-related enterprises in which a faculty member is engaged as a faculty member and should explicitly invoke ideas and explore their consequences in the world of ideas, *the world of action*, or both"

(162; emphasis mine). Validating intellectual work in the world of action is, I think, a radical new stance for the MLA.

In any case, here is my take on the future of "English."

Literature as Belles Lettres

I have argued that distinguishing between "imaginative" and "non-imaginative" texts is destructive and epistemologically indefensible. To that discussion, I now add a few words.

First, reading theory is the juncture at which rhetoric and literary theory have met and are becoming one, and reading theory came into literary theory via reader-response criticism with Jane Tompkins's collection as the landmark.

And second, an anecdote that for years I have used to illustrate the futility of differentiating imaginative and inventive works involves the following text:

Lift receiver.
Listen for dial tone.
Deposit coin(s).
Dial number.

On a plaque in a phone booth this text is utterly colorless; its voice is that of a machine, a badly executed, recorded announcement.

With the title "AT&T," in a book with a bright, multi-colored cover and the title *Now Poetry*, the text is quite another matter. In the first place, the "voice" is now a wry takeoff on the mechanical monotone in the set of instructions. The whole text is a satire on the impersonality of American industry—that and much more. The sexual imagery is so blatant as to be almost embarrassing. Coins in slots. Fingers in —. Well, the text is so obviously pornographic, and I am so diffident about anything off-color, that I refuse to go further in my analysis.

Here are some examples of the spectrum of non-imaginative works:

Instructions for *The Snow Leopard*
Assembling a barbecue
"Hickery Dickery Dock"
The Wings of the Dove

Where does one draw the line between non-imaginative and imaginative? Does one want to draw such a line? Certainly I don't, even though the institution of English has obdurately done so since, at least, the rise of the New Criticism.

The master question that guides me as a teacher of composition is also the master question that is beginning to animate the study of literature: What does this text do? (Implied, of course, is the modifier "for the reader.")

The distinction between "imaginative" texts and "other" is one of the destructive myths that have created the English department mess. In the coming Utopia the canon will be reunified.

A Writing Program resulting from reunification of the canon will be the inevitable reunification of writing, abolishing the distinction between creative writing and composition. The Utopian writing program will be broad-based with options such as poetry workshops and technical writing. The juncture between, say, the business report and the short story will be the value placed on *craft* rather than *imagination*.

Some years ago, a craftsman named Harold Smith enlarged and remodeled our kitchen. His was a solo operation. He did the cabinetry and the tile work, the plumbing and the electrical wiring. On the day when the job was finished, Harold stood back and admired his work. "I enjoy taking a final look at my jobs," he said, obviously and justifiably satisfied with his impeccable craftsmanship.

At the very least, every writer should experience the satisfaction that comes from a job well done: a memo skillfully planned and executed, a business letter, an argument in favor of ungraded general education classes, a poem, a fictional narrative, an epic.

"Creativity" and "imagination" are such exalted terms that they must daunt most writers, but "craft" is homely and comfortable.

The Utopian writing program would be a hub-and-spoke operation, a *writing center* being the hub—a site where writers could congregate, talk about their craft, get help with problems, help others solve problems. The center would be a hub for all writers, from "basic" freshmen to upper-division students to faculty members. Genres would include every conceivable kind of writing: research papers, fictional stories, limericks, scientific reports, theses and dissertations, meditations–the sublime and the outrageous.

The "spokes" would lead to destinations (depending on institutions and demand) such as basic composition, advanced composition, writing for business majors, the essay, research writing, and so on. When demand for flights to a destination falls, airlines cancel the spoke; such would be the case in the ideal writing program.

In the writing center and the program, words such as "imagination" and "creativity" would be *infra dig*, replaced by "craft." The basis of all art is craft, and when the focus is on craft, when craft is honored, such lowly concerns as sentence structure and document design (typography, effective subheads, organizational strategies) gain value that they do not have when imagination is the god-term, yet it is often craft that makes the difference between an effective and an ineffective text, a text that does what its author intends, and a text that does not accomplish its purpose.

The writing center is a place for craftspersons to assemble. Instructors in the writing program teach the craft of writing—and, of course, in many fortunate instances a good deal more.

Teaching

I realize that I am repeating myself, but I feel strongly about this point. I find it hard to understand why the history, theory, and criticism of literature should be more challenging and interesting than the history, theory, and practice of teaching literature and composition, but, of course, I know why such "applied" scholarship is taboo among literary people, and my book *The English Department* is my attempt to explain.

In the Utopia of which I dream, however, teaching would be a primary concern. If literature is somehow good for people, then "delivering" that boon should be an important concern, as should defining the ways in which literature is salubrious and evaluating to determine whether or not the claims for the value of literature are valid or are simply chimerical rationalizations that enable English department faculty members to wander their ways undisturbed in the garden of poesy.

English departments need to define what they are attempting to accomplish, posit the best ways of achieving their goals, and evaluate results in relation to methods. One of my colleagues, for instance, argues that studying literature gives students the ability to think critically. Now that may or may not be a valid claim, but until she defines "critical thinking" and then demonstrates through evaluation that she has accomplished her purpose, her statement is merely one of those chimerical English-department rationalizations.

On the other hand, think of the post-revolutionary English department—coffee room talk concerning the human results of the literary enterprise and how best to achieve those results.

Outreach

The University of Southern California is an island fortress of learning, culture, propriety, prosperity, and entrepreneurial spirit in a sea of poverty, crime, grime, and hopelessness. As my colleagues write their literary papers on the Gothic novel or lesbian themes in nineteenth-century fiction or cross-dressing and the problem of identity in Restoration drama or (a title that, I must confess, I find wonderfully inventive) "Tropical Fruits," the world just outside the well-patrolled perimeters of the University seethes with anger and frustration; children learn early that their only possible hustle (and, after all, everyone has a hustle, even my colleagues and you and I) is peddling dope or doing burglaries. The balm of literature, the healing properties of poetry, the ennobling effect of great novels never seeps out of the university, to cross its boundaries into the community which, the English-department creed would hold, so desperately needs what the texts discussed by the term papers in the journals can bring to humanity.

There are noble exceptions, but, by and large, English departments are so preoccupied with scholarly papers with "new readings" and ontological knowledge that they have no time or energy to give to the world around them. In my department at USC, one faculty member is a remarkable exception to the rule. James Kincaid has, for several years, been working with kids in a program called the Neighborhood Academic Initiative. Jim teaches literature and composition to public school children, who, if they successfully complete a course of study in the Initiative, are assured of full-ride scholarships at USC. But I stress: this is the exception.

The Utopian English department would, of course, value outreach, perhaps even more highly than the production of literary term papers, or at least just as highly.

What an exciting world it would be, this English department.

One of my young colleagues was, justifiably, aglow with pride over having signed a contract for a book with Stanford University Press. Suppose a faculty member could experience the same glow of satisfaction, having increased the scope of reading and appreciation (and, perhaps, critical thinking) in a junior high school. And suppose this faculty member would receive as many kudos as the faculty member who had published a book on Mrs. Gaskell. It would be a wonderful place in which to spend one's career—or even the last part of one's career.

I am *not*—and I say again *not*—suggesting that traditional literary scholarship should be abandoned or devalued. *One*, but just *one*, of the important functions of an English department is producing new readings and new ideas about literature. I am merely arguing for an expansion of what we mean when we speak of the discipline we call "English."

As professors of English, not merely as citizens, we should gaze up from our texts and look at the teeming, tragic world around us. As professors of English, not merely as citizens, we should go out from our academies into the communities of which we are a part. We should be intensely concerned with making English *do* something.

Note

1. Members of the Commission are Robert Denham, Roanoke College; Claire Kramsch, University of California, Berkeley (Chair); Louise Wetherbee Phelps, Syracuse University; John Rassias, Dartmouth College; James F. Slevin, Georgetown University; Janet Swaffar, University of Texas, Austin.

Works Cited

Commission on Professional Service. "Making Faculty Work Visible: Reinterpreting Professional Service, Teaching, and Research in the Fields of Language and Literature." *Profession 1996*. Ed. Phyllis Franklin. New York: MLA, 1996. 161–216.

Frye, Northrop. *Anatomy of Criticism*. Princeton: Princeton UP, 1957.

Greenblatt, Stephen, and Giles Gunn, eds. *Redrawing the Boundaries: The Transformation of English and American Literary Studies*. New York: MLA, 1992.

Lentricchia, Frank. *After the New Criticism*. Chicago: U of Chicago P, 1980.

Martin, Biddy. "Teaching Literature, Changing Cultures." *PMLA* 112 (1997): 7–25.

Miller, J. Hillis. "Literary Study in the Transnational University." *Profession 1996*. 6–14.

Ransom, John Crowe. *The World's Body*. 1938. Port Washington, NY: Kennikat, 1964.

Scholes, Robert. *Textual Power: Literary Theory and the Teaching of English*. New Haven: Yale UP, 1985.

Shelley, "A Defence of Poetry." *Percy Bysshe Shelley: Selected Poetry and Prose*. Ed. Alasdair D. F. Macrae. London: Routledge, 1991. 204–33.

Winterowd, W. Ross. *The English Department: An Institutional and Personal History*. Carbondale: Southern Illinois UP, forthcoming.

Chapter 5

Ethics, *Ethos*, Habitation

James Comas

The Emergence of "Ethics" in the Academic Marketplace

What should we make of the sudden emergence of "ethics" in the discourse of North American composition studies?

Ethics, it could well be said, is never far from teaching nor from the philosophy of education. In the tradition of Western thought, this connection is made explicit in Plato's *Gorgias*, where Socrates proposes "a life of philosophy" *(ton bion ton en philosophia)* in opposition to the rhetorical education offered by Gorgias, which Plato represents less in the figure of the aging Gorgias than in the self-serving politics of Callicles. Two millennia later, in 1708, Vico explained to an audience at the University of Naples that "the greatest drawback of our educational methods is that we pay an excessive amount of attention to the natural sciences and not enough to ethics." By "ethics" Vico had in mind that "which treats of human character, of its dispositions, its passions, and of the manner of adjusting these factors to public life and eloquence" (33). And because "human events are dominated by Chance and Choice," Vico believed that, unlike Plato's rejection of a rhetorical-based *paideia*, an "ethical" reform of education should be grounded in the study of rhetoric.

We are thus the inheritors of a complex, if not inconsistent tradition regarding the purposes of education. Not only does this tradition struggle with the debate of scientism versus humanism, but the very concept of the humanities is strained by the ambiguous relationship between ethics and rhetoric. Nevertheless, we can see that the core of this tradition consists in a profound concern with the ethics-rhetoric relationship. And as we see by comparing Plato to Vico, this concern transcends differing views on how this relationship should be understood.

It is not yet clear, however, what we might do with this inheritance; that is, it is not clear how the recent surge of interest in "ethics" is related to this tradition. In fact, we should be greatly surprised if our relationship to this tradition were unambiguous, given the complexities not only of the tradition but of our discipline's recent history. We are receiving a tradition within a disciplinary institution that is still struggling to legitimate its intellectual prerogatives within the North American academy. The situation is complicated further by the fact that, in the last few years, "ethics" has come to be associated with "postmodernism."[1] To the extent that postmodernism is understood as a critique of the tradition of Western thought (e.g., the Cartesian subject, humanism, etc.), it would attempt to separate itself from the tradition of educational philosophy I sketched above. But this is yet to be thought through.

There is another aspect of our discipline that has yet to be thought through in relation to "ethics." Actually, this is an aspect that encompasses North American literary studies in addition to composition studies, and has affected other disciplines in the humanities and social sciences, as well. I am referring to the increasing influence of a "market logic" in the shaping of academic professions. This is not a new concern. One might recall Northrop Frye's wry comparison of literary fashions to the dynamics of the stock market:

> [Meaningless criticism] includes all casual, sentimental, and prejudiced value judgments, and all the literary chit-chat which makes the reputations of poets boom and crash in an imaginary stock exchange. That wealthy investor Mr. Eliot, after dumping Milton on the market, is now buying him again; Donne has probably reached his peak and will begin to taper off; Tennyson may be in for a slight flutter but the Shelley stocks are still bearish.[2]

With a couple of simple adjustments to Frye's conceit, we shift the focus from literary studies to composition studies and from the literary canon to a canon of theoretical concepts: the key terms of composition studies boom and crash in an imaginary stock exchange; "social constructionism," for example, has reached its peak and has begun to taper off; "hypertext" and "webbed classrooms" may be in for a slight flutter; but the "political" stocks are still bearish. And what about "the fate of ethics" in this academic marketplace?[3] Maintaining Frye's ironic tone, one could caution that while "ethics" appears to be a good short-term investment, it is not yet clear whether its performance is likely to continue into the long-term. Perhaps the current interest in ethics will continue to parallel another unprecedented explosion of growth—that of the real stock market; or perhaps one might want to consider, like Alan Greenspan, the possibility that what we are witnessing, in composition studies, is only an irrational "exuberance."

Frye, of course, offered his analogy as criticism of the failure of academic literary studies to establish a disciplinary foundation, a foundation consisting of basic principles of scientific inquiry, including the empirical study of specifically literary phenomena (e.g., symbols, modes, myths, genres). The analogy was intended, however, as a taunt, a provocation; and Frye did not entertain seriously the possibility that the epistemological infirmity of North American literary studies was related to a "market" ideology or any other aspect of its socioeconomic setting. Nor did any of his colleagues explore systematically the possibility that larger social forces impacted their hallowed institutions (in spite of being painfully aware that federal funding for education, after Sputnik, was tied to national defense).

We, however, have witnessed a dramatic reversal of perspective over the last 15 years. During this period, the disciplines of literary studies and composition studies have cultivated a professional *ethos* that not only acknowledges the impact of socioeconomic forces on the academy, but prizes its comprehension of these social forces. Moreover, this *ethos* proffers the profession's intellectual work as a project of politics. This is the well-known "political turn," in which disciplinary practices, both scholarly and pedagogical, have been retooled for ideological critique. The continuing force of this *ethos* is clearly visible in the mimetic process of assimilating graduate students into the profession, a process framed by a canon of theoretical texts that, in spite of differences, all assume the priority of political analysis.[4] Another crucial aspect of this *ethos* is its censorious attitude toward its own disciplinary past, an attitude best represented by the influence of two works in disciplinary history: James Berlin's *Rhetoric and Reality* (1987) in composition studies and Gerald Graff's *Professing Literature* (1987) in literary studies. Both histories rely on and promote an historiographical opposition in which our disciplinary past is characterized as politically naive in order to establish the sense of our own political sophistication.

Given the condition of political self-consciousness that characterizes contemporary composition studies (a condition, it seems to me, often verging on political narcissism), one might expect my paraphrase of Frye's analogy to cut much differently than Frye's original. But in spite of the differences of 30 years, there remains a crucial similarity. Both Frye's scientific *ethos* and our current politicized *ethos* presuppose a resistance to what I will call the logic of capital. This is hardly a new concept; I simply mean the kind of transactions we have in mind when we use phrases like "cultural capital," "intellectual capital," and other forms of symbolic capital, including "professional capital."[5] To a significant extent, professional capital in both composition and literary studies consists of theoretical terms and the names of theorists, the value of which is established in relation to a kind of gold standard called "the political." Of course, these terms and names are deployed as a kind of shorthand to designate more complex theories and positions; and they are chosen typically to produce rhetorical effects. Citing Jean-François Lyotard quite obviously produces effects different from citing, say, Northrop Frye. But not the least of these effects is the "portfolio factor," the list of proper names and theoretical concepts in which one has invested. Epigraphs, quotations, works cited—all these features of academic writing comprise one's investment portfolio and, thus, contribute significantly to one's professional standing.

Viewed from the perspective of this political paradigm, the recent emergence of interest in "ethics" could be interpreted in one of two ways: either it constitutes a development that furthers the progressive political work of our disciplines or it constitutes a reactionary gesture that nostalgically seeks a return to an imagined state of apolitical intellectual work.

But what if we view the emergence of "ethics" as an opportunity to step outside the political paradigm, to gain some critical distance on the trend that has dominated our disciplines for almost two decades? That is, how might we understand the emergence of "ethics" within a period of disciplinary history that has witnessed the relegitimating of our disciplinary practices as political practices? Should we understand this emergence as part of the disciplines' political project; or is it possible that the exuberant rush to "ethics" embodies a tacit acknowledgment of the limitations of "the political turn"?

A definitive answer to these questions cannot be found by looking to those texts most responsible for establishing ethics as a key term in both composition and literary studies. I'm referring to J. Hillis Miller's *An Ethics of Reading* (1987) and Wayne Booth's *The Company We Keep: An Ethics of Fiction* (1988). The problem is that these books advocate mutually exclusive conceptions of ethics and thus stage (as an effect of the authors' professional reputations) conflicting uses of the word. Miller, for his part, posits an ethics of reading that he hopes could controvert the politicizing of critical practices, a recent development that reduces literary studies to a "relatively trivial study of one of the epiphenomenon of society, part of the technological assimilation or assertion of mastery over all features of human life which is called 'the human sciences'" (5). Booth, on the other hand, understands "ethics" as political, more specifically, as the individual's expression of values, which, for Booth, are necessarily political. Moreover, at an early point in his discussion, he suggests that we replace the word *politics* with *ethics* and regard the work of Terry Eagleton and Fredric Jameson as "ethical" criticism. (It is not clear from Booth's remarks, however, how one would then use the word *politics*.)[6]

Ethos: Kenneth Burke's Deferral of "Ethics"

In response to these complex questions, I offer this initial study, part of a larger project that will examine how the concept of "ethics" was used by past American critics. Being a student of the work of Kenneth Burke, I have become intrigued by his constant reformulation of key terms for the investigation of human motivation, terms that designate the focus of his Motivorum studies: grammar, rhetoric, symbolic. And being a student of rhetorical theory, I'm interested in how these reformulations affect Burke's theory of rhetoric, especially the way in which they suggest limits to the rhetorical dimension of language. A bit more specifically, I have noticed that Burke, after using ethics as the central term for his 1935 book, *Permanence and Change: An Anatomy of Purpose*, drops it for nearly 20 years. Then, following the publication of the second volume of his three-part Motivorum in 1950, *A Rhetoric of Motives*, Burke plants evocative statements here and there that promise a fourth volume that will clarify how "ethics" has been the goal of his entire life's work. Yet in spite of these statements, Burke's study of ethics was postponed indefinitely. I hope that an inquiry into the problematic nature of Burke's interest in "ethics" will assist us in elucidating complexities that our profession, perhaps, is overlooking in its rush to embrace this word.

The Role of "Ethics" in Burke's First Theory of Motives

Even though "ethics" functions as the central concept in *Permanence and Change*, it is not immediately obvious how Burke uses the term, in large part because there is no discussion of the concept until the third, concluding part of the book. A reading of Burke's discussion thus requires two preliminary stages: first, one must examine the way in which Burke presents the book as an intellectual project, that is, the way in which he conceptualizes the problem that he wants to address; second, one must discern the three-part conceptual structure, or trajectory of the book.

Although Burke is rather explicit in defining many of his goals in *Permanence and Change*, the coherence of the project is masked, ironically, by a dominating theoretical discussion on the nature of interpretation, a discussion that overshadows the social problems he wishes to address. Burke begins by designating the object of his theoretical study as judgment; that is, the mental faculty through which we relate ourselves to the external world. When I characterize this study as "theoretical," I simply mean that the type of question guiding Burke's inquiry is the *ti esti?*" of traditional philosophy, or translated from the Greek, "what is the nature of . . .?" Thus, the general theoretical question that Burke raises is, What is the nature of the process of judgment? And, of course, he responds to this question by arguing that this process is grounded by interpretation of the world around us.

Because Burke titles Part I of the book "On Interpretation" and devotes much of his discussion to the relationship between interpretation and world-view, it is not surprising that students of *Permanence and Change* typically give their attention to this theoretical component of the book. I think, however, that an examination of the book's second study provides a much fuller understanding of Burke's own motives (and provides a glimpse into Burke's transformation from a literary critic to a social critic and philosopher). The object of this second study is the condition of contemporary society; that is, the quintessential modernist *topos* of a post-religious world where the center no longer holds, a plaint intensified for Burke's generation by the market crash, consequent economic depression, and the embrace of fascism in Italy and Germany (a return of the center with a vengeance). Burke is interested especially in defining the modern substitutes for the organizing force of religion; and he does this by elaborating John Dewey's concept of "occupational psychosis," which Burke defines as a pronounced character of mind resulting from the patterns of work that a society makes available to its members. Dewey's concept, Burke continues, thus corresponds roughly to "the Marxian doctrine that a society's environment in the historical sense is synonymous with the society's methods of production" (38). Burke identifies several "occupational psychoses of the present," including the capitalist, or free-market psychosis, the force of which is best revealed, Burke claims, in "the professionalization of sports, and in the flourishing of success literature during the late-lamented New Era" (41). Burke also identifies an "investor's or creditor's psychosis," which "is not tied down to a concern with tangible, physical properties, manual or mechanical operations—but is a highly speculative occupation, dealing in such diaphanous things as forecasts, prospects, futures, such metaphysical bewilderments as valuation, and requiring a whole new astrology of graphs, statistics, indices, crop reports, and tables" (42).

But it is not until Burke discusses a final psychosis that we discern the project of his book. This is "the technological psychosis," which Burke claims is "the center of our glories and our distress." This distress, Burke explains, results from "the doctrine of use," which, as a central feature of eighteenth-century Utilitarian philosophy, transformed thinking about the nature of values:

> The doctrine of use, as the prime mover of judgments, formally established the secular as the point of reference by which to consider questions of valuation. The transcendental accounts of moral origin, in accordance with which truth had been revealed by God to chosen representative and thence transmitted through priestly ordination by the laying on of hands, now gave way to the notion that consideration of service or interest both do shape and should shape our religious, ethical, esthetic, and even cosmological judgments. (45)

For Burke, the problem with this secular grounding of values is that it reduces human experience to the attempt to control the forces of technology and, thus, overlooks human needs that were more clearly expressed in earlier periods of human history; for example, the attempt to control specifically human forces through religion. Thus, the project of *Permanence and Change* is to theorize a mode of interpreting/engaging the world that will moderate the excesses of modernity's technological psychosis. And this corrective, Burke believes, lies "in the direction of the anthropomorphic or humanistic or poetic" (65). However, Burke explains, the overwhelming influence of scientific rationalization makes poetic, or literary discourse ineffective:

> the poetic point of reference is weakened by the fact that the poetic medium of communication itself is weakened. The center of authority must be situated in a philosophy, or psychology, of poetry, rather than in a body of poetry, until the scene itself becomes sufficiently stabilized for linkages to acquire

greater spread and permanence throughout the group . . . The corrective of the scientific rationalization would seem necessarily to be a rationale of art—not however, a performer's art, not a specialist's art for some to produce and many to observe, but an art in its widest aspects, an art of living. (66)

These are the words that end Part I of *Permanence and Change*. Burke, however, does not explain how this "poetic" project is related to the concept of ethics until the reader moves through a "transitional" Part II and into Part III, in which Burke stages a dialectical transcendence of the modernity's psychoses.[7] Burke presents his conception of ethics as, itself, a transcendence of what he understands to be the two major theoretical options offered in the history of Western philosophy—Kantian Transcendentalism and Utilitarianism:

We may, like Kant and the theologians, locate ethics in a transcendental source. Or we may, like the Utilitarians, consider ethical weightings as hardly more than an epiphenomenon of buying and selling. But whether we discuss the moral as an outgrowth of the economic, or the economic as merely a low order of transcendental moral insight, the same ethical relationship between the individual and his group can be disclosed. (195)

It appears that Burke's dialectical move beyond Kant and the Utilitarians consists of nothing more than the proposition that "ethics" concerns the relationship between "the individual and his group."[8] But Burke, aware of the linguistic turn overtaking philosophy by the 1930s, proposes that the ethical relationship must be understood as a linguistic phenomenon.

Of greater interest is the fact that Burke describes the linguistic phenomenon of ethics in terms that he will associate later with rhetoric. For example, in his summary of Part III, he observes that "poetic" language (that is, the language meant to correct the technological psychosis of modern society) uses "weighted" words; but, Burke continues, "such weightings in themselves are not poetic but ethical (being derived from the partisan nature of practical action) which is guided or deterred by 'censorial terms'" (167). This is precisely the language Burke uses thirteen years later to define rhetorical discourse in *A Rhetoric of Motives*, as we see in an early section of that book where he distinguishes the study of rhetoric from the other two studies of the Motivorum, the completed Grammar and the projected Symbolic: "The *Rhetoric* deals with the possibilities of classification in its partisan aspects [Burke underscores "partisan"]: it considers the ways in which individuals are at odds with one another, or become identified with groups more or less at odds with one another" (22). Burke's interest in rhetoric first becomes apparent in his 1924 essay "Psychology and Form." But in that essay, along with his elaboration of its key ideas in "Lexicon Rhetorics" (1931), Burke's conception of rhetoric focused on the psychological effects of discursive form. The complete absence of the term rhetoric in *Permanence and Change* suggests that Burke, while working on the manuscript in 1932–33, had not yet rethought the concept of rhetoric in terms of the "partisan" relations that would characterize his later theory.[9] It also suggests the difficulty of distinguishing rhetoric and ethics, a difficulty that Wayne Booth resolved fifty years later by conflating ethics and politics.

The Return of Ethics

As I have just shown, sometime following the publication of *Permanence and Change*, Burke comes to realize that the concept of rhetoric is a more appropriate name for the "interested," "partisan" relationship that he had called "ethics."[10] Just as "rhetoric" is the missing term in *Permanence and Change*, ethics has lost its status as a key term in the Rhetoric. Yet in 1953, three years after the publication of the *Rhetoric*, in a summary of the development of his thinking written for the second edition of *Counter-Statement*, Burke sketches the Motivorum project thus: "These three Motivorum books deal with linguistic structures in their logical, rhetorical, and poetic dimensions respectively. And they will require a fourth volume, probably specifically entitled "On Human Relations," stressing the ethical dimension of language." Then Burke adds parenthetically, "(As things thus turned out, the devices that were to be the beginning of the project are postponed until its end)" (218). Burke continues this sketch with brief descriptions of the Grammar, the Rhetoric, and the Symbolic; yet nothing more is said about the "ethical" fourth volume, "On Human Relations."

Burke again gives special status to "ethics" in a brief passage from "On Catharsis, Or Resolution" (1959). His comments are part of his explanation of why this particular essay is a study in "Poetics"; and in order to explain what he means by "poetics," he locates it in relation to what he now regards as the other three "aspects of language":

> Poetics as here considered is part of a scheme involving what I take to be the four aspects of language. Besides Poetics there are: Logic (or 'Grammar'), the universal principles of linguistic placement; Rhetoric, language as addressed,

as hortatory, and as designed for the stimulating or transcending of partisanship; Ethics, language as a medium in which, willy nilly, writer and reader express their identities, their characters, either as individuals or as members of classes or groups. The Poetic dimension of language concerns essentially the exercise of linguistic resources in and for themselves. . . . (340)

The category of "ethics" has, in this passage, replaced the earlier category of the "Symbolic," which Burke had reserved for expressions of the individual qua individual, as elucidated by psychoanalytic techniques. Here, it seems as though Burke is ready to subsume the specific interests of the Symbolic under a broader category of identity, or character, that is, the typical translation of the Greek *ethos*. But it strikes me that the most important phrase in this definition of ethics is "willy nilly," the silly rhyme which draws so much attention to itself in the midst of philosophical prose. An emphasis on this phrase makes ethics the study not merely of expressions of identity, but of the haphazard nature of such expressions. The phrase itself appears to be an expression of Burke as inveterate punster, comically locating "ethics" between the human will and the Latin "nothing." This space is not at all the scene of decision or judgment that interests Burke in *Permanence and Change*. Perhaps this impossible space is similar to Heidegger's conception of *Gelassenheit*, which the Jewish philosopher Emmanuel Levinas has defined as "the will that wills not to will," that is, as the fundamental gesture of generosity.

Intellectual Habitation

Heidegger, in his "Letter on Humanism" (1947), draws attention to the Greek words *ethikos* and *ethos* in order to mark the difference between the discrete discipline typical of Platonic philosophy (i.e., *ethikos*) and what he believes is an ontologically more profound concept found in the thought of the tragedians and presocratic thinkers (i.e., *ethos*):

> Along with 'logic' and 'physics,' 'ethics' appeared for the first time in the school of Plato. These disciplines arose at a time when thinking was becoming 'philosophy,' philosophy, *episteme* (science), and science itself a matter for schools and academic pursuits. In the course of a philosophy so understood, science waxed and thinking waned. Thinkers prior to this period knew neither a 'logic' nor an 'ethics' nor 'physics.' Yet their thinking was neither illogical nor immoral. But they did think *physis* in a depth and breadth that no subsequent 'physics' was ever again able to attain. The tragedies of

> Sophocles—provided such a comparison is at all permissible—preserve the *ethos* in their sagas more primordially than Aristotle's lectures on 'ethics.' A saying of Heraclitus which consists of only three words says something so simply that from it the essence of the *ethos* immediately comes to light. (232-33)

Heidegger's reference, here, is to Heraclitus fragment 119: *ethos anthropoi daimon*. Typically, this fragment is translated with *ethos* rendered as "character," as we find in Kathleen Freeman's *Ancilla to the Pre-Socratic Philosophers*: "Character for man is destiny."[11] Heidegger, however, objects that such a rendering of *ethos* is not at all Greek but, instead, a modern projection onto ancient thought. The ancient meaning of *ethos*, Heidegger insists, is "abode," or "dwelling place."[12] He continues, "The word names the open region in which man dwells. The open region of his abode allows what pertains to man's essence, and what in thus arriving resides in nearness to him, to appear. The abode of man contains and preserves the advent of what belongs to man in his essence" (233). I am not interested, here, in the ontological thesis that Heidegger attempts to support with etymological arguments. His observations, however, do point toward a fascinating semantic field in which "ethics" is linked to a relationship between one's existence and places of habitation, a relationship designated by the Greek word *ethos*. In its earliest usage, *ethos* refers to the haunts or abodes of animals, as we find, for example, in a passage from the *Iliad* where Homer compares Paris with a stalled horse who, breaking free of his rope, "gallops over the plain in thunder to his accustomed bathing place in a sweet-running river and in the pride of his strength holds high his head. . . ." *Ethos*, in this older usage, is not so much the expression of character, or identity; instead, it is a revelation, or manifesting of character in a place of habitation. And by the time of Hesiod, the word's reference is extended to human habitation.

A modern idea similar to the ancient concept of *ethos* appears in the ethical philosophy of Emmanuel Levinas. I characterize Levinas's work as an "ethical philosophy" because he argues for the priority of ethical thought in philosophy, a project he refers to as "ethics as first philosophy." In his most expository book, *Totalité et Infini* (1961), Levinas treats "habitation" as the very condition of contemplation, which he posits as the core of human subjectivity: "the subject contemplating the world presupposes the event of dwelling, the withdrawal from the elements (that is, from immediate enjoyment, already uneasy about the morrow), recollection in the intimacy of the home."[13] Moreover, Levinas reasons, this "intimacy of the home" presupposes an intimacy with someone, with an other: "The intimacy which familiarity already presupposes is an *intimacy with someone.* The interiority of recollection is a solitude in a world already human. Recollection refers to a welcome" (155). And this welcoming other, Levinas claims, has the special character of "femine alterity": "The woman is the condition for recollection, the interiority of the Home, and inhabitation" (155).

Without engaging in the issue of the appropriateness of Levinas's feminization of habitation, it is interesting to return both to the concerns of Frye's stock-market analogy and to Burke's analysis of occupational psychoses. Both critics, I think, were primarily interested in raising the question of how our intellectual identities, or self-understandings, are related to our professional abode and, thus, to the dwelling of our intellects. Are our "dwellings" characterized by the sense of welcoming intimacy that Levinas describes? Or have we become accustomed to dwelling within what Burke will call "the Scramble, the Wrangle of the Market Place, the flurries and flare-ups of the Human Barnyard, the Give and Take, the wavering line of pressure and counterpressure, the Logomachy, the onus of ownership, the Wars of Nerves, the War"?[12] Burke, here, is characterizing the human condition that calls forth rhetoric. But it is clear, I think, that Burke is attempting to speak about rhetoric from a non-rhetorical space, from a space within which one can maintain a distance from the temptations of the Logomachy, the temptations of Callicles's "political" life. This is the space of ethics. And our recognition of such space leads us, morally and intellectually, to rethink our embrace of rhetoric.

Notes

1. See James E. Porter, "Developing a Postmodern Ethics of Rhetoric and Composition," in *Defining the New Rhetorics*, ed. Theresa Enos and Stuart Brown (Newbury Park, CA: Sage, 1993), 207-26.

2. Northrop Frye, *Anatomy of Criticism: Four Essays* (Princeton: Princeton University Press, 1957), 18.

3. An early draft of this paper was presented as part of a panel on "The Fate of Ethics in Postmodern Theory" at the Annual Convention of the Conference on College Composition and Communication, Phoenix, Arizona, 13 Mar 1997.

4. Typically, the canon of theoretical texts functions as a list-of-authors-one-should-cite. The practice of citation deserves more critical attention. There have been, of course, studies of the rhetoric of citation as well as comparative studies of the differences between the conventions of various disciplines. I am thinking, though, of a study that would compare the practice of citation to the practice of criticism since students typically learn that certain texts are meant to be cited while certain other texts are meant to be criticized.

5. The work of Pierre Bourdieu has been, perhaps, the most influential in elaborating a critical analysis of "symbolic capital." See, for example, the essays collected by Randal Johnson.

6. I have written at some length on Miller's and Booth's books as well as other major contributions to the topic of "ethics and criticism." See *Theoretical Communities: Studies in the Ethics* and *Rhetoric of American Criticism, 1921-1994* (Urbana: NCTE Press, forthcoming).

7. Burke, of course, was preoccupied with questions of form, whether it was theorizing dramatic form as a manifestation of desire or mapping trajectories of psychological and historical development.

8. Burke's statement relies on a common assumption regarding ethics: ethics pertains to the relationship between individual and group. Although this assumption hardly seems problematic, I will show later that, in fact, it is.

9. "*Permanence and Change* was written in 1932-33." Kenneth Burke, "Curriculum Criticum," in *Counter-Statement*, 216.

10. In developing this study of Burke, I plan to determine more precisely when Burke rethinks the concept of rhetoric. Obviously, this shift takes place by the time of "The Rhetoric of Hitler's 'Battle,'" published in 1939. And this famous essay provides, perhaps, a clue that Burke's reconsideration of rhetoric was prompted by the rise of fascism and yet another war engulfing Europe.

11. See the translation in G. S. Kirk and J. E. Raven, *The Presocratic Philosophers*. "Man's Character is His Daimon" (213).

12 Heidegger's definition of *ethos* is verified by the entry in Liddell-Scott-Jones, which cites passages from the *Iliad* and the *Odyssey*, as well as later texts. The use of *ethos* to designate the rhetorical interest in a speaker's delineation of character is, according to Liddell-Scott-Jones, not found until Aristotle's *Rhetoric*.

Works Cited

Berlin, James A. *Rhetoric and Reality: Writing Instruction in American Colleges, 1900–1985.* Carbondale: Southern Illinois UP, 1987.

Booth, Wayne. *The Company We Keep: An Ethics of Fiction.* Berkeley: U of California P, 1988.

Burke, Kenneth. *A Rhetoric of Motives.* Berkeley: U of California P, 1969.

———. *Counter-Statement*, 3rd. ed. Berkeley: U of California P, 1968.

Enos, Theresa and Stuart Brown, eds. *Defining the New Rhetorics.* Newbury Park, CA: Sage, 1993.

Freeman, Kathleen. *Ancilla to the Pre-Socratic Philosophers: A Complete Translation of the Fragments in Diels.* Cambridge: Harvard UP, 1948.

Frye, Northrop. *Anatomy of Criticism.* Princeton: Princeton UP, 1957.

Graff, Gerald. *Professing Literature: An Institutional History.* Chicago: U of Chicago P, 1987.

Heidegger, Martin. "Letter on Humanism." Trans. Frank A Capuzzi and J. Glenn Gray. *Basic Writings.* Ed. David Farrell Krell. New York: Harper, 1977.

Johnson, Randall, ed. *The Field of Cultural Production.* New York: Columbia UP, 1993.

Kirk, G. S. and J. E. Raven. *The Presocratic Philosophers.* Cambridge: Cambridge UP, 1957.

Levinas, Emmanuel. *Totality and Infinity: An Essay in Exteriority.* Trans. Alphonso Lingis. Pittsburgh: Duquesne UP, 1969.

———. *Proper Names.* Trans. Michael B. Smith. London: Athlone Press, 1996.

Miller, J. Hillis. *An Ethics of Reading.* New York: Columbia UP, 1987.

Vico, Giambattista. *On the Study Methods of Our Time.* Ed. Elio Gianturco. Ithaca, NY: Cornell UP, 1990. *De Nostri Temporis Studiorum Ratione*, 1709.

Chapter 6

Encountering the Other: Postcolonial Theory and Composition Scholarship

Gary A. Olson

Theorists of the postmodern have often asserted that now that we have entered what has been termed "the postmodern age" ethics is dead, that no system or code of moral values can universally regulate human behavior. Those who make such assertions typically point out that prior to modernity, ethics was a product of divine will as invested in and regulated by the social institution of the Church. With the advent of the Enlightenment and the apotheosis of "reason," monitoring and enforcing moral behavior switched from the priests to the philosophers, from the Church to the State. Thus, ethics became a distinctly humanist project. As Zygmunt Bauman points out in *Postmodern Ethics*, ethics as legislated by the philosophers was based on two criteria: universality, in that all ethical prescriptions were assumed to be immediately recognized by all human beings as "right" (and therefore obligatory), and foundational, in that such prescriptions were well founded in reason and so all rational humans could be expected to follow them (8–9). Of course, postmodern theory has radically challenged the premises of such a concept of ethics, including the notions that distinguishing right from wrong is somehow an inherent capacity, that a system of ethical prescriptions can somehow justly regulate behavior in specific, local contexts, that "reason" is the most appropriate (or even an adequate) source of ethical behavior, and that prescriptions established prior to specific moral dilemmas can universally and reliably produce "proper" outcomes independent of local contingencies.

Such critiques of traditional notions of ethics make a great deal of sense, but, unlike Bauman, numerous theorists of the postmodern have unfortunately concluded that there can be no such thing as ethics in a postmodern age: ethics is a system of values; all systems are undependable and illusory; therefore, no system of ethics can justly and reliably regulate behavior. This position has become almost axiomatic among many theorists. An increasing number of scholars such as Bauman and various feminist theorists such as Luce Irigaray, however, are taking issue with this conclusion. In fact, to many of us, far from being irrelevant, ethics takes on more importance in the postmodern age than ever before. Once we dispense with externally provided ethical structures (be they from priests or philosophers, faith or reason), and once we believe that preestablished prescriptions are inadequate given local contingencies, then the responsibility for ethical behavior falls squarely upon the shoulders of each individual. That is, no longer can we conveniently rationalize our behavior by appealing to rules, rule books, priests or philosophers; each individual is responsible and accountable for his or her actions—the bulky, impersonal apparatus of official ethics can no longer support, defend, rationalize, or direct our individual choices.[1]

Perhaps the most useful way of conceiving ethics is in the same terms that several postmodern thinkers do: *ethics is the encounter with the Other.*[2] By definition, all human interactions entail various encounters with an Other, and because we all bring to these interactions our own agendas—our own wishes, desires, needs, motivations—and because these agendas are often in conflict (or at least not in perfect concordance), we are constantly negotiating and renegotiating our interactions. Further, few if any interactions are between "equal" players; power differentials invariably are at play.[3] Consequently, how we interact with an Other—how we balance our own needs, desires, and obligations with those of the Other—is precisely what ethics is about. Absent external, preestablished rules of ethics, how we effect this balance of needs, desires, and obligations, how we negotiate our encounter with the Other, is a weighty responsibility. Thus, far from being dead, ethics is perhaps more alive than ever, for now we must actively participate in our own moral decision making, no longer abdicating our responsibility to external forces.

In many ways, the current trend in composition studies to introduce into the writing class discussion of and writing about issues of gender, race, or "contact zones" is a supremely ethical move, in that such discussions foreground interaction with an Other. That is, contemporary composition theory and pedagogy are increasingly more concerned with ethical questions, regardless of whether ethics as a concept is introduced directly into the discussion.[4] This development seems to be a healthy one (even if you do not subscribe to the cognitive-developmental thesis that cognitive and ethical growth are inextricably interwoven) because students are learning to engage the world in substantive ways, to think and write about issues of importance to themselves and others. However, the scholarly examinations of these issues often fall short of presenting the ethical dimension in its fullest complexity. Scholarship on contact zones is a good example.

Scholars in rhetoric and composition have invoked Mary Louise Pratt's concept of contact zone to examine questions of teacher authority in pedagogical situations and to devise multicultural-focused pedagogies.[5] Pratt uses the term to refer to "social spaces where cultures meet, clash, and grapple with each other, often in contexts of highly asymmetrical relations of power, such as colonialism, slavery, or their aftermaths, as they are lived out in many parts of the world today" ("Arts" 34). She further describes the contact zone as a "space in which peoples geographically and historically separated come into contact with each other and establish ongoing relations, usually involving conditions of coercion, radical inequality, and intractable conflict" (*Imperial* 6). Pratt's discussion emerges from a strong postcolonial perspective. Her "Arts of the Contact Zone," the essay that began the conversation about contact zones in composition, draws heavily on the example of a seventeenth century manuscript written by Felipe Guaman Poma de Ayala, an unknown indigenous Andean, written "some forty years after the final fall of the Inca empire to the Spanish" and addressed to the king of Spain.[6] This work, *The First New Chronicle* and *Good Government*, attempts to re-present the colonized world of Peru from the eyes of the colonized, the Other, rather than, as was traditional, from the official perspective of the colonizer. Pratt uses this example to discuss classroom dynamics from the perspective of contact zones, and throughout the article she relies heavily on postcolonial discourse to construct her argument.

The term "contact zone" is highly evocative. On the one hand, it is an adaptation of the sociolinguistic concept "contact language," "a sort of creole or pidgin that speakers of differing languages develop when forced into communication with one another" (Harris 31). However, as Stephen Brown points out, the term *contact* itself carries numerous connotations, being coded with military, historical, anthropological, and psychological meaning. Contact is used by the military to describe violent clashes with the Other, the enemy; by historians to describe "not only the dynamics of initial encounters between indigenous peoples and their colonizers, but the epochs preceding those encounters" (as in describing the period of Hawaiian history prior to Captain Cook's "discovery" of the islands as "pre-contact"); by anthropologists to evoke "nostalgic images of an Edenic moment when the native lived in a state of communion with nature, uncorrupted by 'contact' with Western civilization"; and by various theorists to signify "an attempt to reclaim, recolonize, or reterritorialize lost realms of the indigenous self" (2–3). Thus, the term *contact* and the concept "contact zone" are imbricated with associations related to encounter with the Other, especially from a kind of postcolonial perspective.

While Pratt's notion of contact zone has been useful in interrogating how teachers exercise power and authority, especially in the multicultural classroom, some compositionists have tended to deploy it in such a way as to defend a kind of liberal pluralism, thereby subverting attempts to come to terms with the truly colonizing effects of the pedagogical scenario. As Joseph Harris comments, such discussions frequently devolve into a kind of "multicultural bazaar" where students "are not so much brought into conflict with opposing views as placed in a kind of harmless connection with a series of exotic others" (33). What's problematic about such a stance is that it undermines the very objective of postcolonial discourse, which is to analyze and articulate the dynamics of systems of domination and oppression, to highlight "difference" as an important, even central, aspect of political relations (be they on the micro or macro level), to focus, that is, on the crucial importance of Otherness. The stance taken in much contact zone scholarship effects the opposite: it deemphasizes systems of oppression and attempts to flatten out difference in order to strive for some mythical, elusive harmony.[7]

Now, while my main concern here is with how compositionists have used—or, more to the point, diluted—Pratt's concept of contact zone, Pratt herself could be criticized for not fully developing the postcolonial aspects of her own work. Harris provides an excellent critique of Pratt in his "Negotiating the Contact Zone." He claims that while Pratt calls for classrooms where the voices of the marginalized get heard, she is vague about how this can be accomplished other than through simply introducing class readings written by authors from diverse cultures. What can we do to truly hear the voices of the subaltern and avoid engaging in cultural and intellectual tourism—an Epcot Center approach to culture that amounts to a process of recolonization? And how can we ensure that diverse student voices get heard in the classroom? In the eyes of Harris and others, Pratt undermines her own theory by calling for a kind of unified, utopian community—a "safe house"—where students can articulate differences in a nonthreatening environment. Richard Miller describes the writing generated by such a contact zone as "oddly benign" (390).[8]

While such critiques merit attention, Pratt, working from a strong postcolonial perspective, was at least attempting to interject into the discussion an awareness of how systems of domination and oppression threaten effective pedagogy. She points out, for example, that teacher-pupil language

> tends to be described almost entirely from the point of view of the teacher and teaching, not from the point of view of pupils and pupiling (the word doesn't even exist, though the thing certainly does). If a classroom is analyzed as a social world unified and homogenized with respect to the teacher, whatever students do other than what the teacher specifies is invisible or anomalous to the analysis. This can be true in practice as well. ("Arts" 38)

The question Pratt is attempting to answer is, "What is the place of unsolicited oppositional discourse, parody, resistance, critique in the imagined classroom?" ("Arts" 39). Yet, these are not the dynamics often investigated in composition scholarship.[9] What is most unfortunate is how contact zone theory, having entered our professional vocabulary, has come to signify a multicultural melting pot approach to pedagogy: it's *au currant* to be concerned with cultural representativeness in our pedagogies, so let's introduce the writings of "exotic" others, but, we seem to be saying, let's not be overly concerned with real issues of conflict; let's, instead, paper over difference since we're all the same inside—can't we all get along?

Implicit, then, in the way contact zone is being theorized are serious theoretical and pedagogical dangers. I believe that an effective way to elaborate and perhaps even improve such practices is to introduce postcolonial theory into composition theory. Postcolonial theory can illuminate how despite students' attempts to "empower" themselves by learning to inhabit subject position, and despite our own efforts to facilitate this process, we construct students as Other, reinforcing their position in the margins where it is doubly difficult to gain the kind of empowerment we ostensibly wish to encourage. It also illustrates how colonial impulses come into play between students and teacher as well as between members of different races and ethnic groups, affecting how learning occurs, or doesn't, how students relate to peers and to teachers. And it emphasizes that the exotic readings we assign to students are often more than simply examples of different kinds of "art"; frequently, they are vocal acts of resistance against the kinds of oppression and even treachery perpetuated by the West. I'm positing, then, that postcolonial theory, given its rigorous concern with encounters with the Other, can reinvigorate our theorizing of contact zones as well as present substantive implications generally for composition theory and pedagogy.

The literature of postcolonial theory is especially relevant to our own scholarship specifically because it is so frequently concerned with articulating the interactions of discourse, ideology, and authority—interactions compositionists have been analyzing for well over a decade. For example, those postcolonial theorists who are most concerned with the ideological power of discourse, such as Gayatri Chakravorty Spivak, are particularly useful. In her noted "Can the Subaltern Speak?" Spivak argues that despite well-intentioned efforts to give voice to the subaltern, there is little possibility for recovering the subaltern voice, in that hegemonic discourse constitutes and disarticulates the subaltern. This "epistemic violence" is a means by which the oppressed subject, through a process of internalizing the discourse of the master, learns to construct his or her identity as Other, to rewrite the self as the object of imperialism. Spivak concludes that "For the 'true' subaltern group, whose identity is its difference, there is no unrepresentable subaltern subject that can know and speak itself" (285).

Discussions such as Spivak's are relevant to our own theorizing about whether we as teachers of discourse can help students take on subject position, to have agency in their own worlds, and they also shed light on questions of the balance of power and authority in the classroom. While it would be a stretch, if not a kind of violence, to liken the college student to a Third World subaltern, discussions of hegemonic discourse and power dynamics in relation to the latter can nonetheless illuminate similar dynamics in our classes and can do so in a much more powerful and useful way than the current liberal version of contact zones and utopic safe houses.

As another example, consider the work of Homi Bhabha. In "Signs Taken for Wonders," he explores how the colonizer uses "the book" as an instrument of control of colonized peoples because it carries with it a logocentric and "civilizing" power that displaces the subaltern's authority of experience. The subaltern copes with the colonizer's presence through imitation and mimicry, an ambivalent position involving the attempt both to become like the oppressor and to resist the imperial presence.[10] The colonized at once adopt the master discourse and simultaneously rewrite it in their own key, imitating while parodying, appropriating while subverting. Such subtle misappropriation of the dominant discourse is thus an act of resistance, both against the Word of the oppressor—the logos, law, language—and against the power over the oppressed that the Word authorizes.[11]

The colonial space, then, is agonistic, oppositional; yet, according to Bhabha, resistance is "never entirely on the outside or implacably oppositional. It is a pressure, and a presence, that acts constantly, if unevenly, along the boundary of authorization" (152). In fact, such resistance is just as effective (if not more so) than more overt forms in that it works imperceptibly from within the heart of colonial authority: its discourse. Benita Parry calls this "a textual insurrection against the discourse of colonial authority":

> The argument is not that the colonized possesses colonial power, but that its fracturing of the colonialist text by re-articulating it in broken English, perverts the meaning and message of the English book ("insignia of colonial authority and signifier of colonial desire and discipline"), and therefore makes an absolute exercise of power impossible. (42)

Unlike Spivak, then, Bhabha believes that the subaltern can speak, can adopt subject position, but does so in indirect ways, through a kind of "sly civility." The subaltern does not escape hegemonic discourse, but speaks from within it, turning it on itself. And in this very act of resistance, colonial power is diminished, altered, and thus, ambivalent, limited, never complete, never entirely successful.

What is especially valuable about work like Bhabha's is that it often addresses concerns similar to our own and does so rigorously and from a fresh perspective. It sheds light on several lines of scholarly inquiry in composition, from those concerning the power of our classroom texts to indoctrinate students, often through students' own complicity, into particular ideological perspectives, to the numerous recent discussions of the nature of resistance; from debates about the uses and misuses of teachers' authority in the classroom, to debates over whether our role as composition teachers is to replace students' home discourse with "official" academic discourse or to empower students to move in and out of multiple discourses with facility.

If, in theorizing about contact zones and about the power dynamics of pedagogical scenarios, we are serious about attempting to comprehend how power operates in our classrooms on both political and psychological levels, then postcolonial theory may be able to enrich our understanding of as well as our own discourse about these subjects. For example, Abdul JanMohamed has much to say about the intricacies of power relations, and while his discussions deal specifically with colonial domination, they are also relevant to how domination works in lesser contexts, such as in our classrooms. In "The Economy of Manichean Allegory," for instance, he explores how the imperialist uses difference—racial, social, cultural, linguistic—as the basis or rationale for domination and control of the Other. Assuming that the Other is "irremediably different" provides less incentive for the imperialist to adopt or try to understand such alterity than to retreat "to the security of his own cultural perspective" (65). In fact, there is considerable psychological pressure to avoid coming to terms with alterity:

> Genuine and thorough comprehension of Otherness is possible only if the self can somehow negate or at least severely bracket the values, assumptions, and ideology of his culture. However, this entails in practice the virtually impossible task of negating one's very being, precisely because one's culture is what formed that being. (65)

Furthermore, the colonial site provides the perfect opportunity to satisfy a deep emotional need to dominate: "If every desire is at base a desire to impose oneself on another and to be recognized by the Other, then the colonial situation provides an ideal context for the fulfillment of that drive" (66). What's at play here, according to JanMohamed's Lacanian analysis, is that in the very act of domination, the one who dominates is able "to compel the Other's recognition of him and, in the process, allow his own identity to become deeply dependent on his position as a master" (66). Thus, the imperialist's own identity and "narcissistic self-recognition" are dependent on the Other, on the power imbalance that constitutes the relationship. Once such a relation of dominance and submissiveness is constituted, the one who dominates derives "affective pleasure" from the perceived moral superiority over the Other, further perpetuating and even intensifying the need and rationale to dominate, to "civilize," and thus to exploit. Once the relationship has arrived at this point, the move from paternalism to hatred seems effortless.

Of course, compositionists, many drawing on the work of Freire, have long been concerned with examining how systems of domination are manifest in pedagogical situations. Most notable is the debate over whether teachers should relinquish part or all of their classroom authority in order to help students gain subject position, some level of agency and autonomy both in their discourse and in their pedagogical interactions.[12] Another related debate concerns the extent to which teachers' role is to indoctrinate students, to champion their own particular perspectives to the exclusion of other viewpoints—some scholars insisting that teachers are ethically bound to adopt a so-called objective stance, others arguing that such a stance is impossible. All such discussions involving teacher authority are germane to recent work on contact zones and to the ethical obligations of instructors.[13] The work of such theorists as JanMohamed, however, can contribute substantially to these discussions and may even encourage us to interrogate the extent to which we may use difference as a tool of control; the extent to which we may then ignore difference and retreat to the comfort of our own perspectives; and the extent to which we as teachers derive affective pleasure from our positions of authority over students, constructing our identity, at least in part, from our position as master over the uncivilized. All such questions may well help us come to terms with the deeply ethical content of our work as teachers, with how we encounter Otherness.

These brief sketches of some of the postcolonial work of Spivak, Bhabha, and JanMohamed are necessarily cursory, incomplete, and even somewhat reductive, but they are meant to be suggestive, to draw attention to a rich avenue of inquiry that can contribute substantially to our own scholarship, especially that related to deeply ethical concerns such as encounters with Otherness, as contact zone theory attempts. There are many other postcolonialists we can draw on. Edward Said can illustrate how we construct an Other in order to define ourselves. That is, Otherness is defined by those in the center and is defined over and against those doing the defining. In a way, defining Others (students? members of other social, ethnic, or racial groups?) as different is a strategy of self-definition, in that by holding up to ourselves a "contrasting image, idea, personality, experience" we thereby carve out what we are not and, thus, what we are (2). Sara Suleri, by unpacking the "peculiar intimacy" of the colonized and colonizer, can help us avoid unsophisticated notions of alterity that construct Otherness as a simple center/margin binary—a project Freire was concerned with as early as *Pedagogy of the Oppressed*. After all, comments S.P. Mohanty, "Just how other, we need to force ourselves to indicate, is the Other?" (58). Certainly, a nuanced notion of Other is necessary if our theorizing of contact zones is to be truly useful. And Linda Hutcheon can contribute to our debates about how feminist theory can illuminate questions of agency and subjectivity despite postmodern deconstructions of the notion of subjectivity: "The current post-structuralist/post-modern challenges to the coherent, autonomous subject have to be put on hold in feminist and post-colonial discourses, for both must work first to assert and affirm a denied or alienated subjectivity: those radical post-modern challenges are in many ways the luxury of the dominant order which can afford to challenge that which it securely possesses" (168). These and other theorists of the postcolonial can provide substantial insight into the various discursive practices that we examine in composition as well as give us a conceptual vocabulary for better interrogating our encounters with Otherness in the contact zone.

Furthermore, postcolonial theory is even relevant to our own purposes on a more general level. Much of our work has involved drawing on postmodern discourses to articulate discursive practices, and postcolonial theory has numerous affinities with postmodern theory: both find value in oppositionality, in deconstructing master narratives, in interrogating systems of representation, in determining the availability of agency in discourse, in understanding power dynamics, in examining the role of ideology in the construction of self—and these very projects are central to much recent scholarship in composition. Engaging the postcolonial can help us further such projects in substantive ways.[14]

In short, then, the trend in composition scholarship to interrogate how gender, race, ethnicity, and power relationships manifest themselves in discursive practices is in effect a move toward the ethical, toward understanding the encounter with the Other. However, if discussions such as those about contact zones are to contribute fully to this effort, it is incumbent upon us not to allow a weak multiculturalism or an ineffectual liberal pluralism to diminish that effort. Turning difference into a "multicultural bazaar" and avoiding the thorny problems of conflict even while saying we valorize it only serve to conceal the underlying power dynamics of discursive practices. As Min Zhan Lu writes, the field is finally taking seriously two notions of writing: "the sense that the writer writes at a site of conflict rather than 'comfortably inside or powerlessly outside the academy' (Lu) "Writing as Repositioning" (20) and a definition of 'innovative writing' as cutting across rather than confining itself within boundaries of race, class, gender, and disciplinary differences" (888). It is important not to undercut these efforts with a "residual distrust of conflict and struggle" (910). Postcolonial theory, if we allow it, will give us the conceptual vocabulary we need in order to encounter the Other, both in our scholarship and in our classrooms.[15]

Notes

1. I'd like to make clear that I am not advocating a form of ethical relativism or a return to a neo-romantic individualism that is incognizant of the power of culture, ideology, and social context; rather, I am referring to the notion that within the social contexts of our interactions we constantly make choices, and what choices we make, despite the absence of external strictures, situates us firmly in the ethical domain.

2. This position is particularly associated with the work of Emmanuel Levinas and is elaborated in the work of Luce Irigaray (see Hirsh and Olson).

3. One of the finest works I know on the subject is Evelyn Ashton-Jones' "Collaboration, Conversation, and the Politics of Gender."

4. Of course, direct discussion of ethics is becoming more common, as indicated by this book and by the work of James Porter. Also see Moore and Kleine.

5. Interestingly, Patricia Bizzell has even argued that the contact zone can be used as a way to reorganize literary study: "This concept can aid us both because it emphasizes the conditions of difficulty and struggle under which literatures from different cultures come together (thus forestalling the disrespectful glossing over of differences), and because it gives us a conceptual base for bringing these literatures together, namely, when they occur in or are brought to the same site of struggle or 'contact zone'" (166).

6. A revised version of Pratt's "Arts of the Contact Zone" serves as the introduction of her book *Imperial Eyes: Studies in Travel Writing and Transculturation.*

7. Giroux makes a similar point about how compositionists and literacy scholars have appropriated the work of Freire: "What has been increasingly lost in the North American and Western appropriation of Freire's work is the profound and radical nature of its theory and practice as an anti-colonial and postcolonial discourse" (193).

8. A telling indication of the deradicalizing of a potent concept like contact zone is that textbooks are beginning to emerge that attempt to "apply" contact zone theory in their overall pedagogy. If, as Kathleen Welch argues, textbooks are the most conservative repositories of our knowledge at any given moment, then one wonders what the implications are of contact zone theory being packaged in textbooks. I'm reminded, too, of C.H. Knoblauch's observation about social construction: "One can be quite sure, however, that when roving, and normally warring, bands of cognitive psychologists, text linguists, philosophers of composition, historians of rhetoric, Marxist critics, poststructuralists, and reader response theorists all wax equally enthusiastic about 'the social construction of reality,' there is a good chance that the ex-

pression has long since lost its capacity to name anything important or even very interesting" (54).

9   There are, of course, notable exceptions, but few if any draw on the kind of postcolonial theory I will be discussing shortly.

10 In *Pedagogy of the Oppressed,* Freire discusses the dynamic in which the oppressed desire to become like the oppressor, and he warns literacy workers to be prepared for such desire as the oppressed gain critical consciousness (Chapter 1 *passim,* especially 29).

11 The story that Pratt tells of Guaman Poma's *New Chronicle* illustrates this very point, in that Poma provides a revisionist history, "written in a mixture of Quechua and ungrammatical, expressive Spanish," that imitates and parodies the official discourse: "Guaman Poma constructs his text by appropriating and adapting pieces of the representational repertoire of the invaders" ("Arts" 34, 36).

12 In a recent interview, Freire addresses misreadings of his position on teacher authority and the ethical obligation of teachers to exercise their authority (Olson).

13 A notable recent work on the subject is Xin Liu Gale's *Teacher Authority in the Postmodern Classroom*, a winner of the W. Ross Winterowd Award for the most outstanding book on composition theory.

14 One encouraging development is the special issue of *JAC* (1998) on postcolonial theory and composition.

15 I'd like to thank Evelyn Ashton-Jones, Julie Drew, Debra Jacobs, and Todd Taylor for reading and commenting on earlier drafts of this essay.

Works Cited

Ashton-Jones, Evelyn. "Collaboration, Conversation, and the Politics of Gender." *Feminine Principles and Women's Experience in American Composition and Rhetoric*. Ed. Louise Wetherbee Phelps and Janet Emig. Pittsburgh: U of Pittsburgh P, 1995. 5-26.

Bauman, Zygmunt. *Postmodern Ethics*. Cambridge: Blackwell, 1993.

Bhabha, Homi K. "Signs Taken for Wonders: Questions of Ambivalence and Authority Under a Tree Outside Delhi." *Critical Inquiry* 12 (1985): 144-65.

Bizzell, Patricia. "'Contact Zones' and English Studies." *College English* 56 (1994): 163-69.

Brown, Stephen. *Words in the Wilderness: Ideology and Resistance in the Contact Zone*. Unpublished monograph, 1996.

Freire, Paulo. *Pedagogy of the Oppressed*. Trans. Myra Bergman Ramos. 1970. New York: Continuum, 1989.

Gale, Xin Liu. *Teachers, Discourses, and Authority in the Postmodern Composition Classroom*. Albany: State U of New York P, 1996.

Giroux, Henry A. "Paulo Freire and the Politics of Postcolonialism." *Composition Theory for the Postmodern Classroom*. Ed. Gary A. Olson and Sidney I. Dobrin. Albany: State U of New York P, 1994. 193-204.

Harris, Joseph. "Negotiating the Contact Zone." *Journal of Basic Writing* 14 (1995): 27-42.

Hirsh, Elizabeth, and Gary A. Olson. "'Je—Luce Irigaray': A meeting with Luce Irigaray." *Women Writing Culture*. Ed. Gary A. Olson and Elizabeth Hirsh. Albany: State U of New York P, 1995. 141-66.

Hutcheon, Linda. "Circling the Downspout of Empire: Post-Colonialism and Postmodernism." *Past the Last Post: Theorizing Post-Colonialism and Post-Modernism*. Ed. Ian Adam and Helen Tiffin. Calgary: U of Calgary P, 1990. 167-89.

JanMohamed, Abdul J. "The Economy of Manichean Allegory: The Function of Racial Difference in Colonialist Literature." *Critical Inquiry* 12 (1985): 59-87.

Knoblauch, C.H. "Some Observations on Freire's Pedagogy of the Oppressed." *Journal of Advanced Composition* 8 (1988): 50-54.

Lu, Min-Zhan. "Conflict and Struggle: The Enemies or Preconditions of Basic Writing?" *College English* 54 (1992): 887-913.

Miller, Richard E. "Fault Lines in the Contact Zone." *College English* 56 (1994): 389–408.

Mohanty, S.P. "'Us and Them': On the Philosophical Bases of Political Criticism." *New Formations* 8 (1989): 55–80.

Moore, Sandy, and Michael Kleine. "Toward an Ethics of Teaching Writing in a Hazardous Context—The University." *Composition Theory for the Postmodern Classroom.* Ed. Gary A. Olson and Sidney I. Dobrin. Albany: State U of New York P, 1994. 93–104.

Olson, Gary A. "History, Praxis, and Change: Paulo Freire and the Politics of Literacy." *(Inter)views: Cross-Disciplinary Perspectives on Rhetoric and Literacy.* Ed. Gary A. Olson and Irene Gale. Carbondale: Southern Illinois UP, 1991. 155–68.

Parry, Benita. "Problems in Current Theories of Colonial Discourse." *Oxford Literary Review* 9 (1987): 27–58.

Porter, James E. "Developing a Postmodern Ethics of Rhetoric and Composition." *Defining the New Rhetorics.* Theresa Enos and Stuart C. Brown. Newbury Park, CA: Sage, 1993. 207–26.

Pratt; Mary Louise. "Arts of the Contact Zone." *Profession 91* (1991): 33–40.

———. *Imperial Eyes Travel Writing and Transculturation.* New York: Routledge, 1992.

Said, Edward W. *Orientalism.* New York: Random, 1978.

Spivak, Gayatri Chakravorty. "Can the Subaltern Speak?" *Marxism and the Interpretation of Culture.* Ed. Cary Nelson and Lawrence Grossberg. Urbana: U of Illinios Press, 1988. 271–313.

Sulleri, Sara. *The Rhetoric of English India.* Chicago: U of Chicago P, 1992.

Welch, Kathleen E. "Ideology and Freshman Textbook Production: The Place of Theory in Writing Pedagogy." *College Composition and Communication* 38 (1987): 269–82.

Chapter 7

Ethos and Ethics: Ancient Concepts and Contemporary Writing

Rosalind J. Gabin

In his finely detailed commentary on Bk. II of Aristotle's *Rhetoric,* William Grimaldi asserts (1) that *ethos* as Aristotle uses it is a complex term that includes the *ethos* of the audience along with that of the speaker; (2) that the Romans, lacking an equivalent (as Quintilian openly acknowledges in VI, 2, 8), translated it as *mores* or social customs, which overlaps in part with the meaning of the Greek term in Aristotle but does not do it justice; and (3) that the Romans further diluted the sense of *ethos* by tending to conflate it with *pathos* (see p. 183–189). "In its strict sense as moral character," Grimaldi concludes (p. 188), "Aristotelian *ethos* [the moral character of both the speaker and the audience] does not appear to have been understood in the Latin tradition."[1] Given the impact of Roman rhetoric on the history of rhetorical theory and practice, and especially on education, such a provocative statement deserves some sustained attention, as does the question of what kind of rhetoric we get with Aristotelian *ethos* and what kind without it. *Ethos* is crucial to Aristotle's idea of rhetoric as audience-centered discourse—the discourse in which the speaker's awareness of and response to the temper and values of the listener is paramount in the image that he or she projects in the act of speaking, yet many reputable writers on rhetoric over the centuries seem to do quite well without *ethos,* or with a thin or misconstrued concept of it. This complex legacy of classical rhetoric, with *ethos* present, or absent or attenuated, yields a tradition that is far from coherent, and this lack of coherence, combined with the postmodern complication of the idea of the human subject—the agent of both *ethos* and its etymological sibling ethics, has led to the present moment, full of important questions in rhetorical theory and in our analyses of social practices. Certainly it has led to important questions about the discourse community we call the writing classroom—itself an important social practice—since workshopping and collaborative learning, which require regular and often intense student interaction, have come to shape classroom practice.[2] My interest in *ethos*, and in ethics, ultimately rests here, in the classroom. First, however, I want to review the varied fortunes of *ethos* over time and discuss the relationship of *ethos* to ethics. Then I take up the question of how the presence or absence of *ethos* as a guiding principle in the contemporary interactive writing classroom can change the nature of classroom practice in crucial ways, especially in our postmodern age in which students often meet in the classroom largely as strangers.

The varied fortunes of *ethos*, and with them the incoherence of the rhetorical tradition, emerge with startling clarity in two of the many good books on rhetoric to appear in the last twenty years in the United States, and I use them as my point of departure: Richard Lanham's *The Motives of Eloquence* (1976) and James Boyd White's *Heracles' Bow* (1985). Lanham uses Cicero (and with him the sophists) as representative of the rhetorical view of life, while White uses Aristotle (in combination with the Judeo-Christian tradition and Kant) in his representation of rhetoric. Taken together their books collide, yet both are solidly based in the history of rhetoric and in *ethos* variously conceived. The consequences of their ideas are especially interesting in the way they might play themselves out in the writing classroom, and I will take up these consequences after reviewing Lanham's and White's ideas and accounting in some measure for their complex antecedents.

For Lanham, guided by Cicero, the rhetorician is a role-player, a stylist, a projector of images and appearances; if he or she has a self at all it is a de-centered self with an *ethos* that is more speaker- and language-centered than audience-centered, for the speaker is above all an actor propelled by his or her own discursive and histrionic powers. (Lanham speaks of "that huge and exuberant Ciceronian egotism," p. 13.) "The rhetorical stylist," asserts Lanham, "has no central self to be true to . . . At his center lurks a truly Ciceronian vacuity. He feels at home in his roles . . . Rhetorical man is an actor and insincerity is the actor's mode of being" (p. 27); "Whatever sins the rhetorical person might register," says Lanham at the outset of his book, "stylistic naivete would not be one" (p. 3). White, guided on the other hand by Aristotle, sees the rhetorician as someone who forms his or her own character in the act of speaking; he or she is a profoundly ethical being in this sense. White's concern is who we become in our conversations with one another. White connects *ethos* with ethics directly and seems to answer in an equally direct way Lanham's Ciceronian characterization of the rhetorician: in the dialogue that ends *Heracles' Bow*, the interlocutor to whom White gives the final and decisive word asserts, "I want audiences to take seriously what I have to say. . . I am not a chameleon or an actor. . . In any case in which I act, my own sense that I am speaking properly and functioning out of a sense of fairness to others . . . is essential to my *ethos* and therefore to my success" (p. 234-235). For Lanham, rhetoric is speaker- and language-centered play, for White it is a serious audience-centered endeavor. Play is possible, implies Lanham, because Cicero (and with him the sophists, especially Gorgias, p. 14-15) taught us that play (the dramatic playing out of roles) was the essence of both rhetoric and social life; being serious and building character in what you say and do, implies White on the other hand, is the essence of rhetoric and social life because Aristotle (and Plato, the Bible and Kant, p. 5) showed us that the individual is not a means to an end (not to be "played" with) but an end in him- or herself, the foundation for White of the "standard ethical position" and of all moral experience (p. 5). The consequences of each of these positions for shaping social practices and the social reality of the interactive writing classroom are yet to be examined, but first I ask: what are the historical antecedents that permit Lanham and White, both well versed in the history of rhetoric, to differ so profoundly from one another?

The Fragile Fortunes Of *Ethos*

The evidence from the Romans is clear for a largely language- and speaker-centered view of rhetoric—a view which provides Lanham with his model. (Some of the details I offer here come from Grimaldi's elaboration of his notes to Aristotle's *Rhetoric* II in "The Auditor's Role in Aristotelian Rhetoric.") Cicero asserts in the *Orator*, for example (XXXVII, 128), that "Duae res sunt . . . quae bene tractatae ab oratore admirabilem eloquantiam faciant." All the stress here is on the way the orator arouses admiration for his eloquence and, while we cannot take any single statement in the *Orator* at face value—without reading it, that is, with reference to its context and with reference to who is speaking in the dialogue (in this case the patrician Crassus who is acknowledged to be Cicero's spokesperson)—what Cicero goes on to say about the winning of cases in the law courts imposes upon the reader the absolute centrality of the speaker and the peripheral nature of the audience. He recounts his own victories over Hortensius, Catiline, and others, emphasizing all the while (and in addition to his own successes) the ornaments of speech as crucial to the ends of bowling over the audience, keeping them breathless with admiration for his eloquence, controlling them as he plays on their feelings and plays out the proper role of the speaker. This role is nothing less than divine, he tells us in *De Oratore*: "oratoris vis illa divina virusque"; the role confers on the speaker a godlike power. Yet Cicero is also adamant about the importance of the speaker's moral goodness; see, for example, *De inventione*, I, 16, 22; *De Oratore*, II, 79, 321; and *De officiis*, III, 30. Grimaldi is correct, I believe, in his comments on these passages: that even while speaking of the moral goodness we associate with *ethos*—with, i.e., the projection of an image on the part of the speaker of good sense, good will, and above all good moral character—Cicero is clearly referring to the appeal to feeling, the arousing of the emotions of his listeners, the controlling of those emotions through stylistic means. The probative nature of *ethos* slides into the appeal through style, and the heuristic value of *ethos*—finding your arguments and your general stance through considering the values, beliefs, and frame of mind of the listeners—slides into finding the right "ornaments" of speech and donning the right mask in which to address them. Cicero aims above all at powerful performance, a performance which brings personal honor and public glory to the speaker (see Enos, "Cicero Hellenizes," p. 205). As James May explains, the Romans believed that "an individual cannot suddenly, or at will, change . . . his *ethos*" (p. 6); *ethos*, i.e., cannot be adjusted to the situation at hand. This view of *ethos* is in complete opposition to Aristotle's: for Aristotle, *ethos* must be formed in the speech itself in direct response to the values of the listeners, i.e., to the context of situation. For the Romans *ethos* is a permanent characteristic much like some conceptions of character, not formed by experience but inborn. The tactics left to the speaker like Cicero, therefore, have to do with arousing feeling and of course gaining consent through argument. As a result, what Grimaldi refers to as the "psychological proofs" of *ethos* and *pathos* (Grimaldi, *Commentary on Rhet* II, p. 186) collapse into *pathos* alone.[3]

In Quintilian, the blending of *ethos* and *pathos* is as apparent, perhaps more so. Notwithstanding his assertion in the famous passage in Bk. XII of the importance of moral goodness above all else in the formation of the perfect orator—the crowning achievement of rhetoric framed as the "vir bonus peritus dicendi" or, as Kenneth Burke put it, as the union of "right acting and right speaking" (*Rhetoric of Motives*, p. 60)—Quintilian also makes much of the training of the Roman schoolboy in the techniques of the actor at the outset of his long work (see Bk. I): techniques of posture, gesture, facial expression, eye contact, tone of voice, etc. Decrying excessive histrionics and staginess here, Quintilian still advocates that the Roman schoolboy learn to declaim speeches from the theater, learning them by heart for practice in order to develop good delivery and voice along with good memory.[4] And we have the even more telling passages from VI, 2, 8, where Quintilian explains that *ethos* and *pathos* are of the same nature—are "ex eadem natura"—and differ only in degree and use different levels of style: *pathos* is violent emotion, *ethos* a more gentle and calm feeling; the former employs the grand style, the latter middle style to produce an upright and serious appearance (Grimaldi makes much of this passage). Quintilian speaks too of the skillful exercise of feigned emotion (the stock in trade of the actor), of "virtus simulationis." One could also cite the *Ad Herennium* (which Grimaldi does not), dominated by stylistic concerns but with *ethos* part of the picture in an oblique and unexpected way. In IV, 37, on Frankness of Speech, not only is pungency or wit praised as effective under the right circumstances (here, curiously, a discussion of wit falls under frankness) but so is pretense or the guise of Frank Speech: this is a discussion, in essence, of what has been called the "rhetoric of anti-rhetoric" (see Valesio, p. 41-60), the attempt to disarm the listener by openly asserting guilelessness and truthfulness. (As Valesio puts it, p. 59-60, the rhetoric of anti-rhetoric is the attempt, forever doomed, of the word "to detach itself from its mechanism," a practice "more sophisticated and more devious than the rhetoric from which it pretends to shy away.") So we clearly find among the Romans flat assertions of the moral principles which should guide the speaker and alongside these assertions the constant undercutting of those principles as oratorical composition and delivery, conceived as theatrical practice with pathetic intention, guide the speaker toward powerful performance.

The Romans clearly handed down a largely stylistic view of rhetoric as opposed to an ethical one, a view which shows up in texts as diverse as Martianus Capella's *Marriage of Philology and Mercury* and St. Augustine's *On Christian Doctrine* and which comes to dominate European rhetoric through the Renaissance and beyond. Martianus Capella, who depended on Cicero indirectly (he depended on Varro who depended on Cicero), offers us his famous figure of rhetoric as a woman ornamented with tropes and figures and armed for battle: style will clearly do the fighting in the battle of words. And St. Augustine, Martianus Capella's rough contemporary, submerges *ethos* and exalts style, not only because he was partly Ciceronian in his rhetorical orientation but also because, above all, the Christian preacher has lost his probative function for he has nothing substantial to prove. Conversion and belief were the result of God's grace and did not depend on the sermonizer, whose function it was to confirm and intensify belief and to interpret the Bible for the listener. Augustine's Christian preacher is often preaching to the converted so he needs no proofs, only the ability to arouse to more intense belief by stylistic means a listener already committed. Small wonder then that we find in Bk. IV *of On Christian Doctrine* a discussion of the three styles as Cicero discusses them in the *Orator*. Despite Augustine's serious commitment to a serious and ethically demanding belief, his advice to the Christian preacher is to produce above all else powerful performance. He even advocates "faking it" if necessary, i.e., speaking fine words for their good effects on the audience even when the life of the speaker gives the lie to the principles of those words (IV, 59, 60). And, while truth is exalted above error, and the sincerity of the speaker above the mere mouthing of the "right" words, Augustine asserts without reservation that "to contend in words is not to care how error may be overcome by truth, but how your style may be preferred to another's" (IV,61). As Kenneth Burke puts it in *A Rhetoric of Motives* (p. 53), "Augustine is concerned . . . with the *cajoling* of an audience . . . and held that every last *embellishment* [emphasis added here but not above in "cajoling"] should be brought to the service of God."

In subsequent history, *ethos* is largely eliminated from the distinction made increasingly in the sixteenth century between the appeal to reason through logic and the appeal to feeling, to the "affections," through rhetoric (the term *ethos* scarcely appears in the treatises of the period although *ethos* is still present in Renaissance practice; see Baumlin and Baumlin, p. 229). The rhetorical appeal through a combination of Aristotelian *ethos*, *pathos*, and *logos* is fractured, as in Thomas Wilson's *Rule of Reason* of 1551, in which rhetoric is characterized in purely stylistic terms (and in terms we all recognize) as using "gay painted sentences . . . fresh colors and goodly ornaments" to achieve its purposes. Brian Vickers got it right when he asserted in "On the Practicalities of Renaissance Rhetoric" that

> What is striking as one follows . . . rhetoric between 1500 and 1700 in England, France, and Germany is . . . how . . . success is measured by striking power . . . The Renaissance valued rhetoric . . . because it could move people . . . by mobilizing the will . . . The route lay partly through reason . . . Yet the more effective route lay through the passions. (135)

And the route to the passions lay through *elocutio*, through the artful deployment of the tropes and figures—"the power of the figures of rhetoric to move the feelings," as Vickers puts it (p. 137).[5] *Ethos* is also conspicuously absent in Ernesto Grasssi's superb discussion of the Roman-Latin tradition of rhetoric in *Rhetoric as Philosophy: The Humanist Tradition*. Grassi is concerned here with explaining the logic of images, of figurative language, as the basis for the construction of the human world, and clearly sees the Roman-Latin tradition, which, he asserts, stems from Cicero and culminates in Vico, as rhetorical precisely because it assigns to figuration in language—and especially to metaphor—a foundational value. It is figuration, the product of human ingenuity, which makes rhetoric. Grassi explains, for example, in his chapter on "Rhetoric as the Ground of Society," that "as far as poetry is concerned we must note that it makes use of metaphors and images that affect the passions and lend it a rhetorical character" (72). This summation of the Roman-Latin tradition, with the pathetic resonance of images and the general play of figuration as the essence of rhetoric, with *ethos* totally absent, validates Grimaldi's conclusion (and my starting point) that the Romans and the Roman-Latin tradition mistranslated, misunderstood, or eliminated *ethos* from their discussion of rhetoric, and assimilated *ethos* to *pathos*.

The eighteenth and nineteenth centuries are ones to linger over in this brief survey, for they are complex in their approach to *ethos* (in this they foreshadow the twentieth century). On the one hand, as Edward Corbett asserts in "Classical Rhetoric: The Basic Issues":

> Since many of the schoolmasters in the English and American schools during the eighteenth and nineteenth centuries were clergymen, they seized on . . . *ethos* as the justification for their making the teaching of religion and ethics a regular part of the curriculum of the schools. The popular Chatauqua movement, and other enterprises in the United States for the education of the masses, stems from this tradition. (3)

But Corbett adds thereafter that "[t]he public-school system that developed in America in the nineteenth century reversed this tradition by adopting the policy of excluding religious instruction from the classroom." So completely did *ethos* disappear from American schooling that Nan Johnson could assert in 1984 when speaking of the 1970s and early 80s in an article on *ethos* that "the majority of instructors in rhetoric clearly view the issue of ethical intention in rhetoric to be a concern that falls outside the sphere of pedagogy . . ." (p. 114). This tendency was further enhanced by the eighteenth and nineteenth century transformation of mass education into a practical training of functionaries for business and the civil service: little regard remained for moral character or for the importance of *ethos* as a crucial component of any utterance, for stating the bare facts (positivism at work) was the aim. Not only does *ethos* disappear, but so does *pathos*.

Kenneth Cmiel points out in *Democratic Eloquence* that in the effort to train the masses to serve the interests of government and business in the nineteenth century, education saw the ideal of the citizen-orator overtaken by the idea of the working man and woman asked simply to do a proper job in the mechanisms of the company or later the bureaucratic corporation, or in the special (and also bureaucratic) offices of government. Translating Cmiel's discussion into other terms, we could say that *ethos* becomes *persona* (a term from the theater), the playing out of the role one assumes in the everyday world of work, what we have come to call today "impression management," or what Erving Goffman calls in the title of his well-known book "the presentation of self in everyday life." "The speech of the best soul" has yielded to efficiency and pragmatic correctness, with little if any attention paid until relatively recently to the larger social implications of the activities of the functionary within a company or corporation or branch of government or in society at large. This marks the beginning of what we have come to think of as the "bureaucratic mind" (whose dangers have been so sharply analyzed by Hannah Arendt in her examination of Adolf Eichmann and by White in *Heracles' Bow* [see ch. I for his analysis of the dangers of ends-means thinking[6]). Nan Johnson describes the consequences for us of an education in bureaucratic thinking when she describes modern writing texts, which "advise students to correlate 'persona' with assessments of the reader and the writing situation. Such advice presents *ethos* as a skill of *stylistic* adaptability [emphasis added] mode and audience, and typically eschews moral implications" (p.113). Gregory Clark and Michael Halloran, in the introduction to their recent *Oratorical Culture in Nineteenth-Century America* (p. 3), make virtually the same point when they speak of "the new public morality of expertise" that came to dominate American values in the nineteenth century: the experts take care of their special areas without reflecting on the larger social implications of the larger project of which they are a part. The whole dissolves into its parts and collective moral authority vanishes.

At the same time *ethos*, the term itself, continues to form part of several eighteenth century rhetorics (whose influence extended to nineteenth century pedagogy), but in attenuated form. Both George Campbell and Richard Whately saw *ethos* as a strategy for gaining "sympathy" but only so that the passions would then be more deeply affected. As Johnson asserts nicely: "This notion of sympathy is closely related to what Aristotle and Cicero meant by good will [one of the three components of Aristotelian *ethos*], yet Campbell and other eighteenth century rhetoricians bring a slightly different philosophical perspective to what is involved in eliciting sympathy. Campbell perceives the gaining of sympathy as a necessary step in affecting the passions, which in turn engage the will so as to effect persuasion" (p. 107–108). This blending of *ethos* and *pathos*, or the sliding of *ethos* into *pathos*, is reminiscent of the Roman-Latin tradition in which *ethos* conflates with *pathos* and largely disappears as a firm principle that can stand on its own. As James Berlin explains in *Writing Instruction* (p. 8), Campbell ignores the "appeal from character" while retaining "the emotional appeal" through style, because "style becomes central . . . in reproducing the content of the speaker's or writer's experience in the minds of the audience." In this regard, Hugh Blair is especially interesting, for Blair's emphasis on tasteful speaking as the aim of rhetoric links taste with virtue: what Blair calls in his pre-Romantic way "the unassumed language of the heart" will ultimately persuade the listener, for the goodness of the speaker and the truth of his or her words are made manifest through this "natural" language.[7] While the eighteenth and nineteenth centuries continued to stress the importance of truth and sincerity, *ethos* in the Aristotelian sense was fading, for audience mattered less, if at all, as the speaker concentrated on transmitting to the listener as closely as possible the stirrings of his or her own heart.

By the nineteenth century, education in rhetoric came to be dominated by some combination of Campbell and Blair along with Richard Whately's emphasis in his *Elements of Rhetoric* (1828) on argumentation. Techniques of style, and of delivery, might have overtaken all sense of social responsibility were it not for the work of the German Franz Theremin and his translator William Shedd. Theremin's work on rhetoric, which was ethically based and offered a much needed corrective to the "style and rule" rhetorical education offered by the triumvirate of Campbell, Blair, and Whately, appeared in Berlin in 1814 and was translated by Shedd into English in 1844. It was to go through ten editions by 1897 (see Johnson, "Three Nineteenth-Century Rhetoricians," p. 106) and to foreshadow the New Rhetoric of the twentieth century in its concern for the education of students in a rhetoric that was socially and personally responsible (James Boyd White's aim). *Ethos* and ethics as the ground of all communication—awareness of the social and moral context within which we speak and write—clearly dominate Theremin's thinking; yet the ethical paradigm was not to prevail in the way students were trained in the nineteenth century, nor was it to prevail in the twentieth even after the process revolution of the 60s. If we look at textbooks today we can see that stylistic concerns, along with invention, overshadow *ethos*, giving rise in composition to the "current-traditional paradigm" in composition in the United States, the paradigm that stresses above all else patterns of arrangement and grammatical correctness (see Berlin, *Rhetoric and Reality*, p. 9). To be sure, as James Kinneavy and Susan Warshauer explain in "From Aristotle to Madison Avenue" (p. 171), "*ethos* has became an increasingly important focus of modern rhetorical theory" because of the modern interest in persuasion, yet they also acknowledge that "contemporary composition instruction gives the ethical argument perfunctory attention at best," in part because "composition pedagogy has yet to work out a systematic presentation of the ethical proof."

Aristotle himself is somewhat responsible for the difficulties theoretical and practical rhetoric has had with the concept of *ethos*, for he devotes relatively little space to explaining the ethical proof, and what he does tell us is open to interpretation. While "[r]hetoric owes its technical use of the term *ethos* to Aristotle," asserts James Baumlin (Baumlin and Baumlin, p. xvi), ". . . his *Rhetorica* is at the same time the most problematic of discussions." As Kinneavy and Warshauer note (p. 172), Aristotle "devotes only one chapter to *ethos*, whereas he devotes nine to logos, sixteen to *pathos* and eleven to style. Suggestive though this chapter is, it does not constitute a fully developed and applied theory of ethical argument." And they go on to observe that the chapter is especially difficult on the "'ethical,' or moral, intention of *ethos*." It is abundantly clear that in using the term *ethos*, which has a range of meanings in Greek and which shares a word root with "ethical," Aristotle opened up more questions than he answered. The crucial question on the moral intention of *ethos* is simply: what is the relationship of *ethos* to ethics? Before we go on to the complexities of the twentieth century in this brief survey of the antecedents of Lanham and White and of the fate of *ethos*, we must pause to consider this question, especially because, in the preceding discussion, I have referred to and quoted some who link *ethos* and ethics rather carelessly.

Ethos And Ethics

Aristotle encourages us to assume a connection between *ethos* and ethics: in the *Nichomachean Ethics* (1103a) he tells us that "moral virtue comes about as a result of habit," whence its name *ethike*, which is formed by a slight variation from the word *ethos*. *Ethos* meant originally a haunt or habitual place and came to mean habit or habitual practice.[8] (This is the sense it had for the Romans when they translated it as *mores*). Yet, while resting on a shared word root, *ethos* and ethics are difficult to connect if we look at what Aristotle says about *ethos* in the *Rhetoric*.

Many have commented on the tenuousness of the relationship between *ethos* and ethics precisely because Aristotle, while asserting that *arete*, or good moral character, is an essential component of *ethos*, makes clear that *arete* does not inhere in the speaker's performance but in the audience's *perception* of the performance. "*Ethos* and ethics are," as Jasper Neel puts it, the "effects of discourse" (p. 165) and not their cause. The speaker may therefore effectively project an image of moral goodness that is just an image and nothing more. As Kinneavy and Warshauer explain, speaking of the amorality of Aristotle's theory of rhetoric "and especially his theory of *ethos*," "[e]thical appeal . . . as Aristotle describes it . . . combines elements of compromise and manipulation" (p. 178). And they say earlier that Aristotle's theory of *ethos* "admits the expediency of manipulation and appearances" (p. 172). Because the perception of the listener is everything in the act of rhetoric as Aristotle described it, whatever helps to project the "right" image for the speaker's success is admissible. Aristotelian *ethos* therefore has for Kinneavy and Warshauer no connection with ethics; it is amoral in the same way that the whole *Rhetoric* is amoral. Paolo Valesio sees the lack of connection in an even more serious way in *Novantiqua* (p. 83), albeit without directly addressing the concept of *ethos*, when he comments this way, and rather trenchantly, on the well known passage near the outset of Bk. I of the *Rhetoric* (1355a, 29-38) in which Aristotle advocates that the speaker argue both sides of a question in his or her mind as preparation for argument but choose (ethically) the way of right and justice if only because these are more plausible and therefore more effective than their opposites in making the desired impression on the listener:

> What is taking place here is nothing less than this: a mercilessly sharp critical discovery is being masked . . . under a protective veil of moralism. This is something more than an intellectually fascinating performance—it is a turning point in the history of ideas. For the discovery which serves as background to this passage is that the house of human discourse cannot be built on solid rock, that . . . its only possible foundation is ever-shifting sand.

The "protective veil of moralism" here leads us to question not only the link of *ethos* to ethics but Aristotle's own rhetorical strategy: is his idea of *ethos*, which is a construction of language and which he calls at a famous point in Bk. I perhaps the speaker's most effective means of persuasion (1356a), when combined with the stress he places on truth as important in making your own case plausible, part of his own "ethical image" and nothing more? Can *ethos* and ethics be linked at all by the careful reader of Aristotle?

For Grimaldi, certainly one of Aristotle's most careful readers and whose comments on the attenuation of *ethos* in Roman rhetoric are my starting point, *ethos* and ethics are clearly linked because Grimaldi reads Aristotle as a moral Platonist, as a true believer in the moral imperative of the speaker and in the reality of truth and justice. Grimaldi explains ethics in Aristotle's *Rhetoric* most ingeniously: borrowing a key term from the *Poetics*, he asserts that rhetoric is *mimesis* for Aristotle (commentary on *Rhetoric* I, p. 27), and so "if truth and justice are defeated [in the rhetorical act], it is because rhetoric has failed in its function as mimesis" and the rhetorician has failed in his moral imperative to "mimic" reality and tell the truth. It would seem here that despite Grimaldi's careful notes on Aristotle's concept of *ethos*—that the speaker creates his *ethos* through an adjustment to and a negotiation with the *ethos* of the audience, Grimaldi departs from Aristotle's idea to some degree when he suggests that the speaker should be guided more by the truth of the matter than by the audience's values and expectations. I part company with Grimaldi on this point, for reality and truth are not appropriate concepts here. What matters in Aristotelian rhetoric is the listener's perception that the case has been stated and argued or an action has been urged or a value has been celebrated in accordance with that listener's perception of the appropriateness or the rightness of the discourse (the rightness, i.e., of everything in that discourse: its arguments, its style, its examples and images, and the *ethos* the speaker projects). Kenneth Burke hit the nail on the head when he commented in *A Rhetoric of Motives* (p. 54) that

> the relation between "truth" and the kind of opinion with which rhetoric operates is often misunderstood. And the classical texts do not seem to bring out the point we have in mind . . . The kind of opinion with which rhetoric deals . . . is not opinion *as contrasted with truth.*

What Burke means is that in rhetoric we have one opinion coming up against another, not, as in Plato's *Gorgias*, *doxa* competing with *episteme*. If we knew for a certainty what to do or how to judge, if we possessed, i.e., *episteme* or unshakable knowledge of the truth and of reality in contingent matters, we would have no need for opinions and therefore no use for rhetoric, as Aristotle clearly indicates in the *Rhetoric*. And, if "truth" plays no part in the rhetorical process, does the ethical (in the sense of the moral) play a part? Can *ethos* lead us to its etymological sibling, ethics?

With all due respect to Grimaldi, the clear consensus is that Aristotle's *Rhetoric* is amoral. Kenneth Burke, who shares in the consensus, says further that, while "*in general* the truer and better cause has the advantage" according to Aristotle's *Rhetoric*, Aristotle still demonstrates that "no cause can be adequately defended without skill in the tricks of the trade. So Aristotle studies these tricks from the purely technical point of view, without reference to any one fixed position" (*Rhetoric of Motives*, p. 52). Consequently the *Rhetoric* is, among other things, a handbook of tactics for both sides in an argument or a discussion: it describes and analyzes, according to Burke, "the holds and the counter-holds, the blows and the ways of blocking them, for every means of persuasion the corresponding means of dissuasion, for every proof the disproof, for every praise the vituperation that matches it." We have here total moral neutrality. There are many ethical statements to be reckoned with in the *Rhetoric*, to be sure, but they are always outside the rhetorical process. Jan Swearingen gets it right when she asserts in *Rhetoric and Irony* (p. 99–100) that "Aristotle . . . posits . . . that a separate discipline, ethics, will take care of the abuses of rhetoric." *Ethos*, however, does not belong to a separate discipline but is integral to the rhetorical process as Aristotle explains it. Can it have some positive ethical content even if we accept that the ethical is a perception of the listener? I believe that it can and that the late twentieth century, in an oblique way, has helped us to see that.

The Ethical Turn In The Twentieth Century

The present century would seem for many unlikely to interest itself in *ethos*. The New Rhetoric reshaped classical rhetoric and in the process often ignored the terms and concepts of ancient theory, as in the case of I. A. Richards, or often renamed them, as in the case of Kenneth Burke. Mikhail Bakhtin thought of rhetoric as a dying discipline and replaced it with dialogism. Chaim Perelman discussed at length the logic of informal argument, as has Stephen Toulmin, but *ethos*, while hovering about the edges of their writing on argumentation, does not figure in an important way in their considerations. Ethics does, however. And postmodernism might be redefined, asserts James Baumlin (Baumlin and Baumlin, p, xxi), "as an age after *ethos*, since the very notion of the sovereign individual [the agent of *ethos* and of ethics] now falls under question." In addition, the triumph of electronic technology has only intensified the demise of the individual and the "disappearance of the . . . human voice . . . behind symbolized words," according to Michael Heim's *Electric Language* (p. 212). In our postmodern climate, individual choice and responsibility have been undercut in favor of seeing the individual as the effect, not the cause, of historical and cultural forces. So great has been the assault on the idea of the individual that Tobin Seibers could assert in 1988 (p. 10) that "the character of language promoted by theory today makes extremely difficult the type of consciousness necessary to moral reflection," and Manfred Frank in 1984 (p. xxiii), in his discussion of the work of German social theorist Niklas Luhmann, that the individual receives from the cultural systems of which he is a part the ethical message of *mimesis*: total and automatic conformity to the logic of the system.[9] Yet, in the midst of this culture of forces and systems in which the individual is crushed or simply eliminated from consideration—and with the individual, human choice, both *ethos* and ethics have emerged as focal points for important discussions of language and social relations and have helped us to come to terms with postmodernism's dehumanization of the human world. *Ethos* has also become a focal point for the teaching of writing if we are to believe a recent review of Baumlin and Baumlin's *Ethos: New Essays in Critical and Rhetorical Theory* (CCC, 46:3 [Oct 1995] p. 456), which asserts that "[w]hat 'invention' was to discussions of rhetoric/composition in the 1970s . . . 'ethos' has become for the 90s."

We can look at two recent volumes for evidence of a resurgent interest in *ethos* and in ethics: Aarons and Salomon's *Rhetoric and Ethics: Historical and Theoretical Perspectives* (1991) and Baumlin and Baumlin's *Ethos: New Essays in Rhetorical and Critical Theory* (1994). While these volumes appear to differ in their general orientations, with ethics the focus of one and *ethos* of the other, their overlaps are significant and their common insights, once sorted out, are suggestive of some links between *ethos* and ethics. Both are collections of essays by various authors, but both, taken as a whole, are concerned with responding to postmodernism's more extreme positions on the individual and on human freedom or its lack; both draw heavily on the classical tradition of rhetoric either directly or indirectly; and both are concerned with human relations and language. What emerges from taking them together is a deeper understanding of the self as a social being formed by culture and yet still able to act and to speak as something far less than an automaton. "Although various forms of the self change over time," asserts one of the writers for the Baumlin and Baumlin collection (Marshall Alcorn, p. 6), "the particular selves formed by historical conditions have relatively stable self-structures" even as these selves project "different sorts of *ethos*" (p. 7) over time and in varying situations.

Both *Rhetoric and Ethics* and *Ethos: New Essays* reject style as the essence of rhetoric—reject, i.e., the Ciceronian legacy as Lanham framed it—and define rhetoric in a more Aristotelian way as social engagement through language and specifically through the crafting of *ethos* and the practice of ethics. Both volumes suggest, that is, that in social engagements there are always ethical entailments. Rhetoric is constituted by "the activities and language of our mutually engaged sensibilities, presumptions, judgments, and justifications," asserts Lawrence Kimmel, for example (p. 2). And Kimmel goes on to explain that, in social engagements, we make meaning with each other through selves which are distinguishable entities while shaped in part by social values, by language, and by material forces. In *Ethos: New Essays* (p. 14), Marshall Alcorn defines rhetoric similarly: "Rhetoric," he asserts, "might be defined as a well-focused and carefully crafted strategy for changing self-organization as it seeks to participate in the modification of self-components in order to produce changes in human action or belief." Both volumes deal with persons who have taken into themselves the values and attitudes of others, and in the process refer us to the Aristotelian idea of *ethos*, in which the speaker is subjected to the social and ideological pressures of the group he or she addresses. Both volumes also refer us to what ethics is: the awareness of others as we speak and act, the awareness of not only our own interests but of the interests of others. Both volumes join discourse, selves, and public values for purposes of discussing ethics or for purposes of discussing *ethos*, and both believe that human action is possible even as the human being is subjected to painful and seemingly irresistible pressures from the forces of culture and history. (Victor Vitanza, for example, a thorough-going postmodernist, believes in the possibility of human action in a form that he calls a "transgressive individualization" [Baumlin and Baumlin, p. 393], a concept he takes from both Nietzsche and Foucault.) The authors in both volumes can believe in human action because, thinking "ethically" and also within the parameters of their own postmodern moment, they perceive individuals as both active and passive at the same time in the act of speaking or doing. (Vitanza's idea is to make the agent as active as possible and to eliminate as much as possible passivity or conformity to what is outside the individual, for he seeks to "liberate us both from the state and from the type of individualization linked to the state"; here he quotes Foucault [see Baumlin and Baumlin. p. 393].) Kenneth Burke has explained in his *Grammar of Motives* how this union of action and passion ("passion" to be taken literally here) comes about.

Burke describes the implicit irony in human action as a case of "dialectic substance" (p. 33), explaining that "the motivational properties of communication [which is a form of action] characterize both 'the human situation' and what men are 'in themselves.'" Action, that is, is not wholly "active," but shaped in part by the situation of the actor or the agent. We see "a merger of active and passive," he asserts (p. 40), "in the expression 'the motivation of an act.'" And he continues:

> Strictly speaking, the act of an agent would be the movement not of one *moved* but of a *mover*. . . . For an act is by definition active, whereas to be moved (or motivated) is by definition passive.

Yet actions are motivated, Burke explains, and in large measure by things outside the self, and so are never wholly free or spontaneous.

Burke's idea of dialectic substance (in itself deeply Aristotelian, since Aristotle thought of the free individual in relation to the *polis* as both "subject" and "sovereign"; see MacIntyre, p. 159) suggests both *ethos* and ethics as examples of the dialectical movement between oneself and others. This dialectical movement is not only incorporated by Aristotle into his general idea of rhetoric as audience-centered discourse, it is also named as one of the three components of *ethos* and called *phronesis*. *Phronesis*, which can mean "practical wisdom" or "good sense," is at the same time dialectical, ethical (in the moral sense of the term), and situational, for it can only be exercised in specific circumstances and, in communication, in response to the mood of the audience and that audience's interests (see Kinneavy and Warshauer's discussion of *phronesis*, p. 179). There are no rules to follow in the exercise of *phronesis*, just as there are no rules to follow, for Aristotle, in ethical activity, for both demand the ability "to do the right thing in the right place at the right time in the right way" (MacIntyre, p. 150). The link between *phronesis*, a basic component of *ethos*, and ethics is so strong that in his *Teacher's Guide to Philosophical Hermeneutics* (p. 43), Timothy Crusius calls *phronesis* "ethics in action"; Crusius' understanding of *phronesis* is inherently ethical, for it follows from his understanding of the "free" agent of a discourse or an action as one who is inevitably altered by others and by culture (this is of course a crucial part of the "situated quality" of the self in hermeneutics). And, as we shall see, *phronesis* figures in an important way in the formation of a postmodern ethic.[10] Yet all the links established between *ethos* and ethics still do not erase the moral neutrality of Aristotle's view of rhetoric and the calculated and manipulative quality of his idea of *ethos*. Putting *ethos* into action, however, in a certain kind of classroom can provide, I suggest, an ethical (i.e., moral) education for students if we think of *ethos*, as Aristotle did, as an aspect of discourse that is consciously crafted and therefore susceptible of being learned.

Ethos And Ethics In The Collaborative Writing Classroom

In his book on Cicero, James May, as I noted, asserts that for the Romans "character remains essentially constant . . . and does not evolve or develop . . . rather it is bestowed or inherited by nature" (p. 6). And May continues: "The Romans further believed that in most cases character remains constant from generation to generation of the same family." Roman orators, therefore, often narrated their own actions and those of their ancestors as a form of ethical proof (May, p. 6). The Roman belief in the authority of nature to such a degree in the formation of character makes logical Lanham's reading of Cicero as above all a stylist, and Lanham's consequent interpretation of the Roman legacy to rhetoric as the cultivation of style and social surface. An Aristotelian framework, on the other hand, which we find in White, appears a more fruitful way to approach moral training because Aristotle, while acknowledging the "natural" component of character, also believed in the importance of habit: as noted from the *Nichomachean Ethics* (1103a), "moral virtue comes about as a result of habit." Habits, once formed, stick to the individual, become ingrained, and help to form the individual's character. In this way, education plays a major role in forming selves and in forming citizens (the legacy of the classical tradition of rhetoric), for what is education for students but the formation of habits of thought and behavior? (Such was the aim of Roman education as well, as it is of all education, but the goals of Roman education were also guided by the Roman acceptance of the overriding importance of nature). Aristotle's *Rhetoric* is amoral in its stress on appearances and effectiveness, but Aristotle's ethical concept of habit formation in the development of character—the idea that people are what they do—can, I suggest, take the immoral edge off his idea of rhetoric if we apply it to *ethos* in the collaborative classroom. Students can learn to craft their *ethos* consciously not only as they write for an imagined readership but also as they speak to each other in their collaboration. Awareness of *ethos* in that collaboration can be a first step toward forming ethical habits.

Kinneavy and Warshauer apply Aristotelian *ethos* to classroom instruction in writing and in analyzing the messages we receive from others (p. 172), advocating that students learn "the full range of techniques that shape and manipulate self-images . . . and their possible moral use and their possible moral abuse." Such an education would include training students in how to shape their self-images in their own written discourse and how to detect and to analyze the manipulation of image and character in the discourse of others, especially politicians and advertisers. I suggest that the collaborative classroom, which has become the current model for writing classrooms, can permit another kind of education in *ethos* as it fosters personal interaction among students over the course of a semester. A collaborative writing classroom can foster an education in human relations as well as in composition when it stresses not only the writing process but also the social process in which students engage as they participate in the maturation of each other's ideas and language. A classroom that used Lanham's Ciceronian framework, even if it were collaborative, would be an exercise in style and in power; one that used White's Aristotelian framework would be an exercise in responsible discourse. The first would be a political classroom, the second an ethical classroom. So much stress has been placed in the past decade on power and the politics of discourse; the stress is now shifting to cooperation and the ethics of discourse.

The shift from politics to ethics is emerging in the literature about the teaching of writing: we can in fact see in that literature a hovering between the political and the ethical. Louise Phelps, for example, In *Profession 93* (1993), asserts that "a discourse of ethics and human agency . . . has . . . been both neglected and assumed in the claim that 'everything is political'" (p. 47). One year later Carrie Leverenz produced, in "Peer Response in the Multicultural Composition Classroom," a highly nuanced discussion of the difficulties of student collaboration and peer response set in a political framework: Leverenz concludes her discussion of peer response by asserting that one group in her class "replicated an uneven distribution of power" (p. 184). In the same issue, however, in the article preceding Leverenz's, "Collaborative Role-Play and Negotiation" by (appropriately) three authors collaborating (Thia Wolf, Lauren Wright and Toll Imhoff), the ethical framework prevails: "all of us believed . . . in an ethics-based education" (p. 149), the authors assert at the outset, and at the conclusion that the classroom experiences they describe "provide students with a learning environment that encourages critical self-reflection and awareness of the positions of others" (p. 164). Clearly there is an ethical framework here, as in Michael Hassett's piece of 1995 in the same journal, "Increasing Response-ability Through Mortification." Concerned with helping his students to became writers who are aware of the views of others as they develop their own, Hassett is also concerned with helping his students to develop an *ethos* which will further their ethical practice (he does not use the term *ethos* but suggests it): "As teachers of composition," he concludes (p. 487), and in words which echo White's socially responsible view of rhetoric,

> the best we can do is to see, and to help our students see, the writer as an actor not in the sense of a person pretending to be something he or she is not, but in the sense of a person seeking to act ethically upon the symbolic world in which we both write and live.

And see as well my own "Ethics Across the Curriculum," 1995, for a discussion of the needed incorporation of ethics into writing-across-the-curriculum programs.

This hovering between the political and the ethical in composition is clear not only in composition journals but also in one of the more substantial recent monographs on teaching writing, Lester Faigley's *Fragments of Rationality: Postmodernity and the Subject of Composition*. Most interesting in Faigley's book is its closing chapter, "The Ethical Subject" (p. 225-239), in which not only is the issue of ethics raised in regard to both writing and classroom procedure, but also the importance of Aristotle in Faigley's discussion of the ethical thought of Jean-François Lyotard. Faigley, significantly, begins his book in a political framework but ends it, as he looks to the future, in an ethical framework. As I read Faigley's book and put it together with the shorter pieces mentioned, I can only conclude that the political aim in composition of empowering students to get what they want from the systems that rule them through powerful discourse is winding down, and that an ethical aim is replacing it—the aim of promoting sounder human relationships through encouraging attention to others and through responsible discourse.

Ethos emerges in Faigley's discussion of this ethical possibility, although Faigley, like Hassett, does not use the term *ethos* but suggests it as he refers to Lyotard's preference in *The Differend* for the term "prudence." "Prudence" is one of the several translations of "*phronesis*," the "good sense" or "practical wisdom" component of *ethos*, and so morally charged that Crusius, as I have noted, calls it "ethics in action." Faigley is clearly using a suggestive set of terms for ethical purposes, yet his most suggestive, as I will show, is not "prudence" but "anonymity," which Faigley explains in regard to language and in regard to community. "Prudence," however, will figure in his discussion of "anonymity."

Referring to Mark Poster's *Modes of Information*, Faigley explains (p. 230) that

> [m]ost acts of reading in our culture—reading signs, reading labels, reading instructions, reading forms, reading most of what's in a newspaper . . . 'feel anonymous,' for rarely are author's names attached to such . . . texts.

This anonymity, technologically determined for Poster by both print and electronics (but especially the latter), pervades our culture as well as our reading experience. I say that it is the opposite of *ethos*, for a message that has *ethos* emanates from a particular speaker (or group of speakers) and is shaped for a particular audience, a shaping which, according to Aristotle, depends on the audience's mood and values. A message has *ethos* when it bears a signature inscribed in the text in some way that indicates the character and the personality, even the mind and certainly the attitude, of both the speaker or writer and the audience. That speaker or writer has been formed, and is being formed in the process of communicating, by cultural and material forces and by the audience's temper, but he or she embodies nonetheless the human and even the personal origin of the message. The message therefore has a face and a voice. Thought of this way—as a kind of signature—*ethos* can become the antidote to the faceless and voiceless language of many of the messages that circulate today and that have the force of authority precisely because they lack the specificity of a signature, for such messages seem to emanate from a superhuman source.

Faigley goes on to develop the pervasiveness of anonymity in contemporary culture in yet another way: in his explanation of the disappearance of community and the consequent rise of what he calls "urban spaces" peopled largely by strangers. In this urban anonymity, the group consciousness on which traditional ethics has always depended (the *ethe* or traditional haunts and customs which for the Greeks and for others had great cultural and therefore ethical force) gives way to another kind of consciousness, Faigley suggests, dependent far less on communal affiliation and shared values and more on individuals who run across each other as they do in a modern city: as total strangers. And, since education reflects society, no longer are classrooms, believes Faigley, groups whose coherence of purpose, attitude, and background we can take for granted but "urban spaces bringing together a range of differences even when students are relatively homogeneous in race and class" (p. 230). He concludes that words he borrows from Mike Rose's general description of UCLA in *Lives on the Boundary* are in fact the specific description of the contemporary classroom in most colleges today: "the wild intersection of cultures, spectacular diversity, compressed by a thousand social forces." If classes, and especially collaborative classes, are to function at all, and if we are to encourage students to communicate with each other in significant ways, we need a moral and social framework, Faigley suggests, which cannot rest on shared values and community spirit but on a new ethic which can and must deal with diversity and difference.

Faigley's suggestion of the need for a new ethic comes into sharp relief when placed alongside Alasdair MacIntyre's more traditional analysis of ethics in a world shorn of overarching systems of value and left with disconnected fragments of these systems.

MacIntyre perceives the contemporary world as does Faigley (and as do Poster and the others on whom Faigley depends), but suggests in *After Virtue* a different course: the formation of small, local communities in which shared values and purposes can more easily emerge. As examples of such an enterprise, MacIntyre suggests (p. 151) "the founding and carrying forward of a school, a hospital or an art gallery." MacIntyre, in Aristotelian fashion (and in the fashion of all ancient societies), cannot imagine the individual severed from the community, the prototype of which is the Greek *polis*, even when that community with all that it implies in the way of commonality of practices and values has largely disappeared. The individual, asserts MacIntyre, "is indeed intelligible only as a *politikon zöon*" (p. 150). Faigley, on the other hand, basing a good deal of his discussion of a postmodern ethic on Iris Young's *Justice and the Politics of Difference* and then on Lyotard's *The Differend* (Faigley, p. 231 ff.), can imagine a classroom, or any other small group, with an assortment of strangers who can still meet and communicate because Lyotard has guided him in the direction of an Aristotle whose ethical ideas are still functional even without the idea of the Greek *polis*, i.e., the idea of community. Aristotle's ethical ideas can still guide us, Lyotard believes, because they contain the concept of *phronesis*. *Phronesis* is important to Lyotard because it depends on the immediate context of situation and not on preformed communal values. Lyotard believes that in his thinking he is closest to Aristotle

> insofar as Aristotle recognizes—as he does so explicitly in the *Rhetoric* as well as in the *Nichomachean Ethics*, that a judge worthy of the name has no true model to guide his judgments, and that the true nature of the judge is to pronounce judgments . . . without criteria. This is what Aristotle calls 'prudence.' (qtd. in Faigley, p. 233)

The prudent person in the contemporary world, according to Lyotard, has to attend to the present without the guiding principles which a community provides.

We may disagree with Lyotard's appropriation of Aristotle in this way—his separation of judgment from precedent and from principle—but appropriate Lyotard nonetheless for his use of *phronesis* for ethical purposes. *Phronesis* can guide the person who uses it, one might say, toward an ethic which may serve when all else—community, shared values—has disappeared. *Phronesis* may help to connect the disconnected—the strangers who people our classrooms—because it encourages attentiveness to what is outside the self and encourages consequently the expansion of the self if only for purposes of survival in a strange world.

A world like ours did not exist for Aristotle: as Troels Engberg-Petersen points out (p. 138) in "Is There an Ethical Dimension to Aristotelian Rhetoric?," Aristotle did not have to "reckon with what we would call radical conflict of values." Aristotle assumed a community and thought with the *polis* in mind. We, obviously, cannot make his assumptions. We have to deal with the "spectacular diversity" Mike Rose speaks of, "compressed by a thousand social forces" and reinforced by the anonymity of modern life. If we had a community and communal values, we could appeal to them. Many do in political exhortation in a seeming last-ditch effort to deal with social problems and social relations. But Faigley, I believe, is right when he asserts that "[i]n an intensely urbanized society, holding up community as an ideal can be a way of avoiding politics" (p. 232); it can also be a way of avoiding ethics if we think of ethics only in terms of community and of principles rooted in communal values rather than as an activity or a continuing series of performances.

The *Rhetoric* of Aristotle, notes T. H. Irwin (p. 160) in "Ethics in the Rhetoric and in the Ethics," "describes virtue as a capacity (*dunamis*) . . . an active power to perform a certain type of action." Can students develop their ethical capacity to perform ethical actions from which might flow ethical habits? My suggestion is that they can if made aware of *ethos*, of which *phronesis* is a crucial part, for *ethos* compels attentiveness to the present situation and can only be put into play in the moment of action.

I can imagine a collaborative classroom in which students who are strangers to each other engage in discussion about their writing while mindful of *ethos* as a component of their language exchanges. Such a classroom would also engage in a battle against anonymity as students reminded each other, when appropriate, that the language of the discussion was lapsing into stereotypes, into i.e., the faceless, and in its own way anonymous, language that so provokes social hostility. In a computerized classroom in which the anonymity of the sender of a message is often protected as a way of encouraging the kind of honesty direct contact can make difficult, I believe students should at some point face each other and speak directly so as to perceive the differences between communicating through one and the other medium. Such an exercise would drive home the anonymity that electronic gadgets afford us. A classroom with *ethos* present as a live and active principle would be to some degree, therefore, a classroom in cultural studies, a classroom in which students might became aware of where their own language comes from and of how that language affects others. The task would then be a critical one as well as a psychological and ethical one: to account in the measure possible for the "haunts" one unconsciously "inhabits," and to endeavor in the measure possible to consciously craft an *ethos* not anonymously or stereotypically—with no regard for the determinate situation and the specific listener at hand, but with keen attentiveness to the context within which one is operating at a given moment. When strangers meet, paying attention can be the beginning of social relations.

Ethos has proved fragile over the centuries, first overtaken by style and then virtually eliminated by the cult of sincerity and the culture of expertise in the modern world. But it can resurface, indeed it has begun to, in reaction to the anonymity of contemporary life and the power of anonymous language. It can be a powerful tool of cultural study and a powerful social and ethical tool in the collaborative classroom.

James Boyd White's concern, I noted at the outset, was who we become in our conversations with each other.[11] That act of becoming, of shaping our identities in performance, can be part of an interactive classroom with *ethos* present. With *ethos* absent as part of classroom procedure, students may psych out their audiences for purposes of writing but miss the greater adventure: using *ethos* for purposes of living.

Notes

1 See Enos, "Cicero Latinizes," especially p. 192-193, for how Cicero handles *ethos*; and Welch, p. 13 and 17, for more on the poor or mistaken translations of *ethos* into Latin. See also note 3 below.

2 I think of the collaborative classroom as one in which the principal lines of communication are not between teacher and student but between student and student. Collaborative learning has been largely associated with epistemology; see, for example, three recent books by Charles Bazerman, Kenneth Bruffee, and Linda Flower. I am not concerned here, however, with the social construction of knowledge but rather with how students interact in the process of collaboration.

3 James May's position on *ethos* is close to mine: "the conception of *ethos* presented . . . in the *De Oratore* and elsewhere in Cicero's *rhetorica*," asserts May, "is broader and more inclusive than Aristotle's; it is an *ethos* that deals with the emotions (*affectus*), closely related to *pathos* but involving the milder feelings . . . it is an *ethos* attentive to and more intricately associated with style" (p. 5), See also Kennedy (p. 81), who is succinct but clear on this point: "Cicero . . . (*De oratore* 2.183-185) blurs the distinction between *ethos* and *pathos*, a development carried on by Quintilian (6.2)." For another view, see Enos and Schnakenberg, p. 197-200, who explain that Ciceronian *ethos* has three components (as does Aristotelian *ethos*, but only one of the three components is the same)—*ingenium* or *natura*, *prudentia*, and *diligentia*—and that the most important is the first. Cicero, however, also stresses the importance of *prudentia* (the Greek *phronesis*), which helps the orator to adapt to the audience, Yet, I still adhere to the view that Cicero's primary and ultimate aim was powerful performance and the acquisition over time of power and renown, a view which Enos and Scbnakenberg seem to share in their closing words: "For Cicero, *ethos* was not only a 'proof' created within the discourse; indirectly, *ethos* was manifested in the development of personal power and public glory" (p. 206).

4 Aristotle also discusses the importance of the training of the rhetorician in the techniques of delivery at the outset of Bk. III (1403b ff.), for rhetoric, as he explains, comes down to appearances. Yet he apologizes for his discussion of delivery, in his opinion an unworthy subject, because all that should count in rhetoric is stating the case and proving it. A popular audience, however, needs more than reasoning, he adds.

5 Vickers also asserts (p. 136): "The increasing stress on persuasion via the passions led to an important readjustment of emphasis within rhetoric between 1540 and 1640. Of the three goals of rhetoric, *movere*, *docere*, and *delectare*, *movere* became the most sought-after; of the five parts of the compositional process, *elocutio* received the greatest attention." This con-

nection of style to psychology—"the power of the figures to move the feelings," as Vickers puts it—was of course reinforced by Ramism, but its roots go back much further. See Kennedy's discussion of *letteraturizzazione*, for example.

6   See especially ch. 8 of Arendt, where she speaks of the "blind obedience" of Adolf Eichmann (p. 135) and later of the "painstaking thoroughness of the Final Solution—a thoroughness . . . characteristic of the perfect bureaucrat" (p. 137).

7   See Norton on the eighteenth century's development of the Platonist idea of a beautiful soul and of moral beauty, both of which depend on naturalness.

8   See Cherry and Chamberlin for more on the connection between *ethos* and ethics; also Jarratt, p. 96.

9   See note 6 on the "blind obedience . . . of the perfect bureaucrat."

10 *Phronesis* is not a strictly Aristotelian concept; it figures in an important way in Isocrates, among others (see Sipiora, p. 17–19, for example, for a discussion of *phronesis* in the thought of Isocrates).

11 White's view of human life is "radically communal" (p. 25), yet his idea of establishing one's identity in performance is still usable in our world of vanishing communal affiliations and vanishing communal values.

Works Cited

Aarons, Victoria and Willis A. Salomon, eds. *Rhetoric and Ethics: Historical and Theoretical Perspectives.* Lewiston, N.Y.; Queenston, Ontario; Lampeter, UK: The Edwin Mellen Press, 1991.

Alcorn, Marshall. "Self-Structure as Rhetorical Device: Modern *Ethos* and the Diviseness of the Self." Baumlin and Baumlin 3–35.

Arendt, Hannah. *Eichmann in Jerusalem: A Report on the Banality of Evil.* N.Y.: The Viking Press, 1967.

Baumlin, James S. and Tita French Baumlin, eds. *Ethos: New Essays in Rhetorical and Critical Theory.* Dallas: Southern Methodist UP, 1994.

Bazerman, Charles. *Constructing Experience.* Carbondale: Southern Illinois UP, 1994.

Berlin, James. *Rhetoric and Reality: Writing Instruction in American Colleges 1900–1985.* Carbondale: Southern Illinois UP, 1987.

———. *Writing Instruction in Nineteenth-Century American Colleges.* Carbondale: Southern Illinois UP, 1984.

Bruffee, Kenneth. *Collaborative Learning: Higher Education, Interdependence, and the Authority of Knowledge.* Baltimore: The Johns Hopkins UP, 1993.

Burke, Kenneth. *A Grammar of Motives.* Berkeley, Los Angeles: U of California P, 1969.

———. *Language as Symbolic Action: Essays on Life, Literature, and Method.* Berkeley, Los Angeles: U of California P, 1966.

———. *A Rhetoric of Motives.* Berkeley, Los Angeles: U of California P, 1969.

Chamberlin, Charles. "From 'Haunts' to 'Character': The Meaning of *Ethos* and Its Relation to Ethics." *Hellos* 11, 2 (1984): 97–108.

Cherry, Roger. "*Ethos* vs. Persona: Self-Representation in Written Discourse." *Written Communication* 5 (1988): 251–276.

Clark, Gregory and Michael S. Halloran, eds. *Oratorical Culture in Nineteenth Century America: Transformations in the Theory and Practice of Rhetoric.* Carbondale: Southern Illinois UP, 1993.

Cmiel, Kenneth. *Democratic Eloquence: The Fight Over Popular Speech in Nineteenth-Century America.* N.Y.: W. Morrow, 1990.

College Composition and Communication 46:3 (1995): 456.

Conners, Robert J., Lisa S. Ede, and Andrea A. Lunsford, eds. *Essays on Classical Rhetoric and Modern Discourse.* Carbondale: Southern Illinois UP, 1984.

Corbett, Edward P. J. "Classical Rhetoric: The Basic Issues." Gabin, *Discourse Studies* 1-10.

Crusius, Timothy W. *A Teacher's Introduction to Philosophical Hermeneutics.* Urbana: NCTE, 1991.

Engberg-Petersen, Troels. "Is There an Ethical Dimension to Aristotelian Rhetoric?" Rorty 116-141.

Enos, Richard Leo and Karen Rossi Schnakenberg. "Cicero Latinizes Hellenic *Ethos.*" Baumlin and Baumlin 191-209.

———, ed. *Oral and Written Communication: Historical Approaches.* Newberry Park: Sage Publications, 1990.

Faigley, Lester. *Fragments of Rationality: Postmodernity and the Subject of Composition.* Pittsburgh: Pittsburgh UP, 1992.

Flower Linda. *The Construction of Negotiated Meaning: A Social Cognitive Theory of Meaning.* Carbondale: Southern Illinois UP, 1994.

Frank, Manfred. *What is Neostructuralism?* Minneapolis: U of Minnesota P, 1989.

Gabin, Rosalind J., ed. *Discourse Studies in Honor of James L. Kinneavy.* Potomac, MD: SCRIPTA HUMANISTICA, 1995.

———. "Ethics Across the Curriculum." Gabin, *Discourse Studies* 180-189.

Goffman, Erving. *The Presentation of Self in Everyday Life.* Garden City, N.Y.: Doubleday, 1979.

Grassi, Ernesto. *Rhetoric as Philosophy: The Humanist Tradition.* University Park: The Pennsylvania State UP, 1980.

Grimaldi, William M. A. "The Auditor's Role in Aristotelian Rhetoric." Enos *Oral and Written Communication* 65-81.

———. *Aristotle, Rhetoric I: A Commentary.* N.Y.: Fordham UP, 1980,

———. *Aristotle, Rhetoric II: A Commentary.* N.Y.: Fordham UP, 1988.

Hassett, Michael. "Increasing Response-ability Through Mortification: A Burkean Perspective on Teaching Writing." *Journal of Advanced Composition* 15.3 (1995): 471-488.

Heim, Michael. *Electric Language: A Philosophical Study of Word Processing.* New Haven: Yale UP, 1987.

Irwin, T. H. "Ethics in the *Rhetoric* and in the Ethics." Rorty 142-174.

Jarratt, Susan. *Rereading the Sophists: Classical Rhetoric Refigured.* Carbondale: Southern Illinois UP, 1991.

Johnson, Nan. "*Ethos* and the Aims of Rhetoric." Conners 98-114.

———. "Three Nineteenth-Century Rhetoricians: The Humanist Alternative to Rhetoric as Skills Management." Murphy 105–117.

Kennedy, George A. *Classical Rhetoric and Its Christian and Secular Tradition from Ancient to Modern Times.* Chapel Hill: U of North Carolina P, 1980.

Kimmel, Lawrence D. "The Dialectical Convergence of Rhetoric and *Ethos*: The Imperative of Public Conversation." Aarons and Solomon 1–31.

Kinneavy, James L. and Susan Warshauer. "From Aristotle to Madison Avenue: *Ethos* and the Ethics of Argument." Baumlin and Baumlin 171–190.

Lanham, Richard. *The Motives of Eloquence: Literary Rhetoric in the Renaissance.* New Haven: Yale UP, 1976.

Leverenz, Carrie Shively. "Peer Response in the Multicultural Composition Classroom: Dissensus—A Dream (Deferred). *Journal of Advanced Composition* 14.1 (1994): 167–186.

MacIntyre, Alasdair, *After Virtue: A Study in Moral Theory.* Notre Dame: Notre Dame UP, 1981.

May, James M. *Trials of Character: The Eloquence of Ciceronian Ethos.* Chapel Hill: U of North Carolina P, 1988.

Murphy, James J., ed. *The Rhetorical Tradition and Modern Writing.* N.Y.: MLA, 1982.

Neel, Jasper. *Aristotle's Voice: Rhetoric, Theory and Writing in America.* Carbondale: Southern Illinois UP, 1994.

Norton, Robert. *The Beautiful Soul: Aesthetic Morality in the Eighteenth Century.* Ithaca: Cornell UP, 1995.

Phelps, Louise Wetherbee. "A Constrained Vision of the Writing Classroom," *Profession 93* (1993): 46–54.

Rorty, Amelie Oksenberg, ed. *Essays on Aristotle's Rhetoric.* Berkeley: U of California P, 1996.

Seibers, Tobin. *The Ethics of Criticism.* Ithaca: Cornell UP, 1988.

Sipiora, Phillip. "A Rhetoric of Ethics and Cultural Understanding: The Quest of Isocrates." Gabin *Discourse Studies* 11–24.

Swearingen, Jan. *Rhetoric and Irony: Western Literacy and Western Lies.* N.Y.: Oxford UP, 1991.

Valesio, Paolo. *Novantiqua: Rhetorics as a Contemporary Theory.* Bloomington: Indiana UP, 1980.

Vickers, Brian. "On the Practicalities of Renaissance Rhetoric." Vickers, *Rhetoric Revalued* 133–141.

―――, ed. *Rhetoric Revalued: Papers From the International Society for the History Of Rhetoric.* Binghamton: Center for Medieval and Renaissance Studies, 1982.

Vitanza, Victor J. "Concerning a postclassical *Ethos* as Para/Rhetorical Ethics, the 'Selphs,' and the Excluded Third." Baumlin and Baumlin 389–431.

Welch, Kathleen E. *The Contemporary Reception of Classical Rhetoric: Appropriations of Ancient Discourse.* Hillsdale, NJ: Lawrence Erlbaum Associates, 1990.

White, James Boyd. *Heracles' Bow: The Rhetoric and Poetics of the Law.* Madison: U of Wisconsin P, 1985.

Wolf, Thia, Lauren Wright and Tom Imhoff. "Collaborative Role-Play and Negotiation: A Cross-Disciplinary Endeavor," *Journal of Advanced Composition* 14.1 (1994): 149–166.

Chapter 8

Ethics, Rhetorical Action, and a Neoliberal Arts

Kathleen Ethel Welch

All writing practices, including writing pedagogy, involve the transmission of value systems. All writing practices are embedded in ideology. For these and other reasons, even skills-and-drills[1] writing practices and pedagogy derive from and in turn promote value systems, or ethics. The institutions and writing teachers who promote the decontextualizing of writing by demanding skills and drills of their usually captive students unwittingly (or perhaps wittingly) divorce writing pedagogy from ethics. However, since all writing and indeed all language use are inherently ethics-laden and inherently rhetorical, these writing programs and teachers are in fact teaching ethics. They are teaching ethics badly. If this issue were more widely recognized in our universities, then the deprofessionalization of writing pedagogy could not take place. Of all the disciplines and subdisciplines of the postmodern humanities, composition and rhetoric studies have had the most difficult challenge in persuading institutions and their administrators, students, and most of all colleagues in English that the teaching of writing requires training and credentials.[2]

The challenge of persuading the majority of writing teachers and colleagues in the humanities that writing always everywhere necessarily transmits values, including bad ones, remains one of the daunting tasks of the field of composition and rhetoric studies. In this essay, I want to analyze two rhetorical theorists who offer us a way out of the modernist prison that constructs so much of actual university writing instruction and propose a new version of the liberal arts. Next I will offer a gendered and raced Neolilberal Arts that supplements these theories.[3] The two nonmodernist rhetoricians I reread here are Isocrates and James L. Kinneavy.

I must state right away that this juxtaposition is not a traditional, Arnoldian linking of two important writers or that we reach back 2400 years to see ourselves reflected in the still-assumed glory of Greece. Fourth century BCE Greece, particularly Athens, was not glorious. It was constructed to be so by scientific-minded philologists. Instead, I intend to offer historicized juxtaposition[4] that unveils ethical links. Both Kinneavy and Isocrates work from similar assumptions in wildly different cultural and subject positionings. Each writer sees writing as a cultural practice that emanates from a particular discourse theory. Each writer (I emphasize here that Isocrates was above all a writer, not a speaker, and that he occupies an unusual position in the merger of speaking and writing patterns of consciousness in the fourth century BCE) believes that language theory and training are central to education and culture, not merely a decoration or a means to convey information, a stance that characterizes the modern in general and rhetoric (since Ramus) in particular. Each writer constructs a pedagogy that merges *theoria*, *praxis*, and *poiesis*, the last being reflection, contemplation, construction or production.[5] *Praxis* is a doing or an action. Many of you will spot this three-part construction as Aristotelian and so reject it. But I suggest instead that you think about our homogenized, Ramusized, pablumized, formulized, and generally battered formalistic Aristotelianism that we think of as Aristotle and then go restudy George A. Kennedy's new English translation of the *Rhetoric*[6] in order to reconstruct Aristotle's positioning. As Kinneavy has pointed out, the three-part practice-theory-production language issue has usually been shrunk to a theory-practice dualism. Aristotle's predecessor Isocrates[7] relied on the same, more complex three-part model, not on a two-part model. Both Isocrates and Kinneavy, who look at production as central, or action as essential, recognize the importance of deploying writing across a variety of occasions from the most practical to the abstract, including those with no apparent immediate use.[8] Perhaps most importantly, each rhetorical theorist/writer acknowledges and promotes mergers between so-called public and private discourse and so enables their appropriators to avoid the easy and familiar distinctions between the two flexible realms that characterize so much writing theory.[9] This stance leads each of them not only to favor but to take action in favor of what has been called the liberal arts,[10] or the training of the mind across a number of disciplines.

Isocrates and Kinneavy write in contexts shot through with usually unacknowledged difference. Isocrates wrote from a patriarchal, agricultural, slave-based economy with an inherited elite who needed to be educated so that a particular social order could be constructed. The latter writes from a context of mature corporate capitalism whose very different elite also requires education but who also receive subversive education from teachers like Kinneavy.[11] They faintly resemble each other because they propose the reconstruction of a *paideia*. Isocrates wrote as a cultural and economic imperialist who wanted to unite Greek-identified citizens partly by killing Persians. His many good, even revolutionary ideas surrounding *logos* need to be conditioned by an acknowledgement and assessment of his common brand of imperialism.

Kinneavy writes from an entirely different situation, one in which the cultural necessity of a reconstituted liberal arts is urgent. He does not treat the humanities as a decorated, desiccated, boring curriculum that merely reinforces the corporate status quo, a condition that currently afflicts the humanities in much of United States higher education. In this Arnoldian tradition in which Kinneavy does not work, the humanities are segregated, relegated, and disempowered and the teaching of writing almost automatically becomes skills-and-drills, divorced from culture, subjectivity, or anything else that matters. The lunge toward the decorative or the instrumental primary strategies for robbing language of its power is the primary way that this kind of inquiry and production of discourses becomes excluded in the sense that Foucault discusses it.[12] The dominant history of western rhetoric can be seen as its exclusion at particular historical moments—that is one way that its power has been neutralized, in more ways than one—by acting as if its function is the decoration of ideas and feelings that are already here or the transparent conveying of ideas (the instrumentalist version) of rhetoric. It is a dangerous kind of relegation; it is worse than complete erasure.

The exclusion through decoration began most seriously with appropriations of Aristotle (not with Plato's own rhetorical theory and practice as Foucault contends) and is associated with the split between the true and the false. Instruments and decorations seem to be irrelevant to ethics; they in fact seem to be quite secondary. When rhetoric is seen as a decoration, it leaves the realm of ethics. The argument about rhetoric as decoration has always been present, even in Gorgias and the complaints of many of his contemporaries that the Older Sophists were, among other things, decorating language and thus devaluing it. However one works out these appropriations of rhetoric in the ancient eras, the most damaging split was the far later Ramistic cordoning off of rhetoric and the displacement of two of its five functions or canons (or *erga*), invention and memory.[13] Ramus, of course, radically reconfigured the functions of rhetoric and transferred its enormous power to a version of logic. His murder for political reasons in the St. Bartholomew's Day massacre in 1572 was not of course for his dismantling of rhetoric, but he goes on living in writing pedagogy that remains with us in skills-and-drills composition instruction.[14]

Kinneavy has shown how rhetoric as a neutral conveyor of ideas continues to reside in the realm of expository writing and constitutes a major part of academic literacy. This version of literacy has received excellent analysis from Patricia Bizzell and others who have challenged it. The power of instrumental rhetoric (language as a neutral container than transports meaning) has received trenchant criticism from Kinneavy, who recognizes the danger of teaching only expository writing (the genre of choice for pretending that language is neutral and divorced from ethics, an issue I take up below).

Isocrates, competing diligently, even passionately, with his rival Plato saw all language use (he uses the word *logos* repeatedly, and it is unfortunately translated as "eloquence"[15]) as loaded. He understood the power of *logos* that resides in thought and wanted to see that power increased in a particular *paideia*; that education depended on performance (Isocrates was a Sophist, even though he from time to time denied it[16]), on activity, not on passivity. Training in a variety of fields, including mathematics, was based on interior/exterior dialectic, not on the passive consumption that Kinneavy, with his different version of the liberal arts, has had to contend.

While *The Aims of Discourse* remains a historical marker in the history of rhetoric and composition, it is Kinneavy's unusual work on the *pisteis* and on *kairos* that need, in my opinion, to become another focus. His deployment of these classical Greek concepts (his understanding of them historically, and his ability to show how they can be used now) provide central material for a version of language education that is lasting and embraces rhetoric and its inherent relationship with ethics. Like Kinneavy, Isocrates was preoccupied with the construction of ethics and recognized consistently that language study is inevitably merged with value systems, good ones and bad ones or weak ones. The work on *pisteis* in *The Greek Rhetorical Origins of Christian Faith* and on *kairos* in "Kairos: A Neglected Concept in Classical Rhetoric" in *Rhetoric and Praxis* provide important theoretical formulations for rhetoric and writing as activities, as opposed to assumed passivities.

In the *pisteis* book, Kinneavy recognizes that Isocrates' educational plan derived from the *pisteis* (the means of persuasion made well known by Aristotle). The *pisteis* include the interior persuaders[17] *ethos, pathos, logos,* and the external persuaders such activities as taking someone to court or swearing and so on. Kinneavy writes

> possibly the most influential of all the writers who spoke positively of *pistis* was Isocrates. Like the Sophists, Isocrates was convinced that absolute rules of science, promising certainty, were not a human possibility. In speech after speech he inveighed against the type of theory and science represented by Parmenides and Plato." (35)

Kinneavy goes on to write:

> It is this rhetorical idea that became the ideal of higher education in antiquity. At the heart of the ideal are two notions, the importance of persuasion as a methodology and the importance of the practical kind of knowledge that humans have, based on belief, not science. The educational ideal of Isocrates, then, was built on two meanings of *pistis* . . . the notion of persuasion and the notion of belief." (36)

The primacy of belief and persuasion through language as Kinneavy explicates it formed one center of classical Greek rhetoric and should form a center of current theorizing in rhetoric and composition studies, as Kinneavy argues. One of the central issues of the *pisteis* is that their study can lead to a stepping away from simplistic but nonetheless culturally dominant ideas about the nature of thought/discourse/action. The general, educated public bases its ethics on the modern idea that thought and discourse are separate and that thought is both prior to and superior to articulation. In this way, communication acts become imitations of something already in the mind. An utterance or a written text, for example, merely reflects something already there in the mind and so as mere reflections are downgraded in the university. Writing, then, in this assumed secondary status, does not really have much to do with ethics when it is instrumental, neutral, and largely inconsequential. Kenneth Burke, of course, regards thinking as action in his theory of dramatism.[18]

Isocrates and Kinneavy as historical correspondents share this view. While Kinneavy had to resist it, because he was born into modernism and its split between thought as superior and discourse (action) as secondary, Isocrates did not.[19] Isocrates did, however, have to contend with Plato's radically different *paideia* and philosophy, his transcendentalist, power-down construction of the universe that became the standard construction for western metaphysics. A study of the *pisteis*—of the ways that belief is inculcated in decoders, the ways that people's minds are swayed, their *doxa* (valuable conjectures for Kinneavy and Isocrates, not Plato's disreputable opinion)—allows one to interact with oneself and with a wider world. In this way, both Kinneavy and Isocrates offer powerful correctives to the positivist interpretations of knowledge, that it is a thing out there in the world, retrievable, demonstrable, and able to be tested and confirmed. Their understanding of rhetoric transcends this familiar model. Overcoming the idea that language is a neutral container that holds meaning is one of the most pressing issues before all rhetoric and composition theorists and writing teachers. It is a part of the new *episteme* we have entered. It is postmodern, in the sense that Patricia Bizzell and Lester Faigley have deployed it for rhetoric and composition studies.

From their work on the *pisteis* as a center of inquiry and action, both Kinneavy and Isocrates promote a *paideia* that engages whole human beings who need to have training across a variety of fields, human beings who need—and this is crucial for both rhetoricians—to know how to be active producers of discourse, not passive acceptors. At *Antidosis* 278, Isocrates writes about the centrality of *ethos* in constructing belief. As Kinneavy points out in his *pisteis* book, Isocrates differed from Plato and the later Aristotle in rejecting a firm distinction between science and belief, or between *episteme* and *doxa*. Isocrates saw no such rigid distinction and established a rhetorical theory and an educational system with no such rigid distinction. Kinneavy wants to restore the primacy of the Isocratic positivity of *doxa*, its more problematized relationship to *episteme*, and a recognition that training in a wide variety of fields requires exactly this acknowledgment. Of course, Kinneavy advocates rigorous training in the sciences, including scientific writing. However, he argues persistently that this training is not enough. People in all disciplines need vigorous training in rhetoric as persuasion and communication. It is this angle that ties rhetoric to ethics. Each discipline needs to be able to communicate and to do so passionately, as Kinneavy discusses it particularly in the *kairos* article. There he writes:

> If a writing program is to have an ethical dimension, it must take into account the value system of the situational context of the writer and reader. Conse-

quently, the writing in a computer science department must not just be about the mechanics of creating better programs or better computers; it must look at the values implicit in the discipline of computer science and at the place of the computer scientist as a person and as a scientist in the world determined by those values. (98)

Kinneavy recognizes the false neutrality that dominates curricula in virtually all modernist disciplines. He argues strongly against this stance. Kinneavy writes: "A *Kairos* program will demand, therefore, that the student write some papers about the ethical concerns of his or her personal interests and career choices. Consequently, there will have to be a humanistic component to such a program. It cannot simply be a course in what is traditionally called 'technical writing,' although it should include such writing" (98).

One of the most important issues Kinneavy raises for us—in the *kairos* essay in particular and elsewhere—is that the primacy of expository writing in universities and colleges is important but is not enough. Expository writing tends to be presented as neutral, as the container of knowledge or material already there or synthesized from outside sources by the writer or investigator.

Academic literacy tends to be thought of as the ability to write effective exposition in which, as teachers of writing realize, the *ethos* is detached, credible, authoritative, and logic dominant. *Pathos* in this pervasive and overvalorized genre must be erased in favor of a version of *logos*, an appeal to reason, not merely logic. This stance is seen to be the *raison d'etre* of the text. Kinneavy has given one of the most striking analyses of the ethical and social limitations of this privileging that I have seen. Kinneavy and Isocrates offer us major pathways out of what Fredric Jameson calls "the windless closure of the formalisms." They do so through rhetoric as an activity of mind and culture interacting in ways that are taken to be developmental for the person in the educational system and for the culture the person already operates in and is being trained to operate in. It is not rhetoric merely as subject matter that concerns Kinneavy and Isocrates in their very different ways; it is not the ability to persuade to any case whatsoever. Rather, it is the training and the development of aptitude in students (that is, in the two essential parts of education, the interaction of student and the teacher, not the student alone, as many receptions of Kinneavy and Isocrates assume).

It is the incorporation of *kairos* in the sense of understanding the opportune moment as well as the appropriate response (the idea of proportion or what Kinneavy designates situational context). For both Kinneavy and Isocrates, moral persuasion, defense, and conduct, or the ability inculcated through training by teachers particularly to persuade various audiences, are central in education. Kinneavy's *kairos* essay explicates the importance of training students in all disciplines to speak to the general public about their work (in other words, to make difficult material understandable to a wide range of decoders), to examine the ethical issues raised by a particular course, and the ability to discuss with one's peers and segments of the public, the good or harm or just the consequences of a particular action. He states unequivocally that membership in a profession should bring with it training in how to explain what that profession is engaged in, ethical conflicts that derive from it. Training in rhetoric particularly enables one to do this. And it is in expository writing still the monarch of academic literacy, as Bizzell and others have shown us that does not and is not suited to doing this central work. Kinneavy is similar to some process adherents here because he understands the instrumentalist abuse of exposition, its dangerous charade as disinterested discourse. He offers a remedy: study rhetoric and study it everywhere in the university. Know how to persuade people in your own field, other fields, and, crucially, the general public. Know how to defend our position. Study value systems that necessarily reside in the disciplines that have been invited to think that ethics and issues in moral behavior are the province only of the disciplines of English, theology, philosophy, and so on. Kinneavy's and Isocrates' work on this central issue resonates with that of Plato, whose emphasis on morality was of course important. However, Plato, in his promotion of an attitude toward ultimate reality, the Platonic forms, promoted as well an aversion toward rhetoric (tempered, of course, in *Phaedrus*) that did not allow for genuine dialogue between and among peers. (The Socratic dialogues are misnamed because they are, actually, monologues, with prop-like characters who are written by Plato to set up the Socratic character's next strategic move, set up as Plato revised his own prose; control is the central characteristic of this strategy, and the Platonic Socrates has all the control).

Both Kinneavy and Isocrates offer definite programs by which students can train in language use, not just interpretation, to encounter situations of many kinds and to make intelligent judgments about how to respond. Significantly, they both privilege the production of discourse, not just its interpretation, not just reading but writing of many kinds and for numerous audiences with different agendas and values.

This distinction is, indeed, the one that distinguishes rhetoric and composition studies from traditional English studies. Production of discourse brings with it many kinds of interpretation. Most current theorists do not take this into account and appear not to have absorbed it. (For example, Scholes, in *Textual Power* states that reading is writing, a familiar idea in some theoretical circles; my response is: where is the material text? If the student is "writing" while reading Hemingway in Scholes' example, where is the material text?[20]) This issue distinguishes rhetoric and composition studies from traditional literary studies (traditional insofar as fifty years will take you) and some branches of cultural studies.[21]

Ethics as Rhetoric/Action and the Neoliberal Arts: A *Kairos* Program for a New National Curriculum

A Neoliberal Arts is now urgently needed. In particular, a new trivium, the language-based liberal arts (rhetoric, grammar, dialectic) needs to be retheorized and performed. Of course, Isocrates has been the supposed progenitor of the liberal arts in most of its versions because he advocated and reformed in his school (first in Chios and later in Athens, where he resided and worked as a semi-barbarian-in-transition), a successful school of higher education for mostly privileged young men who were drawn to more extensive training than they had previously received.[22] While *artes liberales* are a medieval construction, nearly all versions of it credit Isocrates and his version of *philosophia* (the development of judgment, not Plato's sense of system that we now regard as philosophy), even as many of these same histories quickly dismiss Isocrates and his extraordinarily powerful pedagogy. The liberal arts have ebbed and flowed in the 2400 years of western rhetoric, even before they were named as such. They need to reflow now in quite different ways, as I discuss below.

One of the biggest of the many problems that the humanities face has to do with its representatives in the mass media, or its communication with the general public. Writers such as Dinesh D'Souza have set the agenda for public discussion of the humanities. Defenders—humanists on the defensive—have merely responded to the attacks, most prominently Stanley Fish, whose incisive critical ability has not yet translated to televisual or journalistic communication expertise.

The two brightest lights who explain our situation have been Henry Louis Gates, particularly in the *New Yorker* but in other venues as well, and Kathleen Hall Jamieson, whose appearances before Senate committees, on the Cable News Network, on C-SPAN, and on the News Hour with Jim Lehrer have instructed spectators with her rhetorically-grounded analyses of political discourse.[23] What mostly represents the humanities or postmodernism to the general public is 1) nothing; and 2) mockery.

A Neoliberal Arts would have to consider the histories of the universities, including work in the archives by Winifred Bryan Horner and Thomas Miller, to name two.[24] Rhetoric has always been tied to educational institutions and it has always been tied to power. One of the problems facing a Neoliberal Arts is a confusion of its terms. One example of this problem occurs in *The Politics of Liberal Education*, edited by Daryl J. Gless and Barbara Herrnstein Smith, the proceedings of a 1988 conference at Duke University and the University of North Carolina. The book's editors appear to regard the liberal arts as equivalent to the humanities, and of course they are not. With the exception of the essay by George A. Kennedy, who does, it goes without saying, understand the interaction of the trivium and the quadrivium and their historical interactions and manifestations, and Richard Rorty, the essayists and one editor in the introduction make persistently perplexing assumptions about the liberal arts. Herrnstein Smith, for example, opens the introduction to the volume by writing:

> In view of the recent eruption of reports in the national press of alleged 'attack on the classics' and 'fall of standards' in American education, and in view also of the increasingly strenuous criticism of liberal arts teaching—and teachers—by, among others, officials in he Department of Education and the [NEH], we believe that concerned members of the academic community are eager for occasions to explore these issues responsibly and to discuss them with each other and with the public. (1)

By paragraph two, Herrnstein Smith has substituted the phrase "humanities" for the liberal arts. Her essay continues this substitution. In fact, she goes on to equate the liberal arts with the teaching of literature. The terms "liberal arts," "humanities," and "literary canon formation" appear to be assigned the same meanings. Giroux, who clearly understands historical correspondences of the current critique of educational practice, nevertheless makes a similar equation in "Liberal Arts Education and the Struggle for Public Life: Dreaming about Democracy,"[25] where the phrase "liberal arts" and the word "canon" are semantically similar. While Giroux does refer once to "science" in a way that may refer to the hard sciences, in the other appearances of the phrase "liberal arts," he refers not even to the humanities but to canon formation in literary studies in what must be English departments. The Neoliberal Arts must be based on a trivium that privileges electrified language and a quadrivium (or whatever we construct) that acknowledges the centrality of all kinds of language in the sciences and mathematics. In other words, as Kinneavy recognizes explicitly and Isocrates acknowledges implicitly, rhetoric infuses all the categories. The rhetorical infusion has been denied for perhaps three hundred years (depending on how one dates the rise of science and the concomitant desire for transparent language). The problem is this: the liberal arts have been moribund for at least the twentieth century. There are sound historical reasons for this (see Berlin, for example), but perhaps the most compelling two reasons have been: 1) the apparent inability of the quadrivium to account for the natural and social sciences, most of which came to prominence as disciplines within the last one hundred years; and 2) the ambiguous placement of education as a field.

Although it goes beyond the scope of this essay, the disciplinary histories of the social sciences and their twentieth-century manifestations in universities and colleges need to be more fully written. Any version of the liberal arts will appear to be quaint relics if it does not take account of this branch of the sciences. This issue is a pressing one because the general public (educated in our schools and universities) does not know how to decode mass communication reports that are based on social scientific and hard scientific methods; when a report on, say, the carcinogenic effects of a particular food is widely reported, most of the public does not know how to determine the validity of the study. While some news organizations (the *New York Times* science pages, for example) lead readers through the experimental process involved, most other sources do not. This is particularly so for the electronic sources of communication (television and internet news) because so little depth is provided so far on those sources. Consequently, the general public hears the conclusions of a study but not the evidence of the nature of the procedure or legitimate conflicting interpretations. While part of the responsibility for this issue lies with journalists who do not communicate the process, the bigger problem lies with the audiences who have not been adequately trained in the methods of, say, empirical research.[26] All students in all fields need this training, and they need to receive it from the discipline that conveys it. This is part of Kinneavy's *Kairos* Program.

The second problem of the moribund state of the liberal arts is the placement of education. Clearly, education schools and colleges (until quite recently segregated in their own institutions in the United States) cover many of the disciplines and would seem to be an excellent location for the *kairos* program. However, this has not yet taken place. I contend that this has not happened in most places because education as a field is in fact one of the social sciences. While many might disagree with this formulation, I would respond that they train their students for the most part in empirical analyses of the kind practiced by the social sciences. Using methodologies and the *American Psychological Association Style Manual*, the students are trained to be social scientists. This is fine, but it should be acknowledged and placed historically. In addition, this preference places added burdens on educationists to train their students in communicating with the general public. I recommend overcoming these problems by incorporating the social sciences, including the field of education, into the quadrivium. Obviously the quadrivium has been challenged anyway with the rise of modern science. Instead of geometry, astronomy, arithmetic, and music, we could come up with an arrangement that would account for all these modern changes.

Racing, Gendering, and Technologizing the Neoliberal Arts

The liberal arts should remain moribund if they continue the myth of the universal subject that pretends to include Others such as women, African Americans, and Native Americans (as well as many other Others) but in fact rigorously excludes them. In addition, our current communications revolution (or at least rapid change) requires that all students be trained in electronic literacy *and the consciousness changes that this revolution has brought about and will bring about*.[27] This work is now being done primarily in rhetoric and composition programs.[28] Recent advances in feminist theories, postmodern postmodern theories, and technological change must be incorporated into the Neoliberal Arts. Each discipline must be in charge of locating training in the rhetoric of that field so that all its members can communicate not just with each other but with the general public as well. In other words, part of the educational function for all of us is to educate the general public and not just our students. We must be trainers of citizens, just as we already are trainers of student citizens.

Isocrates, as a committed imperialist who raised his rhetorical fist against Others (Persians) with all the energy of a former Other (he moved to Athens, as did most of the Sophists), presents us with severe limitations. In addition to his unbridled imperialist desire, he showed virtually no understanding of women (as opposed to Plato, who did demonstrate some incomplete intelligence on this matter), whose situations deteriorated with the advance of representative democracy for the privileged male Greeks (non-barbars); the illness of slavery was also a limitation for him.[29]

Kinneavy has been able to appropriate the positive aspects of Isocrates and to promote the potentially powerful *Kairos* Program. And, of course, unlike Isocrates, Kinneavy has trained many women students. Further work on the correspondences between these two thinkers would help us to establish *Kairos* Programs and a Neoliberal Arts. In particular, the association of Kinneavy with Aristotle, so automatic for many, can be revised by reading Isocrates across Kinneavy.

Without elaborate, wide-ranging production of discourse in writing, particularly electronic writing, and without the theorizing of writing, gender, and race, the Neoliberal Arts cannot work. The Neoliberal Arts need Kinneavy's *Kairos* Program, an activity-based, writer-based vision of higher education that recognizes language as central to all human behavior and belief and that applies language training to training in the quadrivium (with the hard sciences, the social sciences, and the field of education included). A Neoliberal Arts curriculum based on the *Kairos* Program could serve many purposes and in the process help to overcome the rancorous debate that has characterized discussions of what constitutes a good education. Too much of that debate has been dominated by the Killer B's (Bennet, Bloom, etc.), reactionaries such as Dinesh d'Souza, and others. It is time for the humanities in particular to reinvent the trivium and the quadrivium so that we have better trained student citizens and citizens.

Notes

1. I include in skills and drills the still-common five paragraph theme that continues to dominate much writing instruction, offering students a watered-down Aristotle that is so dull that no Burkean identification can exist.

2. This story is well known among composition/rhetoric scholar-teachers. See Theresa Enos, "Introduction," in *Learning from the Histories of Rhetoric* on this issue. See also Sharon Crowley, *The Methodical Memory: Invention in Current-Traditional Rhetoric*.

3. I use "supplement" here in the Derridean sense of "supplement," in addition to and in place of.

4. For an example of this move, see Nan Johnson, "Reader Response and the Pathos Principle."

5. Liddell, Scott, and Jones. This stipulative definition can, of course, go only so far, but it is helpful.

6. The Kennedy translation, the first in English since the 1932 Lane Cooper translation, reconstitutes/reconstructs Aristotle in numerous ways. Now the standard translation, the Kennedy Rhetoric compels readers to take account of translation, keywords, the sexism of previous translations, the ubiquity of enthymemes and their relevance, and other issues.

7. The two are about a generation apart, with Isocrates living from 436 to 338 BCE and Aristotle from 384 to 322 BCE. This generational difference is important in the historicizing of rhetoric and writing practices, as I have pointed out elsewhere. See *The Contemporary Reception of Classical Rhetoric*.

8. This issue remains important for the preservation of pure research in the humanities, natural sciences, and social sciences. The intensive study of various phenomena, including language use, should continue unabated and remain as the constriction of higher education in the United States and elsewhere continues. While this case has been made strongly for the natural sciences, including medicine, it has been made almost not at all by the humanities, a rhetorical problem with severe consequences.

9. It is important to maintain the dramatic distinctions between ancient constructions of the public and private and modern (e.g., from the seventeenth century to about 1985) constructions. The differences are more than vast; many of them are unthinkable. The making of direct connections between fourth century BCE Athens and twenty-first century North Americans is a huge undertaking for which we are negatively prepared by the Arnoldian/faux-Aristotelian twentieth-century devotion to form that is decontextualized from ethics, ideology, belief and structures.

10 For traditional treatments of the movement of the liberal arts, see *The Seven Liberal Arts in the Middle Ages*, especially Martin Camargo's "Rhetoric," pp. 96–124 (although the head note by David L. Wagner contains numerous errors). See also H.I. Marrou, *A History of Education in Antiquity*, pp. 17–177, 183, 211.

11 I write here from the interpretation provided by Jean-Pierre Vernant in "The Class Struggle," where he continues his critique against Marx's historicizing: "For Marxists, the ancient world is a class society which in its typical form can be defined as a slave mode of production. But does it follow inevitably that the whole history of classical antiquity can be seen in terms of an opposition between the two conflicting classes of slaves and slave owners? If Marxist theory has to be reduced to such a brief, rigid, and anti-dialectical formula, it will scarcely be capable of illuminating the work of historians" (11).

12 See, for example, "The Discourse on Language."

13 See Welch, "Ideology and Freshman Textbook Production." See also J. Fredric Reynolds, ed., *Rhetorical Memory and Delivery*; Aldo Scaglione, *The Classical Theory of Composition*.

14 The standard work on Ramus is that of Ong, *Ramus: Method and the Decay of Dialogue*.

15 See, for example, Van Hook and Norlin.

16 See, for example, *Antidosis*.

17 See *The Contemporary Reception of Classical Rhetoric* for an explanation of the use of the translation "interior and exterior persuaders" in place of constructions such as "artistic proofs" and "inartistic proofs."

18 See, for example, *A Grammar of Motives*.

19 When I discuss historical correspondence, I resist the idea that rhetorical history has to be read in chronological order. Since the work of so many writers so permeates current articulation, we cannot read without them anyway. Cf., for example, Freud. One of the problems that I address below with the erasure of active women and Others who are not White from histories of many kinds is that they do not permeate our rhetorics. See Catherine Hobbs, ed., *Nineteenth Century American Women Learn to Write* and Andrea A. Lunsford, ed., *Reclaiming Rhetorica* for examples of books that repermeate language action with the actions of women.

20 James Berlin pointed out the irony of Scholes' stated desire to make radical changes in English studies in *Textual Power* and his reliance on one of the male standards of the canon of American literature, Hemingway. Cf. Rhetoric Society of America speech.

21 A stronger cultural studies position is articulated by Henry Giroux, Henry Louis Gates, Jr., Michele Wallace, particularly in *Invisibility Blues*, Michael Berube, "Pop Goes the Academy," and many others.

22 See Welch, "Writing Instruction in Ancient Athens."

23 In fact, her critiques of political advertising in 1988 and 1992 led to the interrogation of television advertisements by many print and electronic news organizations and so improved subsequent ones.

24 See Horner, *Nineteenth Century Scottish Rhetoric*, and Miller, *The Study of English in the British Cultural Provinces*.

25 See especially pp. 126–27.

26 Of course, science remains a god term in our culture. However, naive commonplace statements such as "what's wrong with medicine that it can't cure the common cold" reveal a misunderstanding of the nature of viruses and their complex behaviors. In this case, medical science is seen as either a godlike entity or a source of magic whose practitioners almost willfully deprive the public of something good.

27 See Welch, Chapter Six, *The Contemporary Reception of Classical Rhetoric*.

28 Ironically, technology training has fallen to rhetoric/composition programs because they are viewed as the service dumping grounds by many English departments. Since for us pedagogy and freshman courses tend not to be viewed as negative but, indeed, as wonderful, this is not an intellectual problem. It is, however, a huge staffing problem, since virtually no English department has as yet hired sufficient numbers of professors to train students and other faculty in the new technology. So the chronic understaffing in the teaching of writing now continues into the electronic revolution with the understaffing of faculty trained in the new communication technologies. This additional work is, of course, onerous for already-overworked rhetoric/composition programs. However, it is a gift, since technology is and will be the center of our work as literacy undergoes great change.

29 See Jasper Neel, *Aristotle's Voice*, for a sensitive explication of this issue and its application for our own American time as well as for Isocrates'.

Works Cited

Berlin, James. Roundtable Discussion, "Rhetoric and Cultural Studies." Rhetoric Society of America. Minneapolis, May 1992.

———. *Rhetoric and Reality: Writing Instruction in American Colleges. 1900–1985.* Carbondale: Southern Illinois UP, 1987.

Berube, Michael. "Pop Goes the Academy." *Voice Literary Supplement.* April, 1992: 10–13.

Bizzell, Patricia. *Academic Discourses and Critical Consciousness.* Pittsburgh: U. of Pittsburgh P, 1992.

Burke, Kenneth. *A Grammar of Motives.* Berkeley: U of California P, 1969.

———. *A Rhetoric of Motives.* Berkeley: U of California P, 1969.

Crowley, Sharon. *The Methodical Memory: Invention in Current-Traditional Rhetoric.* Carbondale: Southern Illinois UP, 1990.

Derrida, Jacques. *Dissemination.* Trans. Barbara Johnson. Chicago: U of Chicago P, 1981.

Enos, Theresa. "Introduction." *Learning from the Histories of Rhetoric: Essays in Honor of Winifred Bryan Horner.* Carbondale: Southern Illinois UP, 1993.

Faigley, Lester. *Fragments of Rationality: Postmodernity and the Subject of Composition.* Pittsburgh: Univ. of Pittsburgh Press, 1992.

Foucault, Michel. "The Discourse on Language." *The Archaeology of Knowledge and the Discourse on Language.* Trans. A.M. Sheridan Smith. New York: Pantheon, 1972.

Gates, Henry Louis, Jr. "King of Cats." *The New Yorker.* 8 April, 1996: 70–81.

Gless, Daryl J. and Barbara Herrnstein Smith, eds. The Politics of Liberal Education. Durham, NC: Duke UP, 1988.

Hobbs, Catherine, ed. *Nineteenth Century American Women Learn to Write.* Charlottesville: U of Virginia P, 1995.

Horner, Winifred Bryan. *Nineteenth Century Scottish Rhetoric.* Carbondale: Southern Illinois UP, 1994.

Isocrates. *Isocrates.* Loeb Classical Library. Vols. I and II trans. George Norlin. Vol. III. Trans. Larue Van Hook. Cambridge, MA: Harvard Univ. Press, Vol. I, 1928; Vol. II, 1929; Vol. III, 1945.

Johnson, Nan. "Reader-Response and the Pathos Principle." *Rhetoric Review* 6, 2 (Spring 1988): 52–166.

Kennedy, George A., trans. and ed. *Aristotle On Rhetoric: A Theory of Civic Discourse.* New York: Oxford UP, 1991.

Kinneavy, James L. *The Greek Rhetorical Origins of Christian Faith: An Inquiry.* New York: Oxford UP, 1987.

———.. "*Kairos:* A Neglected Concept in Classical Rhetoric." In *Rhetoric and Praxis: The Contributions of Classical Rhetoric to Practical Reasoning.* Ed. Jean Dietz Moss, 79–105.

———. *A Theory of Discourse: The Aims of Discourse.* New York: Norton, 1971.

———. "Theory, Theories, No Theories." Paper presented at the Conference on College Composition and Communication. Cincinnati, March 1992.

Liddell, George, and Robert Scott, eds. *A Greek-Enqlish-Lexicon.* Rev. Henry Stuart Jones et al. Oxford: Clarendon Press, 1968.

Lunsford, Andrea A., ed. *Reclaiming Rhetorica: Women in the Rhetorical Tradition.* Pittsburgh: U of Pittsburgh P, 1995.

Miller, Thomas P. *The Formation of College English: Rhetoric and Belles Lettres in the British Cultural Provinces.* U of Pittsburgh P, 1997.

Moss, Jean Dietz, ed. *Rhetoric and Praxis: The Contributions of Classical Rhetoric to Practical Reasoning.* Washington, D.C.: Catholic U of America P, 1986.

Neel, Jasper. *Aristotle's Voice: Rhetoric, Theory, and Writing in America.* SIUP, 1994.

Reynolds, John Frederick, ed. *Rhetorical Memory and Delivery: Classical Concepts for Contemporary Composition and Communication.* Hillsdale, NJ: Lawrence Erlbaum Associates, 1993.

Scholes, Robert. *Textual Power.* New Haven, CT: Yale UP, 1986.

Vernant, Jean-Pierre. *The Origins of Greek Thought.* Ithaca, NY: Cornell UP, 1982.

Welch, Kathleen E. The *Contemporary Reception of Classical Rhetoric: Appropriations of Ancient Discourse.* Hillsdale, NJ: Lawrence Erlbaum, 1990.

———. "Ideology and Freshman Textbook Production: The Place of Theory in Writing Pedagogy." *College Composition and Communication.* Vol. 38, No. 3 (October 1987): 269–282.

Chapter 9

The Hermeneutics of Suspicion and Other Doubting Games: Reclaiming Belief in the Writing of Reading and the Reading of Writing

C. Jan Swearingen

Teachers and scholars in disciplines that teach writing and the interpretation of written texts have recently witnessed the revival of an ancient philosophical dispute. Growing discord surrounds the cultural, ethical, and epistemological values assigned to programmatic skepticism and deconstructive hermeneutics within philosophy and, more broadly, throughout the academy. The dispute is as old as Plato's defense of Socrates' dialectic as an analytic method designed to test and perfect true belief. It is taken up again by Cicero, who quipped that although the Stoic philosophers are very good at dissecting arguments they provide no tools for the construction of proofs and arguments. The Stoic academicians, Cicero charged, propound a purely negative dialectic. Augustine found the teachers and teaching of literature and rhetoric in his time so repugnant in their celebrations of obscenity and amorality that he resigned from the teaching profession when he converted to Christianity. In the introduction to the *Metalogicon,* a defense of the study of grammar, rhetoric, and logic in the twelfth century, John of Salisbury writes, "I have purposefully incorporated into this treatise some observations concerning morals, since I am convinced that all things read or written are useless except insofar as they have a good influence on one's manner or life" (6). In the nineteenth century, the philosopher Søren Kierkegaard chastised his fellow Danes for practicing "mere Christianity": a smug, hypocritical businessman's comfort that bore little relationship to the social reforms that were the goals of the earliest Christians. In a number of literary and philosophical works he challenged both the academy and the churches to revive and teach the ability to feel, to restore the ability to be affected by human suffering, and to address human—all too human—failings that they professed to care about.

Once again, we find ourselves in what Stephen Carter has termed a "culture of disbelief." The hermeneutics of suspicion dominates academic models of textual analysis and interpretation. Reading is directed at unmasking hidden and illusory meanings; the best, as Yeats observed, seem to lack all conviction ("The Second Coming"). In the current climate of programmatic doubt the relationship between the life of the mind and the resources of belief receive little attention or affirmation. What can and should reform the current academic methods, pedagogies, and scholarly goals that focus so relentlessly on skepticism and debate? As writers and readers, as teachers of writing and ways of reading, how should we expand the repertoire of analytic methods and practices that we employ? How can we reintegrate the valuable rigors of the life of the mind with the ability to read with the eyes of faith? Debates on these matters flourish within as well as outside of the Academy.

Marxist literary critic Gerald Graff defends "the culture wars" and propounds "teaching the conflicts." Others ask whether recent critical theories—the hermeneutics of suspicion, deconstruction, and postmodernism—mean that the discovery and articulation of truth and meaning is no longer a valid aim of interpretation? (Thurow; Torgovnik). Should criticism and interpretation be devoted exclusively to questioning all bases of judgment and to a hermeneutics guided by suspicion of discovered or constructed meaning, indeed of closure itself? Similar appraisals of the perils of abstract, analytic thought have been advanced by critics from unexpectedly different camps. Feminist language scholars, postmodern theorists, and proponents of multicultural curricula have converged on one point. For very different reasons, they warn that outside of carefully defined purposes, such as criticism, understanding, and the examination of belief, the practices of skepticism, debate, and negative dialectic as they are conducted today lead scholars and students alike to become "expressionless, pitiless, unteachable . . . incapable of belief"(Wolf 136). Still others ask whether in an increasingly multicultural academic environment, the goals and tacit traditions of argumentation, dialectic, and criticism are simply too foreign to be sustained as models for thought and language.

As in the past, when academia becomes increasingly multicultural and interdisciplinary, it expands and realigns its repertoire, and diversifies its models of thought, identity, ways of thinking, knowing, interpreting, meaning, and writing (Gates "Identities"). The educational psychologist Jerome Bruner proposes that the Western educated self is only one among many possible "canonical images of selfhood" within as well as outside of the academy (130). An individualist model of self and voice contrasts sharply with a social, collective phenomenology of speech. Individuals accustomed to learning and acquiring knowledge in groups implicitly understand—indeed believe in—the individual's voice as willingly and consciously partaking of collective consciousness, and as drawing on the shared common beliefs of a people. Where Socrates' "know thyself" came to mean "separate yourself from the Other" (Kierkegaard 202), Epictetus understood the same enjoinder in an irreducibly collective sense: "Bid a singer in the Chorus 'know thyself' and will he not turn to the others for the knowledge to the others, his fellows in the chorus, and to his harmony with them?" (3.14). There are Western academic paradigms such as dialogue and hermeneutics that have emphasized interactional and collective models of mind, discourse, self, and meaning. These, however, have often held a minority position in relation to the practices of skepticism, programmatic doubt, and hyperindividualism that since Descartes have dominated Western academia and its values. Although our repertoire of ways of knowing include notions of collective and dialogical consciousness, these are at many points incompatible with Enlightenment canons of individualism and related Romantic, post-Freudian, and postmodern depictions of thought and language as implements of separation, analysis, and epistemological and moral autonomy.

Further compounding the emphasis on doubt rather than belief, the individual rather than the collective, the legacy of Marx and Freud has left us with a hermeneutics of suspicion, the habit of interpretive skepticism that questions any apparent or received meaning as possibly and even probably illusory. In keeping with this hermeneutic habit, Freudian theories of individual identity and Marxist theories of cultural structure and development regard religion as delusory and narcotic. Recent scholars in developmental psychology and cultural theory (Bruner, Norris) have increasingly warned against the oversimplified models of Freud and Marx, that have been adopted in theories of language, and in pedagogical and curricular formulas. However, old hermeneutic habits die hard; the cultures of disbelief still outweigh the cultures of belief within academia and have been joined only recently by debates about academic styles, models of consciousness, ways of knowing, and ways of writing. Reappraisals of academic modes have in turn sparked renewed attention to the nature of argumentation, conflict, and controversy, extending the ongoing dialectic between controversy and dialogue within philosophy and philosophical hermeneutics (Maranhão, Swearingen). Conflict and controversy, like "the culture wars," pose no threat to individualist skeptical models of identity. By the individualist measure of intellectual rigor, dialogue and reading for understanding are typically deemed "soft" and epistemologically incorrect. Related notions of classroom dialogues and of the reading of literature as dialogic assume that there can be authentic exchanges between individuals, and edifying discourses (Marino), models that have been repeatedly questioned and even scorned in postmodern theory. However, as an instrument of classroom learning and discussion, the dialogic paradigm is far more comfortable than debate and programmatic skepticism to many students, to many women in Western culture (Belenky, Clinchy, Goldberger, and Tarule), and to many non-Westerners (Gates; Ong *Faith*; Said).

Despite its reputation for spawning culture wars, the multicultural academic setting is proving particularly hospitable to dialogue and dialogical hermeneutics, ways of knowing and ways of learning in the academy that have long provided alternatives and complements to skepticism, analytic dialectic, and doctrines of linguistic contingency (Gates "Pluralism"). These truth-building modes of discourse have always informed academic models; they illustrate that faith need not, indeed should not, be regarded reductively, or as an enemy of reason (Ong "God's Known" 249, and Carter). Reading with the eyes of faith is an activity that secular Romantic aesthetics borrowed from Protestant hermeneutics in the late eighteenth century. The ability to read *with*, and *as*, is a believing game (Elbow) firmly grounded in literary aesthetics such as Coleridge's notion that reading and appreciating poetry require a willing suspension of disbelief, an edifying suspension of skepticism. Dialogue, thus understood, has long functioned as a classroom paradigm without diminishing or impeding the merits of skepticism and analysis. The current climate of conflict within academia makes the task of rehabilitating dialogue, and the belief in understanding that it implies, particularly urgent.

Academic theorists have become dogmatically anarchic in their practices of skepticism. Too often they appear as theatrical exponents of warring theoretical and political orthodoxies locked in ideological debates with each other and with the culture at large (Norris, Torgovnik). Academicians need not correct the problems created by warring theorists by retreating to timidity, and practicing deliberately "weak prophecy" (Hartman) simply to avoid dogmatism. Instead, a dialectical relationship between belief and dialogue, on the one hand, and the discourses of analysis and debate, on the other, is badly in need of rehabilitation. Academia's models can be reshaped as less hostile to the worlds of belief, conviction, and reasoned action where most of the people spend most of their time. In illustrating these proposals, I turn first to an examination of the place that is currently held by literature within the academy, and of the conversion literary study is undergoing both as an object of classroom and scholarly interpretation and as a source of models for alternative classroom and scholarly voices. As literary, social, and cultural studies mingle in a multicultural academic environment, reading with the eyes of faith is not only becoming more epistemologically acceptable, but is also beginning to generate new canons of self and knowledge.

Literature: Object of Academic Discourses, Repertoire of New Academic Voices

Academic study in the humanities is interpretive as well as information-gathering, knowledge-making as well as knowledge-finding. Anthropologists have developed the view that cultures, too, are "texts" to be read by an interpreter who, like the literary reader, brings agendas and understandings that may be quite foreign to the world of the text. Therefore anthropologists, now wary of any claims to absolute knowledge, and fully conscious of their roles as mediating interpreters of one culture to another (Maranhão), are advised to work like literary authors and strive for "thick description" (Geertz). Like modern anthropological ethnographers aware of the mediating, dialogical role they play as interpreters of culture, literary authors and readers can approach texts as instructive representations of alternative modes of discourse and thought. Although modern literary theory and aesthetics have often emphasized literature's strategic indeterminacy and status as beguiling fiction, literature has also been approached in many times and places as a vehicle for understanding the making of cultural and personal meanings on the part of both readers and characters. If cultures through their stories and through adult models provide children with "canonical images of selfhood" (Bruner 130), then the place long held by literature and its reading in the classrooms of Western democracies should be examined as an important and programmatically equalizing resource for the formation of self, particularly the academic self and voice extended to larger and larger, and more diverse, college student constituencies. Approached as a source of images of self, and as a representation of intellectual discourses, literature, and the talk about literature modeled by teachers become more than mere fiction, a diverting belletristic entertainment; they assume the roles of supplements to identity, training grounds for thought, and models for language. Serious attention to literature as a guide to intellectual and moral development is a belief-guided interpretive practice as old as the English and German Romantic concept of the *Bildungsroman*—the novel as a paradigm of character development. The notion of literature as model and guide to the development of identity is assuming renewed importance in a multicultural academy striving to define common grounds and values among its diverse constituencies.

Methods developed for the rereading of women's roles and voices represented in early Biblical and Greek literature provide an example of belief-guided interpretive practice at work at two levels of interpretation. If we adopt a notion of belief as expressly concerned with volitional assent (Kinneavy)—in contrast to blind faith or superstitious belief—I suggest that such literary and indeed much textual scholarship can be observed to follow similar provisions of assent. The problem is determining the often unstated volitional assent, the article of faith or critical doctrine that guides the reading, or, for the scientific investigator, the search. Rereadings of women in Biblical and Greek literature have elected to be guided by contemporary revisionist theory concerning women's language and thought: that women's discourses and thought practices often imbed intellectual substance and work within emotional contents and genres. A number of studies have shown that culturally transmitted beliefs shared by women and men alike hold women's ways of knowing in lower regard than those of men because they manifest associative rather than linear structures, because they locate ideas and judgments in narrative and emotional contexts, and because they are not explicitly stated in terms of general principles and abstract rules (Belenky, Clinchy, Goldberger, and Tarule; Gilligan). Yet, when pressed, many women interviewed as subjects in studies of classroom learning report that they chose not to conduct rational inquiry apart from conviction and emotion, that to do so was dead, or at least so foreign as to be a violation of their sense of identity as intellectual beings. Researchers in this field are extremely cautious to point out that they are making no claims of innate gender natures or innate differences. Rather, they are observing how women style themselves as "knowers" in their descriptions of themselves. Developmental and cultural psychologists such as Jerome Bruner and Walter Ong have postulated that for parallel reasons "story" in many cultures conveys intellectual content that most educated Westerners associate solely with "logic."

The revaluation of women's ways of knowing guides two kinds of reinterpretation of Greek and Biblical stories. Reading "story" for intellectual content enables readers to find more than mere ritual or wordless emotion in women's songs, such as Miriam's song of victory in the Biblical account of the Red Sea, or Cassandra's prophecies in Aeschylus's drama depicting her abduction from Troy. Women readers, and any reader reading as a woman, can encounter such characters in recognition scenes that are both therapeutic and transformative. By reevaluating their own discourse practices as different but not lesser, women and non-traditional students from numerous cultures find in these literary characters: more strength, more intention and agency, and more intellect than they were accorded in the readings shaped by nineteenth-century translators and their nineteenth-century assumptions. Similarly, contemporary interpreters of Biblical representations of women's songs and prophecies are reinstating intellectual content and political agency to genres practiced by women in ancient biblical texts (Meyers; Trible). Antigone, Hecuba, Cassandra, and Clytemnestra in Greek Homeric sagas and plays are being reexamined along these lines, as are Miriam, Deborah, and Mary in the Hebrew Scriptures and New Testament. Many of these women characters' songs were dismissed as incidental, or as vestiges of women's restricted roles as singers and mourners.

Rereadings of women's discourses in the literature of antiquity adopt a second, equally controversial critical apparatus and purpose: of correcting distortions that are assumed to have been introduced by the original authors as a way of suppressing the validity, power, and strength or women's views and voices in the cultures that produced the texts (Frymer-Kinsky vii–6). Readings of the roles and voices of women in ancient texts, then, are openly directed at reclaiming meaning and agency for women and for their voices. Contemporary fiction has become an active instrument in the re-reading, and retelling of ancient texts representing women's discourses, and women's self-understandings of their own discourse practices (Brindel; Chernin; Wolf). In *Cassandra*, a novel refiguring the character of Cassandra that we have always viewed through Athenian drama, German novelist Christa Wolf depicts Cassandra's reflections on the nature of her discourse as a seeress and priestess, and her understanding of the god Apollo's prophecy that although she speaks the truth no one will believe her. Wolf's novel recounts the story of ancient Troy from the perspective of Cassandra in her roles as a daughter of King Priam, thereby a priestess, and therefore a particularly strategic prisoner for the conquering general Agamemnon to abduct. Wolf emphasizes that with the occupation by the Greeks Troy has been invaded by Hellenic understandings of language and religion that are foreign to Trojan experience, belief, and practice. Cassandra reflects upon her own practice of language and how it shapes her belief in herself as a seeress and leader of her people. Wolf's depiction of Cassandra's role as a priestess and seeress provides illuminating details concerning how priestly figures understand what it is they do when they speak as vehicles for a common view, and as the sensibility and voice of the people:

> Words. Everything I tried to convey about that experience was, and is, paraphrase. We have no name for what spoke out of me. I was its mouth, and not of my own free will. It had to subdue me before I would breathe a word it suggested. It was the enemy who spread the tale that I spoke "the truth" and that you all would not listen to me. For the Greeks there is no alternative but either truth or lies. . . . It is the other alternative that they crush between their clear-cut distinctions, the third alternative which in their view does not exist, the smiling vital force that is able to generate itself from itself over and over: the undivided, spirit in life, life in spirit. (107)

She comes to take refuge in her ceremonial role even after despair about the Greek presence and ways of thinking has eroded her beliefs.

> I taught the young priestesses the difficult skill of speaking in chorus, enjoyed the solemn atmosphere on the high feast days, the detachment of the priests from the mass of the faithful, my guiding role in the great pageant; the pious awe and admiration in the looks of the common people; I needed to be present and at the same time unaffected. For by that time I had stopped believing in the gods. (98)

From the perspective of the Trojans, the gods of the Greeks are self-proclaimed lies, fictions in the theatre of Dionysus, mastheads for war and excuses for murder. The great horse the Greeks have brought—the gift or an "Athena" totally unlike the goddess Cassandra reveres under that name—is accepted in a frenzy by the Trojans. Cassandra's voice is no longer heard at all.

> The Trojans laughed at my screeches. I shrieked, pleaded, adjured, and spoke in tongues. Eumelos. I saw the face which you forget from time to time and which for that reason is permanent. Expressionless. Pitiless. Unteachable. Even if he believed me, he would not oppose the Trojans, and maybe get himself killed. He, for one, intended to survive (he said).
> Now I understood what the God had ordained. "You will speak the truth, but no one will believe you." Here stood the No One who had to believe me, but he could not because he believed nothing. A No One incapable of belief.
> I cursed the god Apollo. (136)

There is no name for what speaks through her, but, Wolf's account emphasizes, it is a *vox populi*, a common voice that is the exponent of an undivided life in spirit, spirit in life. It is for this reason that the priestesses Cassandra teaches must learn to speak in chorus, in concert, in harmony. Remnants of this tradition survive in the chorus of the Athenian dramas—those fictions in celebration of Dionysus that the Trojans of Wolf's novel at first found so foreign. In the Greek dramas the chorus functions as the voice of the people expressing and affirming the beliefs of commonly held religious orthodoxy. Where the earlier religious rituals had located a priest or priestess as leader of the people, the Athenian polis celebrated the collective citizenry as exponents of the new Olympian deities, the state gods of Athens.

Wolf emphasizes Cassandra's ability to perform her role and even to be sustained by it as independent of her belief in the gods. After she has lost her faith, she knows her performance to be hollow in terms of her own beliefs, but the voice she speaks nonetheless continues to convey the ritual to the people, and she is willing to conduct that sustaining ritual on their behalf. Her voice ceases to "speak," that is, to be heard with understanding, when the tide of collective belief is turned away from traditional Trojan deities and toward the newer Greek gods, the newer Greek understandings of the gods as false idols, as fictions. In Wolf's rendition, it is this shift, and not Cassandra's individual loss of faith, that undermines the sustaining belief, the world view and values of the Trojan people as a whole. Only within that world, for as long as it is viable, can Cassandra speak and be heard. For as long as she does speak, however, it is as a trained and fully conscious priestess, and not as a raving puppet of ecstatic inspiration and male priests. Wolf's portrait corrects and defends this substantial revision of early Greek women in religious ritual. She reads with the eyes of faith, not with a hermeneutics of suspicion that would doubt everything it cannot prove, and reject everything that is not certain. She assumes rationality, and finds it, contributing much to our understanding of women's discourses in early Greek religion.

A line of inquiry parallel to Wolf's rereading of Greek literature has been advanced in recent studies of pre-monarchic Israel that provide revised accounts not only of its social structure—no central government, no structured politics, no sense of public as distinct from private or domestic domain—but also of roles of women in the tribal political and economic social structures of Exodus, and Judges (Meyers; Murphy 50–5). Elusive remnants of women's discourses appear in these texts of the Hebrew Scriptures. The Song at the Sea, the song of victory after the Egyptians are drowned at the Red Sea, is led by "Moses and the children of Israel" (Exodus 15: 1). In the 1950s, and continuing within the increasingly contextual studies produced by Biblical rhetorical criticism, scholars increasingly began to concur that the Song at the Sea may be attributed to Miriam as much as to Moses (Murphy 50). In a second introduction the Song is "sung by the prophet Miriam, Aaron's sister" (Exodus 15: 21), the same Miriam who finds the infant Moses in the bulrushes and persuades Pharaoh's daughter to raise him as her own. Later, in Numbers, both Miriam and Aaron question Moses' authority: "Has the Lord spoken only through Moses?" While Aaron is not punished for this insubordination, Miriam is afflicted with leprosy and later dies in the wilderness of Zin.

Biblical representations of women as speakers and leaders are obscured by fragmentary preservation—only traces are left of what might have been their greater prominence in the societies of that time (Meyers). However a growing number of classical and biblical scholars now emphasize that it is inevitably the case with ancient texts that we can never know with finality anything save through our interpretation of the fragmentary traces that are left (Fiorenza; Frymer-Kensky: Trible). We guess, guided as much as possible by informed background. Cultural reconstructions provided by anthropology and archaeology are an important background in such understanding (Meyers). Equally important is the knowledge worked at through interpretation, the fundamental goal of the humanist scholar. The task has been newly provisioned by revisionist appraisals of prehistoric societies, and facilitated by recent classical and biblical archaeology, as well as by studies in orality, literacy, and culture. Even revising our idea of story to include truth as well as fiction has aided in understanding the complex role played by story making and story understanding in cultures, and in the lives of individuals. All of these leaps of faith surmount the hermeneutics of suspicion, and supplement its rigorous questions with prudent interpretive conjectures that begin to ring true.

All of this is not to say that questions are not asked in revisionist, belief-guided reading. The role played by ritual, and particularly by priestly proclamatory speech, is rendered problematic in Wolf's characterization of Cassandra. She loses her faith but continues to perform. Wolf's depiction of Cassandra's speech, and of her understanding of its powers, exemplifies but also questions the power of priestly, prophetic, and ritual speech. Performers of rituals past and present are often depicted as invoking and evoking superstition rather than as promoting persuasive discourses of appeal to changes in conscious Volitional belief and assent (Kinneavy). Our received understandings of the role played by these and similar discourse rituals within cultures can perhaps be further challenged—and amended—if belief and ritual are seen at work in the conventions, and conventional discourses, of academic skepticism as well.

Addressing the fine lines that distinguish religious and secular discourses, and what were in the 1920s termed "primitive" in comparison to advanced cultures, Cambridge classicist Jane Ellen Harrison challenged what she charged were rather vague notions of early Greek religion as based on "a sense of the supernatural," as "instinct for mystery," or as "apprehension of an unknown infinite, beyond the visible world" that were being advanced within studies of comparative religion and folklore (488). Instead, she proposed, the mystery, the thing greater than any individual, is not potent

> because it is unintelligible and calls for explanation, not because it stimulates a baffled understanding, but because it is felt as an obligation. The thing greater than man, the 'power not himself that makes righteousness,' is not the mystery of the universe to which as yet he is not awake, but the pressure of that unknown ever incumbent force, herd instinct, the social conscience. The mysterious dominant feature is not Physis [Nature], but Themis [Society]. (490)

According to Harrison's analysis, it is not a foreign and awesome Nature that Cassandra's "primitive" religion dwells in. Nor is it, from within Cassandra's self-understanding that Wolf sketches for us, a mindless herd instinct. Wolfs depiction emphasizes that Cassandra's role is that of sustaining and serving as exponent of a social whole, a unity that Jane Ellen Harrison finds represented by Themis and enacted through ritual as the willing undertaking of obligation of one to another. Whether this interpretation is couched in feminist or social constructionist terms, the emphasis remains the same: collective, consensual, ethically evaluated language; thought and action are among the highest, not among the lowest, exercises of human art and intellect alike. Women's ways of knowing, an ethic of care: these are being reevaluated as among the most conceptually complex, not the intellectually weakest, forms of human reasoning.

Questioning the late nineteenth century enthusiasm for Dionysian and Bacchic rites as ecstatic abandon and even sanctioned violence—enthusiasms that I would note are enjoying a revival in today's academic embrace of Nietzschean philosophy (Cixous; Kristeva; Norris)—Harrison emphasizes the judiciousness, balance, and beauty in what have come down to us as the Greek "mysteries"—rituals that were inculcated and practiced in a range of different modes of consciousness and discourse. Instead of emphasizing that a profound break occurred with the emergence of Western philosophy among the Greeks, Harrison reads Plato's depictions of dialogic education, dialectic, and philosophizing as continuations of social collective and ritual traditions, as a "rationalization of the primitive mysticism of initiation, and most of all of that profound and perennial mysticism of the central *rite de passage*: death and a new birth, social, moral, intellectual" (513).

Double Vision: Belief Seeking Understanding; Inquiry in the Service of Belief

An ancient defense of belief working in accord with intellect that was popular in the middle ages posited that intellectual activity is, and should be, faith seeking understanding, and believing that understanding could emerge: *credo ut intelligam*. Following the poet William Blake's related notion that rationality goes amiss if it avoids belief and poetic vision, Northrop Frye defines a double vision for reading and interpretation: a concerted, dialectical, two-level understanding. Building his model, he proposes that there is both a primitive (his term) and an advanced role for collective aspects of culture, identity, and language, including the consciously undertaken avowal of social contract that Jane Ellen Harrison discusses. Frye writes, "A primitive society is one in which the individual is thought of as primarily a function of the social group. According to this view, in a fully mature society the structure of authority becomes a function of the individuals within it, all of them, without distinctions of sex, class, or race, living, loving, thinking, and producing with a sense of space around them" (8). The prophetic and priestly functions of a Cassandra, of Miriam's song in Exodus, of Hannah's song uplifting the lowly in the Hebrew Scriptures and its echo in Mary's New Testament Magnificat, are to give voice to a common voice, to repeat and recite its beliefs through injunctions to a collective. One interpretation of such societies and ritual practices holds that, "a hierarchical structure of authority has to be set up to ensure that the individual does not get too far out of line" (Frye 9). Frye's exposition suggests how easily and commonly belief has been construed as an implement of social control. Wolf's Cassandra provides us with an example of double vision on this issue. She exemplifies the negative aspect of belief: to be manipulated by powerful priestly figures; she also presents belief's benign alter ego: a reasoned choice of assent. Despite its value as a reminder of our darkest vision of belief as the basis of social repression, Frye's notion that belief within hierarchy is an implement of social control in primitive—but not in advanced—thought should be questioned. Studies such as Harrison's emphasize an alternative interpretation, of social and religious collectivity as both volitional and in a dialectical relationship to one another, rather than as stages in a developmental continuum in which true advancement is marked by the abandonment of belief and superstition. Collective hierarchical societies can be repressive. However, today's academic environment has created an atmosphere that seems equally so. Compulsory skepticism and theoretical abstraction, promoted as ends in themselves, are perceived as mystifying, and as repressive, by many inside as well as outside of academia (Gates "Beyond"; M. Murphy; Phelps). Restoring some balance to the negative dialectic between repressive forms of belief and equally doctrinaire skepticism is certainly in order. Reprisals of the relationships among belief, collective social values, and the many roles played by literary representation can aid in this process.

The embodiment of social qualities—the stuff Jane Ellen Harrison observes in the figure of Themis as a nascent social consciousness in early Greek religion—in the concrete images of the Olympian gods was not in her view necessarily an advance. She links the concrete literalness of these literary images of the gods with a decline in the older social sensibility: "When the religious man, instead of becoming in ecstasy and sacramental communion one with the Bacchos, descends to the chill levels of intellectualism and asserts that there is an objective reality external to himself called Bacchos, then comes a parting of the ways. Still wider is the breach if he asserts that this objective reality is one with the mystery of life and also with man's last projection, *his* ideal of the good" (Harrison 487, my emphasis,). The danger of creating god in the image of man when man no longer conceives of himself as obligated to a group and its values is given similar exposition in the conclusion to Cassandra. The women have been erased from history and public life, reduced to babbling and keening; their words have no meaning other than affect and no sense other than *pathos*. Achilles and Agamemnon go down in history as heroes, as victors who have abducted and raped the Trojan priestesses, and denied to Hector and other slain Trojans a proper burial.

Wolf annotates her novel with three concluding essays on Western literary aesthetics and ethics which provide alternatives to the paradigmatic linear Western Aristotelian plot that is based on crisis, conflict, and resolution. *Cassandra* has been crafted according to an alternative revisionist aesthetic. She develops the view that beginning-middle-end plots, centered in crisis, contest, and struggle are built upon a war and death cult that values separation over collective loyalties, and epistemological and ethical autonomy, even unto death, over participation in collective values. The heroic epic, the plot of the Aristotelian tragedy, and the funeral oration that is the basis of all Western rhetorics all conclude in death and celebrating the death of heroes in war. When women's stories appear within the plot lines created by this aesthetic paradigm they are more often than not depicted in terms of their place in men's life sagas (Gilligan). Commenting on the difficulty—indeed the impossibility—of reconstructing the Greek Cassandra, Wolf illustrates additional instances in which a cultural and aesthetic emphasis on separation and autonomy can be carried to pathological extremes. She selects a passage from the last act of Goethe's *Faust* to emphasize the hyperindividualisation and hypefictionalizing tendencies that Western academia has built upon Greek rationalism: "If, Nature, I stood before you a man alone" (Wolf 283). Wolf asks of Faust's last—death?—wish: "Was it necessary that man should come to stand 'alone' before Nature—opposite Nature, not in it?" (283). Thinking with and thinking against, inside of and opposed to, the collective and the autonomous, each has its virtues and shortcomings, its dangers as well as its capacities for guiding learning and facilitating understanding. Wolf's hermeneutics is one of belief, not suspicion. Her portrait of Cassandra, although it provides a double vision, is guided by the eyes of faith in the premise that intellect can accompany motion and belief within the collective voice that individuals express.

The most fruitful kind of critical thinking models, I propose, encourage dialectical views of intellectual processes and traits, an understanding of their interdependencies, of their reciprocal capacities, in short, a double vision (Elbow; Frye). Our critical and interpretive repertoire, unfortunately, is currently replete with a different legacy. In keeping with the hermeneutics of suspicion advanced within Freudian theories of identity and Marxist theories of culture, most current models of self and society are based on psychological theories that stress the attainments of moral and intellectual self-sufficiency, and encourage an ongoing questioning of any and all received models of meaning, self, and society. Autonomy is regarded as the epitome of developmental achievement; autonomy as an interpretive aim and model is conceived of as the ultimate objective of both maturity and learning. Contemporary literary theorist and practicing analyst Julia Kristeva posits, "As speaking beings, always potentially on the verge of speech, we have always been divided, separated from nature" (8). Her goal as an analyst? To effect a transition "from trust to separation" (56). Ongoing self-examination through psychoanalysis is the modest if tenacious antidote to nihilism in its most courageously and insolently scientific and vitalist forms. It is the superman's shield and protection?" (63). In a manner that seems paradoxical, Kristeva and other postmoderns adopt this Nietzschean defense of skepticism and rationalist autonomy both as a basis for a morality that will be as in Nietzsche's title, beyond good and evil, and as a corrective to the tendency to dominate. The self-questioning self, they claim, will not dominate. Recent pedagogical applications of this defense of skepticism have been challenged on the grounds that denying epistemological and social agency to groups who have long been empowered is hardly an acceptable academic purpose (Gates; M. Murphy; Phelps).

Addressing a group of psychiatrists, Kristeva asserts that analysis annihilates the self in order to foster relationship. Observe the plot and myth underlying her tale, the hermeneutic so different from Wolf's: "The analyst takes another view: he looks forward to the ultimate dissolution of desire (whose spring lies in death), to be replaced by relationship with another, from which meaning derives" (63). Movement from trust to separation, removing desire understood as self-annihilation, will ultimately result in the possibility of relationships, which are the home of meaning. In a concluding segment of her short essay on love, psychoanalysis, and faith—"Who Is Unanalyzable?"—Kristeva reflects upon the receptiveness of different religious and cultural groups psychoanalysis. In her exposition can be viewed the Freudian preoccupation with sexuality as well as the hermeneutics of suspicion that fosters self-questioning and skepticism, and the assumption that religion is an illusion. She asserts:

> Analysis is not less than religion but more—more, especially, than Christianity, which hews so closely to its fundamental fantasies. Protestants *count with* the analyst; they cooperate with their heads more than with their sexuality; Jews *count on* the analyst: they give themselves and attempt to dominate. Catholics *count only for themselves*: hostile to the transference, more narcissistic or perverse than other patients, they are relative newcomers to analysis who pose new problems for the analyst as well as new avenues of research. '*Keep on counting,*' say the Muslims as they get up from the couch. '*Thank you for allowing yourself to be counted* (accounted),' is the polite formula employed by Japanese Shintoists, who avoid the crisis of transference. (53)

In microcosm, Kristeva's litany of selfhoods shaped by religious belief reveals severe limitations in our psychological understandings of how individuals from different religious and cultural traditions enter into participation in Western modes of analysis and discourse, whether on the analyst's couch or in the classroom chair. The psychologist's model of self is both descriptively and prescriptively Cartesian, independent, fully separated, without desire, alone.

Alternative models of metacognitive and metalinguistic self-consciousness are tacit and implicit in many cultures and literatures. "We have no name for what spoke out of me" (Wolf 107). Western philosophy and language theory have made them explicit, mandatory, vehicles of thought and instruction. The Western separated self is able to refer explicitly to *my* identity, *my* position, but it is becoming increasingly clear in cross-cultural studies of identity and intellect that this self is only one among a number possible selves and self images. Augustine's *Confessions* recounts the assimilation of a slightly different kind of generalized Other, an Other who embodies the expression of a self and a voice that is fully conscious of itself and of its responsibilities as an interpreter. That consciousness and that responsibility have been inspired by faith, just as, at the outset, in all but a few of

Kristeva's examples the analysand must give himself or herself over—however temporarily—to the faith, desire, and displacement of self entailed in transference. The proximal learning accomplished by such temporary attachment has been observed in early childhood development. Bruner observes, "An *Anlage* of metacognition present as early as the eighteenth month of Life. How much and in what form it develops will depend upon the demands of the culture in which one lives—represented by particular others one encounters and by some notion of generalized other that one forms" (67). Extending traditional canons of Western individualism that are advanced within psychology, Kristeva posits that trust must be deliberately broken in order to effect separation. In contrast, a number of recent studies of proximal learning, identity formation, belief, and faith underscore a growing awareness, the product of cross-cultural studies, that selfhood and agency are best developed—by many individuals in many different cultures—from within the circles of community and belief, contexts that should never be forcibly removed. What uses can or should the academy make of these insights drawn from cross cultural therapeutic and developmental models?

The Academy: Therapy? Conscience? Identity in the Common Places

Academia, I have proposed, could benefit from an expanded repertoire of models of selfhood and identity, and not just therapeutic models, as it becomes increasingly multicultural. However, an overly literal-minded, reductive panoply of canonical selves and identities—"women," "Black/African/African American," "Asian," or, all lumped together, "non-traditional"—has already produced a fissured politics of identity that is troublingly conducive to a "self-esteem school of pedagogy, a view of education as a sort of twelve-step program to recovery" (Gates "Pluralism" 36). Edward Said warns against the dangers of reductive essentialism along similar lines. "To say that women should read mainly women's literature, that Blacks should study and perfect only Black techniques of understanding and interpretation, that Arabs and Muslims should return to the Holy Book for all knowledge and wisdom is the inverse of saying along with Carlyle and Gobineau that all the lesser races must retain their inferior status in the world" (Said 17). Newly-formed cultural identities that are being shaped within revised academic curricula have been defended primarily on the grounds that they promote self-esteem. This basis for curricular revision confuses the very strong evidence that school achievement is causally related to self esteem with the paucity of evidence that self esteem is related to school achievement. "When Laotian students in California ace their exams it isn't because the curriculum reinforces a rich sense of their Laotian cultural heritage" (Gates "Pluralism" 36). The development of new curricula has grounds other than self-esteem, however, and regardless, it is well underway. Curricular reform needs no further defense: but it begs for orchestration.

A number of writing pedagogies, critical thinking models, and literary critical theories have become engaged in recent philosophical disputes concerning agency, epistemology, and the nature and value of controversy within the academy (Graff; Holmes; Marino). I regard this as potentially refreshing and illuminating because it is a reminder that teaching the conflicts (Graff) is hardly new. Observing contrasts, differences, and dialectical oppositions has long been staple of Western academic practice, especially in the liberal arts and philosophy. I invite a reconsideration of how the commonplaces of ancient rhetoric were regarded as artificial, but useful common grounds for discussing and debating wildly disparate materials, issues, and beliefs. The commonplaces of classical rhetoric included, however, not just difference and contrast, but similarity and comparison, not just dialectic understood as opposing propositions but dialectic understood as dialogical truth seeking. The value of finding common places—in the larger cultural sense—cannot be underestimated in today's academy. The commonplaces of antiquity can help. They are ancient, and were at their inception understood as artificial; they have already proven themselves in the long test of time and shifting cultures and languages within academia.

Humanistic education, I would note, has since the time of the first rhetorical commonplaces been based on the belief that learning critical thought through skepticism and debate prepares individuals to prove, perfect, and defend their views and beliefs in an ongoing dialectical examination. John Henry Cardinal Newman's 19th century essay, "The Idea of a University," extended this concept to incorporate the reading of modern literature as part of the process of criticism. Newman's discussion is a welcome reminder that humanistic study and education have been thought of as cultural criticism for over a century. Among other means, criticism should be taught and earned, he proposes, through reading literature as itself a criticism of culture. The canonical literary authors many would dispense with today—Dickens, Eliot, Twain, Thoreau—were in their own time political activists.

The political and ethical beliefs defended in Newman's "Idea of a University" clearly hearken back to his classical training, but are adapted to modern goals. For a civic, civilized culture to exist, both differences and commonalities among peoples must be recognized. Education should seek to recomprehend the diversity of human cultures in order to promote tolerance and respect, and should establish as a basic premise that tolerance and respect are impossible without knowledge (see Gates 37). Said defines this double movement of the academy's purposes as a dialectic in which discovery is directed at transformation. "In the joint discovery of self and other, it is the role of the academy to transform what might be conflict, or contest, or assertion into reconciliation, mutuality, recognition, creative interaction" (Said 17-18). These are noble, decidedly attractive, familiar, and even pious goals. They are not, however, goals or activities that conform to the paradigms of academic skepticism and programmatic doubt. On what basis can reconciliation, mutuality, recognition, and creative interaction be promoted and established as common ground in the midst of contemporary literary and epistemological theories that regard common ground and its pursuit as politically outdated and ethically incorrect (Holmes)? The most active current movement in academia, observed by many with dismay, is a concerted movement, often under the aegis of multiculturalism and teaching the conflicts, toward pushing the balkanization of academic disciplines and cultures into smaller and smaller warring factions. Among its other alarming aspects, this movement provides ample pretexts for those looking for reasons to further reduce public funding to higher education.

Where in the decidedly Western elite civic and academic tradition is there room for both forging and discovering the common beliefs on which goals like mutuality and creative interaction can be pursued? I hope we can begin to ask this question without apology. What does it mean to read with the eyes of faith—in this sense—in academia, and what can academia teach the eyes of faith? It is encouraging that more questions have been raised concerning defenses of teaching the conflicts, defenses that have perhaps once too often conflated culture with particular theories of culture, confused the political with partisan, and failed to distinguish between teaching students theories and teaching them to theorize with specific purposes (Thurow 51). Liberal arts humanism and a civic minded academia have often manifested a certain tension between the roles of paragon and gadfly, between the aspirations to teach creativity and originality and the responsibility to define standards of taste and correctness (White). Similarly, academia and culture alike have tolerated a commendable range of styles and goals among writers, artists, and critics, some of whom define themselves as makers and readers of literary art and others who define themselves as exponents of political agenda. I advocate a continuation of the practice of encouraging the study and production of literary and critical writing that directly addresses social issues as well as that which does not. However, current practice seems to be a bit more polarized and doctrinaire. Some critical voices teach partisan political commentary; in other quarters critical and theoretical equivocation has led some of the best and brightest critical minds to pull back from commitment to specific positions, and to refrain from morally based action on theoretical grounds: "It is as if someone in a position of power were to issue a policy statement focusing solely on the difficulties of arriving at a policy or to decline doing anything because any action, might, in certain instances, be doctrinaire" (Torgovnick 54).

Marxist cultural critics such as Gerald Graff err in confusing the teaching of (somewhat partisan, doctrinaire, reductive, polarized) theories with teaching to theorize. Geoffrey Hartman errs with similar effect in creating a false dichotomy between deconstruction and political or engaged criticism, as if the two cannot occupy the same critical space. Graff's practice exemplifies what Hartman thinks of as theoretical fundamentalism. A larger, dialectical relationship can be resuscitated to help redefine such oppositions, a double vision of their nature and value that can guard against the formation of doctrinaire master narratives, and what Hartman thinks of as fundamentalist theories and theorists, but that will also place constraints on unlimited, unguided self questioning, and on the ethical and political quietism that tends to result. An eminent exponent of this larger dialectic, and one not at all unfamiliar with the question of the relationship of the life of the mind to the life of faith, was Søren Kierkegaard.

Not So Simple Leaps of Faith

Kierkegaard's views of the inevitably unscientific nature of human reason, and of the inevitably flawed human capacities for faith, including faith in humanity, are expressed and quite deliberately exemplified throughout his works. Much like Plato's dialogues or Gregory Bateson's metalogues, each of Kierkegaard's works takes its contours from its subject. His discourse is openly confessional as well, providing model after model, discursively, of the acts of contrition, self-effacement, and self-creation that he advocates. How many contemporary ethicists, for example, openly employ pseudonyms as a confessional device expressing their belief that they are unable to live out the ethics they propound? Kierkegaard routinely employed pseudonyms for precisely this reason, in order to shear away—through what he depicts as a spiritually therapeutic, self-directed use of literary irony—the festering aspects of himself that impede health and truth. His literary irony is also an irony of selfhood, enacting his philosophical and psychological view that despair is a lack of consciousness of being a self or spirit. Kierkegaard the teacher is at his best in his discussion of achieving spiritual health and of the responsibility each individual has to achieve selfhood and self consciousness. Self consciousness and selfhood are for Kierkegaard not only states received but states achieved: "One can be a wizard of introspection, an expert on one's emotional life, and remain totally unselfconscious in the Kierkegaardian sense. Consciousness of the kind Kierkegaard tried to raise requires conviction—the conviction that one is a self. Kierkegaard counseled that self-consciousness is conditioned by our wider system of beliefs: to be awakened in Freudian terms is to be in a slumber according to Marx, and to be conscious according to Marx is to be comatose according to Kierkegaard" (Marino 112).

Had Kierkegaard's polyvocal, multigenre modes of seamlessly interwoven literary and philosophical discourses come to guide literary practice and theory, we might have ended up with a slightly less suspicious hermeneutic tradition. There is a fine line between acting in bad faith or during a loss of faith, as for example Cassandra does in Wolf's depictions of her priestly performances, and acting antically in order to undermine faith, as do the ancient Cynics, Nietzsche, and some among our more flamboyant modern decon-postmods. In his warnings against destructiveness and its temptations, Kierkegaard implicates literary and philosophical authors, as well as any and all individuals because we are all, he asserts, authors of ourselves. We must therefore beware what characters, plots and stories, what keywords, what general values and concepts, we write into our conceptual and spiritual lives. He sharply characterizes as evil the character that would undermine and question for the sake of destruction, a character that he finds in Socrates. "Socrates' destruction of what is distorted and one-sided does not occur in order that the truth may appear, but merely to begin again with something equally distorted and one-sided. This master is none other than the total irony which, when all the minor skirmishes have been fought and all the ramparts leveled, gazes out upon the total desolation and becomes conscious that nothing remains, or rather, that what retains is nothingness" (143). After deeming Socrates destructive and Hegel somewhat deluded, or at least highly ingenious in his reading of Socrates, Kierkegaard doubles the meanings of his own representations of Socrates and Hegel. In doing so, he reveals and confesses his own destructiveness, his own wishful—or deluded—reading.

Kierkegaard is vividly didactic in his confessional modes; he repeatedly asserts that "the concept" must, and seeks to, take form in the phenomenon. He applies this proviso to academic and non-academic methods of inquiry alike. A concept—an unstated value and model—will always accompany any discussion and find a way of dwelling among us. In this assertion he directs our attention to the continuum that links academic philosophical understandings of concepts and discourse with the experiences and value of everyday conversation. An explicit allusion to incarnation is introduced with the terminology of indwelling/dwelling among us. With the allusion, Kierkegaard quite deliberately, and didactically, addresses the spiritually sickly to awaken from the slumber of pro forma religious belief and practice of his day. I encourage more attention to the use of confessional and polemic images in Kierkegaards's work, for they require as well as model a participatory hermeneutic (Mackey). It takes only a small leap of interpretive faith to see parallels between the academic and cultural environment of his day and that of our own. In a double rebuke of the academy and the religion of his day he assigns to them joint responsibility for a cultural malaise that found its most graphic expressions in limp practices of religion, and philosophical methods and movements bent upon undermining conviction. He offers remedies as well as rebukes—a helpful antidote to his more stentorian voices.

Kierkegaard transforms the Socratic practice of dialectical destruction through relocating it in Hegel's reading of Socratic conversation. However deluded in Hegel's "original conception" it may have been, Kierkegaard forges the model of dialectical dialogue into a paradigm for academic and human discussion always partaking of irony. Life and philosophy are yoked, interanimated: "When irony has been mastered in this way, when the wild infinity wherein it storms consumingly forth has been restrained, it does not follow that it should then lose its significance or be wholly abandoned. As philosophers claim that no true philosophy is possible without doubt, so by the same token one may claim that no authentic human life is possible without irony" (338). And how are doubt, on the one hand, and irony, on the other, to be properly used? Certainly not with the leveling-the-ramparts glee that Kierkegaard finds in Socrates: "There is in every personal life so much that must be sheared away. Here again irony is an excellent surgeon. For when irony has been mastered its function then is of utmost importance in order for the personal life to acquire health and truth" (338).

The Greek *psyche* and the German *Geist* commingle concepts that are held separate in English: mind and spirit. Psychology, we often forget in a post-Freudian and clinically therapeutic era, is an art of studying and healing the spirit that has close ties in earlier eras to art, philosophy, and religion (Maranhão). Welcome warnings remind us that overly therapeutic, psychology-based concepts of philosophizing, or irony, or pedagogy, may lead to a reductive, twelve-step, self-esteem approach to curriculum design and pedagogy (Gates "Pluralism"). A less reductive alternative resides in the model of the mind as spirit, and of belief as the result of reasoned conviction (Kinneavy). These models can rehabilitate belief and faith-sustaining aspects of knowledge, learning, and classrooms while at the same time deterring overly psychologized notions of writing and textual interpretation as fragmentary, eternally incomplete, merely personal, and exclusively therapeutic. Belief oriented intellectual practices can and should be employed to enhance the ability to comprehend diversity as a unity. Even dispassionate analysis, Kierkegaard and Plato long ago recognized, is always directed by interests and purposes, passions and beliefs however well masked these may be by rationalizations and self-denial. Kierkegaard's deliberately personal forms of philosophizing were designed to provide instructive, edifying examples of philosophy as comprising multiple genres and fostering tolerance for many varieties of self while still retaining a common language and common goals. The belief popular today—that objectivity is impossible and even undesirable—may be advanced in either a gleeful or a deeply human spirit. In either case, the defense is itself guided by belief: that we should look for division, or for commonality.

Skepticism, criticism, and debate, regardless of the value that is assigned to them by their diverse reformers and adversaries remain distinctively Western philosophical and academic models that have evolved from agonistic male-to-male rhetorical traditions within the academy and in the forum of public political debate (Ong *Faith*). It is increasingly clear that debate, in this "liberal" and "humane" tradition, has been sanctioned primarily for and by those in positions of power (Holmes). Women and minorities have traditionally not been permitted to dispute, to debate, or even to speak on the public platform (Peaden). Oddly enough, through similar rules of enfranchisement, particularly in the U.S. where church and state are so rigorously segregated, religion has often been excluded from the debate and indeed has been cast as an enemy and not as the ally of education, liberal humanism, and the pursuit of knowledge (Carter; Wills).

Although the conventions—the values—that govern the public presence and power of alternate voices are slowly changing, much remains to be done to broaden the base of tolerance and understanding for the many different kinds of voices that are now seeking to sing together, to forge strengthened common values out of newly discovered common beliefs and together to make just a few simple leaps of faith.

Acknowledgements

A shorter version of portions of this discussion will appear in *The Academy and the Possibility of Belief: Composing Our Intellectual and Spiritual Lives*, edited by Mary Louise Bauley-Meissner, Mary McCaslin Thompson, and Elizabeth Bachrach Tan. Under contract, Hampton Press. Fall, 1999. An earlier version of portions of this discussion was presented at a conference on Advocacy in the Classroom, June 1995, jointly sponsored by the MLA, ACLU, AAUP, and eighteen other professional organizations. It appears in the proceedings of that conference: *Advocacy in the Classroom: Problems and Possibilities*, edited by Patricia Meyers Spacks (New York: St. Martins, 1996). My thanks to the editors of these collections for their encouragement and support for work in this field.

Works Cited

Belenky, Mary Field, Blythe McVicker Clinchy, Nancy Rule Goldberger, and Jill Mattuck Tarule. *Women's Ways of Knowing.* New York: Basic Books, 1986.

Brindel, June Kachuy. *Ariadne.* New York: St. Martin's, 1982.

———. *Phaedra.* New York: St. Martin's, 1985.

Bruner, Jerome. *Actual Minds, Possible Worlds.* Cambridge: Harvard UP, 1986.

Carter, Stephen L. *The Culture of Disbelief.* New York: Basic Books, 1992.

Chernin, Kim. *The Flame Bearers.* New York: HarperCollins, 1988.

Cixous, Helene. "The Laugh of the Medusa." *The Signs Reader.* Elizabeth Abel and Emily K. Abet, eds. Chicago: U of Chicago P, 1983. 279–97.

Elbow, Peter. *Embracing Contraries in the Teaching Process.* New York: Oxford UP, 1986.

Epictetus. *Meditations* 3.14. Trans. A. Lawrence Lowell. *The Practical Cogitator.* Charles P. Curtis Jr. and Ferris Greensleet, eds. Boston: Houghton Mifflin, 1962.

Fiorenza, Elizabeth Schussler. *But She Said; Feminist Practices of Biblical Interpretation.* Boston: Beacon Press, 1992.

Frye, Northrop. *The Double Vision. Language and Meaning in Religion.* Toronto: U of Toronto P, 1991.

———. *The Great Code. The Bible and Literature.* New York: Harcourt Brace Jovanovich, 1982.

Frymer-Kensky, Tikva. *In the Wake of the Goddesses. Women, Culture, and the Biblical Transformation of Pagan Myth.* New York: The Free Press. 1992.

Gates, Henry Louis. "Pluralism and Its Discontents." *Profession 92.* New York: MLA, 1992. 35–38.

———. "Beyond the Culture Wars: Identities in Dialogue." *Profession 93.* New York: MLA, 1993. 6–11.

Geertz, Clifford. *The Anthropologist as Author.* Palo Alto: Stanford UP, 1988.

Gilligan, Carol. *In a Different Voice.* Cambridge: Harvard UP, 1986.

Graff, Gerald. *Beyond the Culture Wars: How Teaching the Conflicts Can Revitalize American Education.* New York: Norton, 1990.

Harrison, Jane Ellen. *Epilegomena to the Study of Greek Religion* [1921] and *Themis, a Study of the Social Origins of Greek Religion,* New Hyde Park: University Books, 1996.

Hartman, Geoffrey H. *Minor Prophecies: The Literary Essay in the Culture Wars.* Cambridge: Harvard UP, 1991.

Holmes, Stephen. *The Anatomy of Antiliberalism.* Cambridge: Harvard UP, 1993.

Kelber, Werner H. "Narrative as Interpretation and Interpretation of Narrative: Hermeneutical Reflections on the Gospels." *The Interpretation of Dialogue.* Ed. Tullio Maranhão, ed. Chicago: U of Chicago P, 1990.

Kierkegaard, Søren. *The Concept of Irony, With Constant Reference to Socrates.* New York: Harper and Row, 1966.

Kinneavy, James L. *Greek Rhetorical Origins of Christian Faith.* New York: Oxford UP, 1987.

Kristeva, Julia. *In the Beginning Was Love: Psychoanalysis and Faith.* Trans. Arthur Goldhammer. New York: Columbia UP, 1987.

Mackey, Louis. *Kierkegaard, A Kind of Poet.* Philadelphia: U of Pennsylvania P, 1971.

Maranhão, Tullio. *Therapeutic Discourse and Socratic Dialogue: A Cultural Critique.* Madison: U of Wisconsin P, 1986.

Marino, Godon D. "Making Faith Possible, Kierkegaard's Writings. *Atlantic Monthly* 272: 1 (1993): 109–13.

Meyers, Carol. *Discovering Eve: Ancient Israelite Women in Context.* New York: Oxford UP, 1988.

Murphy, Cullen. "Women and the Bible." *Atlantic Monthly.* 272:2 (1993): 39–65.

Murphy, Michael. "After Progressivism: Modem Composition, Institutional Service, and Cultural Studies." *Journal of Advanced Composition* 13.2 (1997): 345–64.

Norris, Christopher. *What's Wrong With Postmodernism?* Baltimore: Johns Hopkins UP, 1990.

Ong, Walter J. "God's Known Universe." *Thought* 66:262 (1991): 241–58.

———. *Faith in Contexts.* Vols 1, 2. Thomas J. Farrell and Paul Soukup, eds. Newbury Park, CA: Sage, 1990.

Peaden, Catherine Hobbs, ed. *Nineteenth-Century Women Learn to Write: Past Cultures and Practices of Literacy.* Charlottesville: UP of Virginia, 1995.

Phelps, Louise Wetherbee. A Constrained Version of the Writing Classroom." *ADE Bulletin* 103 (1992): 13–20.

Said, Edward W. "Identity, Authority and Freedom: the Potentate and the Traveller." U of Cape Town: T. B. Davie Memorial Lectures, 1991.

Salisbury, John of. *Metalogicon.* Trans. Daniel D. McGany. Gloucester, MA: Peter Smith, 1971.

Swearingen, C. Jan. "Dialogue and Dialectic: The Logic of Conversation and the Interpretation of Logic." *The Interpretation of Dialogue*. Ed. Tullio Maranhão. Chicago: U of Chicago P. 1990.

Thurow, Sarah Baumgartner. "Illusory Compromise. Review of Gerald Graff." *Beyond the Culture Wars: How Teaching the Conflicts Can Revitalize American Education*. First Things (1993): 50–52.

Torgovnik, Marianna. "Hartman's Dilemma: *Minor Prophecies: The Literary Essay in the Culture Wars*, by Geoffrey Hartman." *ADE Bulletin* 104 (1993): 52–55.

Trible, Phyllis. *God and the Rhetoric of Sexuality*. Philadelphia: Fortress Press, 1978.

White, Edward M. *Teaching and Assessing Writing*. New York: Jossey Bass, 1985.

Wills, Gary. *Under God: Religion and American Life*. New York: Simon and Schuster, 1990.

Wolf, Christa. *Cassandra*. Trans. Jean Van Huerck. New York: Farrar Strauss Giroux, 1984.

Yeats, William Butler. *Selected Poems and Three Plays*. Ed. M. L. Rosenthal. New York: Macmillan, 1986.

Chapter 10

Ethos, Ethical Argument, and *Ad Hominem* in Contemporary Theory

James S. Baumlin
George S. Jensen
Lance Massey

> The man who wishes to persuade people will not be negligent as to the matter of character; no, . . . for who does not know . . . that the argument which is made by a man's life is of more weight than that which is furnished by his words?
> —Isocrates, *Antidosis* 52

> And yet, and yet: I have written as much to hide as to reveal, have written so that I might show the writing to others and not be required to show myself. There's more to me than meets the eye and less. Whatever is in here might be terrible to see, worse to reveal. A piece of writing can be revelatory and exploratory. . . . It can also be a substitute for the unspeakable—a closure, not a revelation.
> —Jim W. Corder, "Hunting Lieutenant Chadbourne," 349

> I seek to make a distinction between attacks on deconstruction as a critical and philosophical entity, and on Paul de Man the man. The two are not identical. . . . The judgment one may wish to make of the character of the man ought not necessarily, without further argumentation, to be the judgment of the ideology. The argument *ad hominem* is rarely useful.
> —Frederick C. Stern, "Derrida, de Man, Despair," 24

We begin with a simple proposition, which we will proceed to view through the vocabulary of Burkean dialectic. For a variety of reasons, composition theory has branded *ad hominem* argument fallacious. On the one hand, humanists dismiss *ad hominem* for criticizing a person's character rather than ideas; on the other hand, poststructuralists dismiss it for presupposing a unified, stable, coherent self—as if person or selfhood were itself a fiction. Yet humanists and poststructuralists alike resort to *ad hominem* attacks in their own professional writing, and it seems that academic discourse cannot function without attempting to identify the author and raise questions concerning his or her competence or character. So we ask, what are the ethical implications of repressing *ad hominem* argument in academic discourse (which includes the teaching of writing)? Can we develop an ethics of discourse that acknowledges the person "behind" an argument, addressing the person as if he or she remained part of the argument itself? Can we, in short, develop an ethics of *ethos*?

Humanism versus Poststructuralism

Taking self-knowledge as the highest form of understanding and the ultimate aim of learning (indeed, of life itself), the liberal-humanist tradition values the individual as the locus of intellect, will, and choice. *Nosce te ipsum* describes this Socratic legacy: "know thyself." A mode of inquiry and critique rather than a political activism, humanism expresses a commitment to ideas, *not* to ideologies: hence its resistance to politically-motivated pedagogy. As a teaching practice, rather, it aims at "students' intellectual and ethical development" (Gregory 42), stressing self-reflection as well as sharpening one's powers of analytical, critical thinking. Granted, twentieth-century theory charts the reduction of the powers and capacities of the "sovereign individual," who is seen to operate within ever-constricting circles of self-knowledge and responsible action; yet the most influential modern theorists—Sigmund Freud, Mikhail Bakhtin, Margaret Mead, Jean-Paul Sartre, Simone de Beauvoir, Julia Kristeva, and Paulo Freire to name a few—remain humanist at their core. For their theories, ultimately liberatory, seek to explain the nature of the individual *in relation to* forces that influence and threaten to limit one's capacities, beliefs, and actions. Their theories, in short, aim to return to the individual the possibility of self-understanding and responsible action. And we might add that human freedom, responsibility, and self-understanding are prior conditions of ethical choice and action. Without acknowledging these values, is a discussion of ethics (much less of the ethics of writing) even possible?[1]

Yet the varieties of postmodern criticism seem, as Howard Felperin observes, to pose "a fundamental threat to the institutional and pedagogical practices" of humanism.² Claiming to be its rival rather than an offspring, Marxist theory begins the assault, proclaiming it "at once largely ineffectual, and the best ideology of the 'human' that present bourgeois society can muster" (Eagleton, *Literary Theory* 200).³ Thus Terry Eagleton faults traditional English departments for remaining part of "the ideological apparatus of the modern capitalist state" (200), in the place of which Marxists have proposed departments of "'cultural criticism,' for which there are no selves," as Harold Bloom complains, "whether in writers or readers, but only politics: gender, racial, class, ethnic" (19-20). While Marxist theory typically subsumes the individual writer within a "collective," poststructuralism offers a more violent assault against humanism: announcing no less than the "death of the author," Roland Barthes and Michel Foucault replace human agency with a theory of textuality. At least in its Isocratean sense, *ethos* reveals an individual giving thought its distinctively unique, human face.⁴ In contrast, privileging writing over speech, much of postmodern theory discovers that the "human face" of language is merely a mask, and authorial presence a fiction. (How can it be otherwise, if language is no more than a simulacrum, a chain of signifiers separated from the material world and exceeding—indeed, subverting—authorial control?) The charge of anti-humanism, often leveled against poststructuralist theory, is accurate in this sense: by denying authorial presence and intentionality, poststructuralism disturbs the ethical relation between writers and their texts.

On one point at least, we can agree with Eagleton: one's pedagogy is necessarily shaped by an "ideology of the 'human,'" that is, a set of assumptions, whether explicit or unexamined, regarding human psychology, social relations, and language. Is the writer (whom we model and attempt to teach) to be seen as an autonomous and ethically-responsible agent, a member of a class (or gender, or race), or an issue of language? Must we choose but one from among these alternatives? Is not the individual writer (yes, we teach individuals, not classes: to this extent we declare ourselves humanist) at once ethical, political, and textual? We do not wish "to understate our disciplinary disunity," as Marshall Gregory puts it (41): as rivals to the humanist tradition, Marxist and poststructuralist theories have thus far resisted assimilation (in effect, their own domestication) by the tradition they seek to displace (Felperin). Still, *within their own discursive practices*, both theories remain grounded in implicitly humanist assumptions, often invoking the very principles that they assault—the most important being the autonomy, intentionality, and ethical responsibility of authors. Their grounding in humanist assumptions should hardly surprise, since the humanist, Marxist, and poststructuralist theories of selfhood are dialectically related: in other words, our "ideology of the 'human'" remains at once ethical, political, and textual, refusing in any absolute sense to separate the social from the psychological, the individual from the collective, the biological from the linguistic.

Doubtless, the problem poststructuralist theory poses to writers and teachers of writing is one fundamentally of *ethos*. By privileging *logos* over *ethos* (hence the term *logocentrism*), contemporary theory generally has sought to de-psychologize and ultimately dehumanize discourse. In effect, such theory operates as if it had "killed off" *ethos* and, by implication, unsettled the ethical connections between authors and their texts.[5] And yet a careful rhetorical analysis of this theory (a deconstruction, as it were, of deconstruction) reveals that poststructuralist theorists inevitably do the opposite of what they claim, by introducing humanist (that is, biographic and "biologic") themes into their writing and seeking to maintain firm control over their meaning—in essence, by establishing their own authorial "presence" within texts.[6] Thus we can explain (and in part justify) the rather extensive criticism directed against poststructuralism, particularly against the writings of Jacques Derrida and Paul de Man; such criticism, inevitably, takes aim at the problematic center of deconstructive argument—that is, at the *ethos* of the theorists themselves. We shall demonstrate, in short, that recent criticism of deconstruction proceeds implicitly and often outright by *ad hominem* attack. Yet we also seek to reappraise the nature and use of *ad hominem*. While argumentation theory assumes that fallacies "render arguments unreasonable" (Herrick 226), we question the conventional wisdom (at least among teachers of writing) that brands *ad hominem* fallacious.[7] So, our essay—which snakes its way through Burke to Foucault, Derrida, and de Man, in order to arrive at a pedagogy of *ad hominem* argument—is motivated by the following question. Can we legitimately give instruction to students regarding the ethics of writing before taking some account of the ethical problems embedded in our own habits of professional discourse?

Time, Death, and the Agon of Academic Discourse

We have termed our essay a "Burkean analysis." Of course, Kenneth Burke provides a dialectical method suited to our complex subject.[8]

No less important, his unique vocabulary allows us to analyze and account for the agonistic styles of academic discourse: it accounts, that is, for the distinctive *rhetoric* of contemporary theory. While Burke has much to say about persuasion, most frequently repeated is his notion of consubstantiation, which is a verbal-symbolic act of communion, a theology of identifying one's cause with an audience's interests (*Rhetoric* 1022)—a praising of "Athenians among Athenians." In contrast with communion, Burke also speaks of "the flurries and flare-ups of the Human Barnyard, the Give and Take, . . . the Logomachy, . . . the Wars of Nerves, the War" (1021). Of course, within the Burkean dialectic, communion and war, identification and division are ultimately one. Explaining how his *Rhetoric of Motives* deals with groups "at odds with one another," he writes:

> Why 'at odds,' you may ask, when the titular term is 'identification'? Because, to begin with 'identification' is, by the same token though roundabout, to confront the implication of *division*. And so, in the end, men are brought to that most tragically ironic of all divisions, or conflicts, wherein millions of cooperative acts go into the preparation of one single destructive act. We refer to that ultimate *disease* of cooperation: war. (You will understand war much better if you think of it, not simply as strife come to a head, but rather as a disease, or perversion of communion. Modern war characteristically requires a myriad of constructive acts for each destructive one; before each culminating blast there must be a vast network of interlocking operations, directed communally. (1020)

Every war against one group relies upon communion with another, as every communion relies upon a division symbolic of an act of war, a killing-off of someone or something. In war—Burke's metaphor for rhetoric—we come together to oppose an enemy. In communion—Burke's metaphor for theology—we kill off someone or something to come together. All persuasion hinges upon acts of identity as they move through a series of dialectics: communion and war, of course, but also similarity and difference, substance and symbol, time and death.

Applying Burke's vocabulary to academic discourse (particularly to the practice and critique of deconstruction), what we find is a warfare that seeks communion. We find Derrida at war with a variety of critics at the same time that he seeks communion with "the profession," a broader audience whom he hopes will join him. We find others at war with Derrida and de Man at the same time that they, too, seek communion with "the profession." And each, we find, accuses the other of academic "war crimes," most commonly of launching *ad hominem* attacks. The dialectic, indeed, is one of time and death, of slaying and being slain, of having an identity thrust upon oneself—and attempting to escape strictures of identity. For "an imagery of slaying (slaying of either the self or another)," Burke claims, "is to be considered merely as a special case of identification in general. Or otherwise put: the imagery of slaying is a special case of transformation, and transformation involves the ideas and imagery of *identification*. That is: the *killing* of something is the *changing* of it, and the statement of the thing's nature before and after the change is an *identifying* of it" (*Rhetoric* 1020). Only death or the killing-off of another (whether in substance or symbol) places a mark in time, allowing us to identify another. But death is also a transformation, enacting what Jung calls the archetype of rebirth: when we kill off an enemy, we initiate a transformation—indeed, we may create a martyr. So the enemy needs to be disinterred, then killed off again and again. Seemingly aware of Jung's notion of the Shadow, Burke realizes that as we kill off the enemy we may also harm ourselves, for the enemy is often no more than a projection of our own dark side.

Though communion and killing seem far from the practices of academic discourse, do we not create our professional identities largely by disinterring and killing off other writers, hoping all the while to escape a similar death? What, indeed, is the "relationship between writing and death"? Treating the literary text as "its author's murderer," Michel Foucault claims that the "relationship between writing and death is . . . manifested in the effacement of the writing subject's individual characteristics . . . the writing subject cancels out the signs of his particular individuality. As a result, the mark of the writer is nothing more than the singularity of his absence: he must assume the role of the dead man in the game of writing" ("What Is" 142-43). So, is the author dead? Not if we think dialectically, projecting ourselves beyond death (suicide, murder, war) to time (being, historicity, rebirth, transformation). Certainly not if we view the text from the perspective of the reader. Imagine reading Foucault's *Birth of the Clinic* in the mid-1970s, shortly after it was translated into English. How might we have read the following passage, part of Foucault's discussion of institutional forces that drive the definition and management of epidemics?

> A medicine of epidemics is opposed at every point to a medicine of classes, just as the collective perception of a phenomenon that is widespread but

unique and unrepeatable may be opposed to the individual perception of the identity of an essence as constantly revealed in the multiplicity of phenomena. The analysis of a series in the one case, the decipherment of a type in the other; the integration of time in the case of epidemics, the determination of hierarchical place in the case of the species; the attribution of a causality—the search for an essential coherence, the subtle perception of a complex historical and geographic space—the demarcation of a homogeneous surface in which analogies can be read. And yet, in the final analysis, . . . the pathology of epidemics and that of the species are confronted by the same requirements: the definition of a political status for medicine and the constitution, at state level, of a medical consciousness whose constant task would be to provide information, supervision, and constraint, all of which 'relate as much to the police as to the field of medicine proper.' (26)

On first reading, we might cross this passage with little thought. If we pause to think it through, we might be puzzled by the way Foucault speaks of the epidemic—as if it were not an empirical fact. Or, we might be intrigued by his pairing of medicine and politics, science and state, doctors and police. We might even come to an intellectual understanding of his argument that disease becomes an epidemic *only under certain kinds of social and political conditions*. Now, imagine rereading *The Birth of the Clinic* more recently, in the midst of the AIDS epidemic. We watched as the disease was largely ignored by the Reagan administration or occasionally dismissed as "the gay cancer." We also witnessed its redefinition, once it affected hemophiliacs. We may have even read *And the Band Plays On* or seen the HBO film, watching as the names of victims scrolled across the television screen—among them, Michel Foucault, reportedly the first person in France to die from AIDS. From the book or film or newspapers, we learned of the early, rapid spread of AIDS in the gay bathhouses of San Francisco, and we read in Eribon's biography that Foucault may have contracted the disease when visiting such a bathhouse. After all this, we are changed. And now we reread *The Birth of the Clinic*. The passage we once glanced over is riveting. What we once understood intellectually, we now feel. We have resurrected Foucault.

But why this talk of resurrecting Foucault, Derrida, or some other author, and how might this pertain to the ethics of writing? Note that the following proceeds from several assumptions that we shall test and develop more fully as our argument unfolds. We assume, first, that writers remain somehow connected to their texts, which is not to say that a writer necessarily *is* or *becomes* the text; perhaps this connection may best be viewed through Bakhtin's notion of "answerability," whereby the author is held to *answer for* the text and the text, reciprocally, for the author. Second, we assume that readers necessarily construct an image of the author, if only unconsciously, and that these imaginary constructions influence the reading. (Concomitantly, Wolfgang Iser and other reader-response theorists have long held that authors construct images of their "implied" reader.) What are the ethical implications of such constructed images? If mere stereotype, such images indeed "kill off" the living, breathing author; yet we argue that readers, once made aware of this projective tendency, might offer some resistance to the construction of stereotypes. (Rather than act as an author's "murderer," as Barthes would have it, might readers not seek a more faithful "resurrection" of the author's image and character?) Our third assumption is that authors—and particularly authors of academic discourse—inevitably construct images of their opponents in argument. (Not just the author, and not just the reader, but a third person is thus constructed: the subject of one's criticism.) And since persuasion, as Burke tells us, hinges on acts of identity, so the current rhetoric of academic warfare turns inevitably to caricature and *ad hominem* attack. Shall we continue, nonetheless, to pronounce such rhetorical practices fallacious and pretend that we do not argue "against the man"? Or shall we admit that identity remains a central, unresolved issue in academic discourse and confront it as such?

Shutter Masks: Derrida and the Deconstruction of *Ethos*

Whether framed by a critique of biologism, psychologism, or some other "ideology of the human," the poststructuralist critique of *ethos* proves incapable of escaping from (and yet refuses to acknowledge) its own humanist assumptions regarding subjective agency—assumptions revealed in its own projective tendency to construct (again, to "kill off") images of authors. Demonstrating this tendency, we turn now to Derrida's deconstruction of "signature," which seeks to reduce authorial "voice" and "presence" to a mere inscription. Even while he wears a series of masks, do we not hear Derrida's own distinctive voice intoned in the reading? (Is it even possible to imagine that he does not hear it himself, that he takes no pleasure in it?) In spite of his habitual posturing, is Derrida not present in the writing? As important, does he not assume—demand—that others, the author-subjects of his critique, be present as well?

The communal rituals of the Nootka of North Alaska employ masks that have two or three levels of shutters, each of which opens to reveal a totem. As the rituals progress, a series of identities is revealed, though the face of the wearer is not (Mauss 9). While we do not wear ceremonial masks in our literate culture, we do wear what Morse Peckham calls a "mask of language" (91). It is through such masks, Peckham argues, that we create ourselves as we create ways of relating to others, for these masks, and not the ego, "hold our personalities together" (94). When we seem to catch a glimpse of "the person" behind the mask, it turns out to be but another mask (92). The persona holds the personality together only for those who view the individual from outside; in fact we never see another individual's ego, and so, when we read another's text, we are working our way through a shutter mask, opening shutter after shutter to see what lies beneath—only to find another mask. The author eludes us. At least, that is what Derrida would have us believe. In "Interpreting Signatures," Derrida deconstructs Heidegger's interpretation and critique of Nietzsche's character. It is the text of a speech that questions what it means for an author to sign his or her name to a text; it questions, in other words, the nature of *ethos*—specifically, the transaction that occurs among authors, texts, and readers.

Let us begin by looking at Derrida's own text as a shutter mask. On the outside of the mask is the traditional view of persona (a writer possessing a unified ego that she displays as she writes, as she plays the role of author) and *ethos* (the reader constructing an image of this author as he reads her text). This is, Derrida seems to say, a naive view of signature, which he derides by means of his own particular devil terms, "biography" and "psychology." Then the first level of the shutter mask opens to reveal the more sophisticated Heidegger. In his *Nietzsche,* Heidegger determines "the essentiality of the name from the 'subject matter of thought'" (62). Heidegger, in Derrida's view, does not assume that the unity of the biographical/psychological Nietzsche is infused in his text; he is not even concerned about the biographical/psychological Nietzsche. Heidegger does, however, infer a Nietzsche as unitary thinker from what he believes to be the consistent system of thought in Nietzsche's texts. Then the shutter mask opens to reveal a new level of sophistication, what we might call Derrida's view of signature:

> Is it correct to say, as Heidegger so positively claims, that this thinking is one?—that Nietzsche then has only one name? Does he name himself only once? For Heidegger, his naming takes place only once, even if the place of this event retains the appearance of a borderline, from which one can get a

look at both sides at once. . . . But who ever has said that a person bears a single name? Certainly not Nietzsche. (67)

In Derrida's view, Nietzsche never possessed a unitary personality, nor do his texts present any unified system of thought. Nietzsche had many names.

Summing up this section of his argument, Derrida compares Nietzsche to a tightrope walker:

> These are the preliminary remarks that I wanted to suggest for a future reading of Heidegger's Nietzsche—for this ambiguous life-saving act, in the course of which one stretches out the net for the tightrope walker, the one who runs the greatest risk overhead on the narrow rope, only insofar as one has made sure that he—unmasked and protected by the unity of his name, which in turn will be sealed by the unity of metaphysics—will not be taking any risks. In other words: he was dead before he landed in the net. (69)

Nietzsche is on the tightrope (*might Derrida see himself up there with him, taking "the greatest risk"?*) and Heidegger has thrown out a net for him. Heidegger is trying to save Nietzsche by shifting from the traditional view of the *biographical/psychological author-as-infused-into-the-text* to the *reader who infers the author-as-thinker* from a series of texts. But in either case, Nietzsche is "dead" before he landed in the net: both approaches to signature reduce "Nietzsche" to a single, static characterization.

Is this the last shutter? We have, after all, reached the end of the text. But what happens if we continue to read, if we begin now to move backwards? In a paragraph preceding the above quotation, Derrida quotes a long passage from Heidegger that describes Nietzsche's abstract thinking as a feast. Interpreting this feast to be a "plurality," a "family of names," Derrida comments:

> The Nietzsches' feast risks tearing [Heidegger's essentialist view of Nietzsche-as-thinker] into pieces or dispersing it in its masks. Certainly it would protect it from any kind of biologism, but this would be because the 'logism' in it would lose its hold from the start. And another style of autobiography would come into being, bursting open . . . the unity of the name and the signature, disturbing both biologism and its critique, so far as it operates, in Heidegger, in the name of 'essential thinking.' (68–69)

What is Derrida saying? Is he unmasking his own critique of Heidegger's interpretation of Nietzsche, "*disturbing both biologism and its critique*" (emphasis added)? Is he admitting that a deconstruction of biologism necessarily lapses into a new form of biologism? What does it mean to say that Nietzsche is not a unified subject and that his texts do not embody an "essential thinking"? Are we back to saying that the author's character (the non-unified subject) is incarnated into the text (which does not contain unified thought)?

But let us continue in our backreading of Derrida's text. Let us open another shutter.

Earlier Derrida had written: "At the time he was teaching his 'Nietzsche,' Heidegger had begun to put some distance between himself and Nazism. Without saying anything in his lecture itself that was directed against the government and the use it was making of Nietzsche (on so much prudence and silence one can certainly put an interpretation—but elsewhere), Heidegger is in the process of overtly criticizing the edition that the government is in the process of supporting" (63). Here Derrida seems to lapse into a traditional form of biologism to save Heidegger and, in the process, perhaps to save Nietzsche as well. In Derrida's own rather essentialist view, Heidegger is putting "distance between himself and Nazism," showing the world that there is another Nietzsche—one who, if he were alive in the 1930s, might not have condoned Nazism.

But maybe Derrida is really trying to save himself. A post-Holocaust Jew who has written eloquently about the hermeneutic tradition of the Talmud, Derrida has spent much of his career writing apologia for Nietzsche (whom some consider to be a proto-Nazi), Heidegger (whom some consider to have been an unrepentant Nazi), and de Man (who hid his support of Nazism). These are issues of *ethos* that seem to be constructed upon a traditional notion of self. Derrida wants to show us the "good" Nietzsche, the "good" Heidegger, and the "good" de Man, perhaps so that we will see the "good" Derrida. And why does Derrida say, within parentheses (so we might pass over it without much thought), that "on so much prudence and silence one can certainly put an interpretation—but elsewhere"? Why does Derrida keep saying, "I could say something here," but "elsewhere" or "later"? Why is he reluctant to speak, to perform an act of identity?

As we continue in our backreading to another shutter, perhaps a hint. Discussing Heidegger's notion that Nietzsche is "nothing other than the name" of his "thinking," Derrida writes, "at this point two paths present themselves. One would consist in taking a new approach to the problematic of the name, at the risk of seeing the name dismembered and multiplied in masks and similitudes. We know what

Nietzsche risked in this respect" (62). Seeing "the name dismembered and multiplied in masks" is Derrida's own path, and, he seems to say, Nietzsche's as well. The second path, "to determine the essentiality of the name from the 'subject matter of thought,'" is Heidegger's. What is interesting here, however, is that Derrida uses the word "risk" in association with developing multiple personae—with wearing, in effect, a shutter mask. Is the risk a loss of identity, a loss of stability? Is this why Nietzsche walks a tightrope? Or is Derrida hiding something else? Perhaps, hiding something even from himself by not speaking something to others? Is the wearing of a shutter mask actually a defense against risk, a means of avoiding being controlled or criticized? After all, if we cannot pin down Nietzsche (or Derrida), how can we critique his (or their) ideas?

And back to the beginning of Derrida's argument, one more shutter? In his introduction, Derrida announces a plan to analyze two chapters from Heidegger's lectures, "The Eternal Recurrence of the Same" and "The Will to Power as Knowledge." He adds,

> In view of the fact that the same interpretation is regularly at work throughout, the risks involved in choosing this strategy are, I hope, quite limited. In each instance, a single system of reading is powerfully concentrated and gathered together. It is directed at gathering together the unity and the uniqueness of Nietzsche's thinking, which, as a fulfilled unity, is itself in a fair way to being the culmination of Occidental metaphysics. (58)

More about risks. Derrida seems to say, "I hope this is not too risky"—that is, "I hope I don't misread Heidegger's reading of Nietzsche." As Derrida works his deconstruction, his saving of Heidegger as he criticizes Heidegger for the futile gesture of trying to save Nietzsche—indeed, even as he argues that there are no unified signatures or texts or systems of thought—Derrida proceeds on the assumption that Heidegger's lectures are themselves consistent and unified, thus allowing him to take chapters out of context *without risk*. But risk to whom or what? The thought of Nietzsche? The reputation of Heidegger's lectures? The signature of Derrida?

In order to guarantee the consistency of Heidegger's argument, Derrida must posit a consistent, unified identity for the author. Heidegger must first be fixed—frozen in time and personality—for, ultimately, he is to be held accountable for his texts in ways that a persona is not.[9]

Even so radical a theory of textuality as deconstruction thus assumes a responsible, intending consciousness standing at a text's point of origin—in a word, an author. Deconstruction does not simply assert the author's death: in grand Burkean fashion, it demands the author's disinterring and killing-off, again and again. In effect, Derrida has read Heidegger—the Other of his text—by employing a rather traditional hermeneutic. Once he has determined what Heidegger has written (*could we say, once he has reduced Heidegger to a sitting duck?*), he can launch his critique (*yes, Derrida both defends and critiques Heidegger*). Or, unfolding in the same moment—if we can think of this text as a narrative—once he has determined how Heidegger has fashioned himself as he is refashioning Nietzsche (*can we say, once Derrida has put out a net for Heidegger so that Heidegger can put out a net for Nietzsche so that they can both put out a net for Derrida?*), he can speak without risk. But is this not the way we all argue? We "essentialize the Other," freezing the Other in time, denying the Other his or her own narrative either to bolster our own persona or to caricature those who are held a threat—even as we claim, in our defense (that is, within the chronology of our own narrative), "You don't understand, I am more complicated than that."[10]

We might even think of Derrida's text itself as "another style of autobiography" (68), a postmodern autobiography. Offering personae (or Derridae) without any progression to sort them out into a "before" and "after," writing a text that can be read backward as well as forward, Derrida strives to efface his presence—and yet reveals something of himself in the process. As one Derrida says, "Don't pin down Nietzsche," we seem to hear another echo, "I will not let you essentialize me, I cannot take the risk." Have we unmasked something essential about the signature (the presence) of Derrida? Is he not the one who writes criticism in stream-of-consciousness (a deconstruction of the literature-criticism binary opposition) as he says, "come into my mind and know that you cannot know me"? Do not his texts about other texts reveal a writer (a deconstruction of the objective-subjective binary opposition) on a tightrope, dancing to avoid imaginary bullets, yelling to those below him, "Throw out the nets, boys, throw out the nets"?

In his essay, "Like the Sound of the Sea Deep Within a Shell: Paul de Man's War," Derrida describes his personal experiences during the opening months of the "de Man affair" in language so thoroughly Burkean it is uncanny.[11] Derrida writes of "the war that broke out . . . around some articles signed by a certain Paul de Man in Belgium between 1940 and 1942" (127), a war that has been "declared"

(127) in newspapers and will soon spread, "if that is what certain people want, *among us*" (128)—that is, among academicians:

> For this deadly war (and fear, hatred, which is to say sometimes love, also dream of killing the dead in order to get at the living) has already recruited some combatants, while others are sharpening their weapons in preparation for it. In the evaluations of journalists or of certain professors, one can make out strategies or stratagems, movements of attack or defense, sometimes the two at once. Although this war no doubt began in the newspapers, it will be carried on for a long time elsewhere, in the most diverse forms. (128)

"So this time I will have to tell" (129), Derrida writes as he begins his defense, adding (in parentheses), "May I be forgiven these 'self-centered' references; I will not overdo them" (129). Of course the essay is entirely "self-centered," a very personal response to the de Man affair, a response motivated not simply by Derrida's past friendship but by the disappointment, confusion, anger, and defensiveness that the affair has raised in him personally. "Today," Derrida writes, "I will speak of my indignation and my worry" (155). Shrewdly, he declares his own innocence by means of self-parody (that is, by saying what he will not—but could—say): "One does not free oneself . . . at a single blow by easy adherences to the dominant consensus,"

> or by rather low-risk proclamations of the sort I could, after all, give in to without any risk, since it is what is called the objective truth: 'as for me, you know, no one can suspect me of anything: I am Jewish, I was persecuted as a child during the war, I have always been known for my leftist opinions, I fight as best I can, for example against racism . . . and so forth.' No, such declarations are insufficient. (155)

In a single, brief paragraph he refers to de Man's (and by extension, his own) critics as "hurried detectives," "symptomatologists in training," and "late beginners," some of whom "may even procure a professional benefit . . . if they take advantage of the opportunity to extend the trial . . . to supposed groups or schools against whom it is advisable to wage war" (153). He condemns a particularly "spiteful and error-ridden article," adding that "one shudders to think that its author teaches history at a university" (160). It is not "Paul de Man's War" but his own that Derrida here fights. Indeed, we might turn back to Derrida's earlier expression, a fear that some might "dream of killing the dead in order to get at the living" (128): surely he refers to his own critics, who would "kill" de Man "in order to get at" Derrida himself.

Some have suggested that Derrida takes criticism too personally and that he protects his texts too closely, though they stop short of using the word *paranoid*—one of the few psychoanalytic terms that contemporary theory has failed to appropriate. We seem unwilling to write a rhetoric of paranoia; maybe we should. Maybe there is a paranoid Derrida who thinks others are against him, who protects his friends and attacks his enemies. But maybe the Derrida behind "Interpreting Signatures" is more like the Derrida of a later text still, one that could be called yet "another style of autobiography." We refer to "Circumfession: Fifty-nine periods and periphrases *written in a sort of internal margin, between Geoffrey Bennington's book and work in preparation (January 1989–April 1990)*." Written in fifty-nine sections (one for each of Derrida's years), the text appears at the foot of Geoffrey Bennington's *Derridabase*, Bennington's contribution to the co-authored *Jacques Derrida*. As Bennington explains Derrida's work in the upper portion of the page, Derrida performs what Bennington describes. We could say it is Derrida's most clearly autobiographical work, if we allow him to deconstruct the very notion of autobiography. Spinning off of quotes from St. Augustine's *Confessions*, Derrida writes about writing (spilling blood on paper—*writing as confession, an act of identity, a moment of vulnerability, a mode of suffering*), circumcision (also spilling blood—*a sign of Jewishness that is inscribed on the body*), his mother's stroke (she can no longer say his name—*what does it mean to be erased from the mother's consciousness, is it also to be erased from "the maternal figure of absolute knowledge"?*), his uncircumcised sons (the first of whom was born close to his first publication, and each his "addressee"—*is he lost to them also?*), his own facial paralysis from Lyme's disease (he seems to lose his face, his persona—*as he becomes like his mother, he cannot identify himself in the mirror*), and, throughout, his concern for what Bennington is saying in the text "above" (how will his name be spoken—*how can Bennington explain his texts without quoting them, how will others react to what is said?*). If traditional autobiography confesses the events of one's life and then reflects on them, Derrida reflects on what he has *not* confessed.[12] Yet even in this, the most autobiographical of his works—even as he seems to confess nothing, to hide the self—we catch glimpses of the young Derrida, "the child about whom people used to say 'he cries for nothing'" (38–39), "the always puerile, weepy and pusillanimous son that I was, the adolescent who basically only liked reading writers quick to tears" (118). Is the Derrida behind "Interpreting Signatures" the sensitive boy who does not want to be hurt and does not want to be forgotten?

We, as readers, can certainly choose which Derrida (or Derridas) we wish to see behind this text or other texts, and there are certainly ethical issues involved in which Derrida we choose and how we represent him in our own writing. What we cannot do is stop thinking about the author, casting him in a body and intoning his voice as we read, for reading entails acts of identity: we, as readers, fashion our own identity as we construct the identity of an author. We can deconstruct various textualized versions of the self, but, inevitably, we will seek (or construct) an authorial identity to stand *in the place of discourse* and be held accountable.

Ethos and *Ad Hominem*: Paul de Man's Past

The debate concerning Paul de Man's "collaborationist" essays illustrates the complex interrelations between identity and ethical argument. As Christopher Norris notes, de Man's essays "talk of the need to preserve national cultures against harmful cosmopolitan influences, and of German literature as a model for those other, less fortunate traditions that lack such an authentic national base. Their language often resorts to organicist metaphors, notions of cultural identity as rooted in the soil of a flourishing native literature" (177). And "it is hard, if not impossible," Norris admits, "to redeem these texts by looking for some occasional sign that they are not to be taken at face value" (177). This last statement echoes a sentiment of de Man's several defenders.[13] While Derrida asks us to wait until the historical record can be clarified, he also searches for silences or subtexts of resistance to Nazism, employing a deconstructionist hermeneutic in order to preserve an ethical de Man. Psychoanalyzing him (Brenkman, Stern, Stoekl), others describe de Man's later deconstructionist writings as an attempt to "wash his hands" of the guilt felt at promoting Nazism. Some critics, indeed, go "so far as to surmise that deconstruction . . . was really nothing more than an elaborate cover-up campaign, an 'amnesty' organized by literary intellectuals who could find no other means to evade or excuse their burden of collective guilt" (Norris 178–79).[14]

In de Man's case, clearly, most critics have refused to separate the thought from the thinker, thus assuming that the ethical failures of an individual are visited upon his intellectual offspring, his ideas: to condemn (or condone) the one is to condemn (or condone) the other. Still we must ask, is a thought tied so intimately to its thinker, that to know one is to know the other? Heidegger suggests as much when he writes, "Who Nietzsche *is* and above all who he *will be* we shall know as soon as we are able to think the thought that he gave shape to in the phrase 'the will to power.' We shall never experience who Nietzsche is through a historical report about his life history, nor through a presentation of the contents of his writings" (*Nietzsche* 1:473; quoted in Derrida, "Interpreting Signatures" 64). By implication, neither critical analysis nor the representations of biography enable us to "know" Nietzsche; rather, we can "know" him *only by thinking his thoughts.* Hence thought, constitutive of consciousness, is presumed to bear traces of the life and psyche of its thinker.[15] Similarly, critics "have found" in his writings a character belonging to and immutable in de Man, thus dismissing de Man's own insistence on the very *impossibility* of such a discovery.[16] (By their reasoning, a person's character remains constant over time and, as a result, one's life's work necessarily represents a consistent, unified system of thought.) Worse, by concealing his collaboration, de Man failed to "own up" to his past. Failing to confess (in contrast with traditional autobiography), de Man apparently sought absolution through his later writings—though without admitting guilt.[17] Like Burroughs' or Ballard's fiction, which cryptically encodes its author's criminal acts (Luckhurst 691), de Man's later, deconstructionist writings become a cryptic text whose complex web of ideas must be read against their decoder "key," the suppressed autobiography of de Man's *Le Soir* essays.[18]

Are such criticisms (and their underlying assumptions) valid? Should we not respond to de Man's later theories on their own merits, separate from their author's life and character? Following de Man's own logocentric assumptions, should we not grant language its own independent capacities for meaning, a textuality divorced from its human origins? Finally, are not such criticisms *irrelevant* to the logic of de Man's texts—just so many fallacies of reasoning? We are now, of course, questioning the validity—the relevance—of *ad hominem* criticism itself. As Charles A. Willard writes, "the historical legacy, largely Aristotle's, has held that *ethos* and *logos* differ in kind and are thus analytically separable" (228), an assumption that not only undergirds such logocentric theories as deconstruction but provides the basis for branding *ad hominem* fallacious, that is, a mode of arguing "irrelevant to the logic of utterance" (Willard 228).[19] It is easy enough to divide *logos* from *ethos*, pitting one against the other. In a relatively early discussion of fallacy theory (1964), Mackie argues, "the ideology behind the *ad hominem* is formalism: the arguments on paper should speak for themselves divorced from personal judgments" (177; quoted in Willard 227). Judged by "formalism" (that is, by a strictly logocentric theory of textuality), "arguments on paper" are "divorced" from their author's voice: they should "speak *for themselves*," which would seem an absolute denial of *ethos* (and a confirmation of the logocentric assumptions of later, deconstructive criticism).Yet, in Burkean fashion, we might instead observe the dialectical transformations that occur between *logos* and *ethos*, the ways *logos* must be judged ethically and *ethos* made the basis of argument.[20] John M. Ellis's critique of "ironic readings" illustrates this effect:

> Deconstruction has evidently become popular in some measure because of its seeming to encourage and legitimize the "ironic reading" (that is, the reading emphasizing the underlying irony of a text). Doubtless, there are many cases in which this is perfectly justifiable. . . . But imagine what happens if we commit ourselves to the ironic reading in all cases, indiscriminately. The first result is that irony loses its meaning. . . . And the practical results will not be so attractive either. Shall we have to believe that Hitler is really a hero? That *Troilus and Cressida* is really Shakespeare in a buoyant, happy mood? I leave it to the reader to find his own example. *Judgment* is needed in each case. . . . (91)

Ellis begins by attacking the logic of deconstruction, only to end by attacking its ethics—specifically, its destruction of a reader's capacity for ethical judgment. While Hirsch suggests that deconstruction turns its back on Auschwitz, Ellis implies that it leads back to fascism by rendering readers incapable of resisting any "ironic reading," however unlikely or unhealthy. Note also how Ellis, appealing to his reader's "good sense," seeks an identification or consubstantiation—an "us" against "them."

We find the same argument repeated against Derrida specifically, whose attempt to deconstruct the most blatantly antisemitic of de Man's writings ("Like the Sound" 143–45) plays directly into his critics' hands. As Stern writes,

> The possibility of applying the methodology, so brilliantly represented by de Man, to an exculpation of his work demonstrates what seems to me a problematic. The deconstructionist effort has placed a limitation on the possibility of *the moral judgment of utterances.* If it is possible to rescue de Man from

the charge of antisemitism, . . . then it is possible to deconstruct any utterance such that it comes to nothingness, or its opposite, or in some way refutes itself. In literary matters, that is of interest and importance. But in the arena of political life, where judgment can lead to the most dire consequences, it is of ultimate importance. . . . Can one so deconstruct the speeches of Rabbi Kahane that his racism toward the Arab world becomes acceptable, if not palatable? If so, one of the charges against deconstruction becomes validated . . . . (31)

We could multiply instances but, like Ellis, perhaps we too should "leave it to the reader to find his own example."

Thus far, the authors of this essay have argued as if with one voice. Having agreed throughout the analysis, nonetheless we diverge in our conclusions. A trio of alternative endings thus follows. But while each stands on its own, they are not entirely unrelated; read together, they establish several of the dialectical possibilities inherent in our subject.

Conclusion I: A Theology of *Ethos*

Whether or not readers agree with our analysis, perhaps we can agree on one foundational point: that a discussion of ethics in writing instruction, like ethical discussion generally, proceeds from an assumption of conscious, responsible, individual human agency. To this, we would add that ethical argument demands a human, a humanized language—that is, a language appropriable and renewable by any speaker, if only partially, thereby revealing the speaker (however partially) within the speech. We can acknowledge the "partial truth" (Colish) of language, the sad fact that our words exceed our grasp, the fact that words conceal as much as they reveal. We need not deny that the crisis of human social relations is a crisis fundamentally of communication, of finding an accommodating language. (I. A. Richards states this succinctly: rhetoric is no more—nor less—than a "study of misunderstanding and its remedies" [3].) Still, we cannot discuss the ethics of writing without assuming that the task of speaking or writing is to incarnate one's words.[21] As the theologian Arthur A. Vogel suggests, our words are (ideally) "extensions of the body" itself, an expression of "meaning in matter, a location of presence." For we are in our words, Vogel argues, "as we are in our bodies, and it is only because we are our bodies that we can 'be' our words—or, as it is usually put, mean what we say. We can stand behind our words because our presence overflows them and is more than they can contain, but we choose to stand behind them with our infinite presence because *we are also in them*" (92). Unless we incarnate our words, we cannot own or control them, *nor can we be held responsible for them.*[22] This ethical relationship between language and individual human agency remains (as we have indicated) a central assumption of liberal humanism. Following such logic, a task of writing instruction in American universities is to teach self-expression as a witness to self-reflection and self-knowledge, to explain (mainly to one's self, though others overhear) the structure of various belief-systems (both one's own and others'), and, ultimately, to stand in an attitude of critique. Indeed, the pedagogy of liberal humanism is grounded not primarily in persuasion, but in explanation and critique—that is, in a fashioning and defense of the grounds of one's own beliefs, bolstered by a reasoned resistance to alternatives. And, needless to say, the ethical relation between language and human agency raises *ethos*—and, we would add, the *ad hominem* argument—to prominence: held personally accountable for the discourse and its effects, the speaker must "stand in witness," as it were, to the truthfulness, sincerity, and good intentions of his or her argument. Platonic in spirit, this is perhaps the most traditional (certainly the most conservative) response to the problem of ethics.

Even before deconstruction's orbit into the American academy—indeed, ever since Aristotle "answered" the Isocratean and Platonic theories in his *Rhetoric*—this traditional theory has pitted its own linguistic theology of selfhood against all textualizations of *ethos*. A Platonic (or Isocratean) theory does not deny that *ethos* can be constructed and manipulated verbally; it demands, notwithstanding, a clear and firm connection—a wedding or troth-plight, as it were—between one's words and one's actions and character. Within this perspective, the Aristotelian techniques of masking and image-making remain a central component of composition instruction but are transformed from strategies of invention into instruments of analysis and critique—and, thereby, implicitly turned against themselves. In their "application of Aristotelian theory to classroom instruction," James L. Kinneavy and Susan C. Warshauer suggest as much, writing that "students need to learn how to shape their self-image in discourse; that is, they need to learn how their character affects an audience and how any change in this character elicits a corresponding change in an audience's response" (172). But "equally (if not more) important, students need to learn how to detect, analyze, and critique the manipulations of image and character that mark so much contemporary discourse." They continue:

> Adherents of Aristotle often downplay the amorality of his rhetorical theory (and especially his theory of *ethos*, which admits the expediency of manipulation and appearances, regardless of a speaker's true moral character and intentions). But we believe that the amorality of the ethical proof should be clearly delineated in instruction. Indeed, we might initially teach the full range of techniques that shape and manipulate self-images and point out their possible moral use and their possible moral abuse. For if students can discover these implications in practice, they will have learned what theory alone might fail to teach: how effective, and how unsettling, the manipulation of *ethos* can be. (172)

True to humanist tradition, Kinneavy and Warshauer teach image-making and its antidote simultaneously, reinterpreting Aristotelian theory as an instrument of critical analysis. By this perspective, we should teach our own students to do the same.

Conclusion II: An Interpersonal Psychology

Though noble and even desirable in its conclusions, the argument of "Conclusion I" hangs crucially "on one fundamental point: that a discussion of ethics in writing instruction, like ethical discussion generally, proceeds from an assumption of conscious, responsible, individual human agency." Here, indeed, is a problem: we hardly know ourselves. We have yet to explain why writers (and writing teachers) have come, if unconsciously, to conceal the role *ad hominem* plays in academic discourse. We might ask, indeed, what ethical issues have we *avoided* by declaring *ad hominem* irrelevant or fallacious? How, and why, have we managed to repress so significant an aspect of our professional behavior?[23] While Freud describes repression as a defense mechanism operating within the individual psyche, a more Lacanian view of the unconscious (i.e., that it is not a location in the mind or brain, but rather a construction that evolves from interpersonal interactions) re-interprets repression as a socio-ideological phenomenon—that is, as a culture's imposition on the ways we collectively talk, *or do not talk*, about the past; seen in this light, our failure to acknowledge *ad hominem* can be viewed as yet another form of culturally-sanctioned repression. Academicians have declared (and, apparently, convinced themselves) that criticism can and should proceed abstractly, impersonally, without acknowledging or raising issues of identity—of the ways a writer constructs his or her identity, the ways a reader is asked to assume (or project) a certain identity, the ways critiquing a text becomes a critique of its author, the ways academic discourse becomes, in the end, an agony over professional reputations and social status. By asking students (and colleagues) to reconsider the role of *ad hominem* in criticism we are seeking, essentially, to bring out the unconscious of a text, thereby working our way through a social repression.

Can this be taught? Just as Kinneavy and Warshauer insist on analyzing authorial *ethos*, so we might call students' attention to the ways one author constructs (that is, disinters, in order to "kill off") another. In *Specters of Marx*, for example, Derrida's summary/critique of Francis Fukuyama's *End of History* takes the form of an elaborate *ethopoeia*:

> To be sure, he recognizes that what he describes as the collapse of the worldwide dictatorships of the right or the left has not always 'given way . . . to stable liberal democracies.' But he believes he can assert that, as of this date, and this is good news, a dated news, 'liberal democracy remains the only coherent political aspiration that spans different regions and cultures around the globe.' This 'move toward political freedom around the globe,' according to Fukuyama, would have been everywhere accompanied, 'sometimes followed, sometimes preceded,' he writes, by 'a liberal democracy and of the 'free market.' There's the 'good news' of this last quarter century. This evangelistic figure is remarkably insistent. (57)

Called to the witness stand, Fukuyama's own words—read ironically as the "good news" (a gospel allusion twice repeated) of an "evangelistic figure"—are intended as self-incrimination. Thus Derrida "kills off" his opponent, naming him the false prophet of global democracy and capitalism. (Note that we have ourselves called Foucault, Derrida, and de Man to the witness stand; we differ from our poststructuralist colleagues, however, by calling attention to the *ethopoeia* and inviting readers to critique our performance.) Can we agree that Derrida's pastiche of quotations entails an *ad hominem* attack? When Derrida "kills off" (and thereby identifies) Fukuyama, does he not also commit suicide, identifying himself? Clearly our teacherly task is to reach beyond caricature when characterizing to another's argument, helping students to do the same.

Surely there are benefits to becoming more conscious of what we have been doing all along: once we have acknowledged that *ad hominem* arguments are typically present, if only implied (often as an enthymemic "hidden premise" and, as such, operant from within a text's "unconscious"), then we can begin to discuss what it means to "kill off" another or one's self (or, indeed, to disinter and kill off again and again). If we are, as writers, stereotyping an opponent (or, as readers, type-casting an author), we can discuss the implications of these largely unconscious, though highly rhetorical strategies. In certain situations, such strategies might be justified; in others, we can learn to move beyond the characterizations (again, caricatures) typical of *ad hominem* argument. Returning to Burke, we can learn to think dialectically about the ways identity enters our texts. When we feel self-righteous about an act of communion, we might ask, "What act of war did I commit in uniting these individuals/theories/ideas?" When we kill off an author, we might ask, "How might she have changed with time?" When we linger in the symbolic, we might ask, "How can I place these words within a living human body?" When we expect similarity, we might ask, "How can I see difference?" When we see difference, we might ask, "How can I see similarity?" Whether as readers or as writers, the following holds: by means of dialectic, we can recover and come to terms with the unconscious (rather, repressed) "other" of our texts.

Conclusion III: A Social (Sophistic) (Re-)Construction

In part, the popular reaction against poststructuralism proceeds from an anxiety regarding the loss of self. This anxiety is understandable: if selfhood is reduced to an effect of language,[24] then what does it mean to say (or write) "we" (or "I") at all? Such questioning might threaten us with a crisis of self-identity, were it not for the fact that we have long ceased to be "innocents."[25] (Identity crises seem even to define the individual in postmodern culture, do they not?) Hence, claims regarding a stable, knowable self sound largely naive. For better or worse, our time is one "of fragmentation and isolation," as S. Michael Halloran observes, a time when *ethos* can succeed only by the degree to which a speaker "is willing and able to make his world open to the other," thus risking "self and world by a rigorous and open articulation of them in the presence of the other" (627–28). So, as we search for an ethical counterweight to deconstructive theory, we are reminded of the sophistic (specifically, Gorgianic) response to the ancient crisis of (self-)knowledge and argument. Affirming a creative opacity rather than an ethical transparency in language, Gorgias claimed for rhetoric a world-building power of persuasion—a power of *apate* or deception, upon which community itself can be built.[26] A radical skeptic for whom immediate and certain knowledge of the external world is impossible,

Gorgias turned away from the philosopher's search for an objective, metaphysical "Truth" to the more humane task of describing the world-as-lived-in—a world which, from the sophistic perspective, is *spoken into being*: what we say (or agree to say) is what is. Perhaps our own task is to speak a world, *and a self*, that is most healthful: that is, most growthful.[27]

Identifying the "early" with the "later" de Man, the fascist with the theorist, we seem to have excluded the possibility of change. Though a common strategy of argument, such an assumption is tragic, if true: presuming that "character is fate," we withhold from the human creature any possibility of transformation. Once a thief, always a thief; an alcoholic remains one for life: despite the partial truth of such old saws, identity—whether externally- or self-imposed—threatens to limit the individual's health and growth. To identify or "fix" an individual is indeed "to kill him off"—that is, to kill off his or her freedom and capacity for growth. Though we are, as a species, hardly likely to cease such practice, we can at least restore to our discourse a rhetoric compensatory to identification, a rhetoric of transformation and change. A more sophisticated approach to autobiography, for example, would reveal the simultaneous presence of two rhetorics. One, a rhetoric of identity, seeks out the stable, knowable characteristics of the self; the second, a rhetoric of transformation, discovers those moments in time, typically crises and "conversion experiences," when the self is changed and *identity thus remade*. Identity ranges across a continuum of transformations. We are, and are not, the same persons as before.[28]

"At the core of a therapeutic rhetoric," Jacqueline Rinaldi writes, "is an assumption that any experience of failure is amenable to being reconstructed in a way that makes that failure tolerable, even beneficial according to a different set of values" (822). Our human frailties can be rewritten as potential strengths and, literally, revised. Gorgianic in spirit, such a rhetoric contributes to the healing of a fragmented, postmodern self: if we are no more than an effect of language, then our task is to become the best stylists possible. As Richard Lanham describes traditional writing instruction, "a self is posited, heart-whole, coherent, located somewhere halfway between the ears. It exists. The task is to develop a prose style fully expressive of it" (115). By this model, however, "half the process is left out," for "two conceptions of the self have prevailed in the West from the time of the Greeks onward. One we might call the central self, or soul. The second depicts the social, dramatic, role-playing self, man as actor not soul.[29] This dramatic self derives its existence from the society surrounding it" (116). "What pedagogy," he goes on to ask, "can accommodate this shifting self?" (116). Lanham seeks his own answer in developmental psychology:

> Erik Erikson . . . sees adolescence as a time of role-experiment. A single self has not yet cohered. In this time of identity crisis, first one role is played, then another. Finally a comfortable dramatic creation falls together into a core self. And around this, the dramatic variations continue to play throughout life. . . . If Erikson's analysis comes close to the mark, traditional 'sincerity' pedagogy should be stood on its head. The adolescent stylist should be encouraged to impersonate other people, not 'be himself.' (116)

Seeming to describe an Aristotelian pedagogy of image-making, Lanham confirms the dialectic between textual and ethical theories of *ethos*. The adolescent's role-playing "falls together into a core self": the mask, it is vital to note, can become face. Whether through impersonation (*prosopopoeia*) or other modes of narrative/stylistic play, we should encourage writing students to pursue experiments in self-making. True, the previous two conclusions affirm an ethics, and a pedagogy, of unmasking—of revealing "what we are"—the first focused specifically on the author's character, the second on an author's characterizations of others. In contrast, this third conclusion affirms an ethics of growth, of asserting "what we may become." Self-making thus becomes a task of writing instruction, and it maintains an ethical dimension.[30] In sum, an ethical (that is, a fully humane) theory of *ethos* and argument must preserve a writer's ethical responsibilities even as it allows for the possibility of transformation and change. And our students should be shown this. Theories that deny either aspect of this dialectic need not be refuted so much as healed.

Notes

1. Our use of "ethical" follows Wayne C. Booth, who writes that the term "may mistakenly suggest a project concentrating on quite limited moral standards: of honesty, perhaps, or of decency or tolerance. I am interested in a much broader topic, the entire range of effects on the 'character' or 'person' or 'self.' 'Moral' judgments are only a small part of it" (8).

2. Heidi S. Krueger notes "the current tendency to polarize deconstruction and humanism" (310), the latter standing for those critical theories (and teaching practices) committed to individual subjective agency—to a "conviction," as Kurt Spellmeyer puts it, "that the self is enduring and real" (907) and that "the body, and not language, is the source of the self and the doorway into the living world" (908). As Jeffrey Nealon writes, "the reemergence of subjective agency as a crucial category in recent literary and cultural studies can be seen as a direct response to the decentering of the subject enacted by the first wave of poststructuralism" (129). While Nealon's Levinasian alternative to "the humanist or Enlightenment subject" (129) reads more like a theorist's wish-fulfillment than an accurate description of lived subjective experience, still we recommend his account of postmodern ethics.

3. "Historically speaking," Terry Eagleton writes, "the idea of the humanities, at least in the modern period, arises at a point where certain kinds of positive human values are felt to be increasingly under threat from a philistine, crassly materialist society, and so must be marked off from that degraded social arena in a double gesture of elevation and isolation" (*Significance* 29). Yet, having historicized humanism, Eagleton dismisses it as "an ideological myth" (30). We could as easily argue that some of the "human values" humanism attempts to save may indeed be worth saving or, paradoxically, that a Marxist critique is not possible without an "ideology of the 'human'"—that is, without some conception of *what it means to be a human being*. Without some stable idea of human nature, how can we say that sweatshops in a third-world country (or Los Angeles, for that matter) are dehumanizing?

4. Among early Greek rhetoricians, Isocrates claims that moral character precedes discourse. For "the power to speak well," Isocrates asserts, "is taken as the surest index of a sound understanding, and discourse which is true and lawful and just is the outward image of a good and faithful soul" (50). Additionally, all persuasion proceeds from the conviction of a prior, private deliberation and self-reflection, for "the same arguments which we use in persuading others when we speak in public, we employ also when we deliberate in our own thoughts" (50). Thus deception and image-making are banished from Isocratean rhetoric. Both Cicero and Quintilian restate the Isocratean tradition, the latter describing the ideal orator famously as *vir bonus dicendi peritus*, "a good man skilled in speaking" (347).

Classical theory, nonetheless, is divided on the subject. In marked contrast, Aristotle asserts that *ethos* is a verbal construct arising out of the speech-act itself: "We believe good men more fully and more readily than others," Aristotle tells us: "this is true generally whatever the question is, and absolutely true where exact certainty is impossible and opinions are divided." Yet "this kind of persuasion . . . should be achieved by what the speaker says, not by what people think of this character before he begins to speak. It is not true, as some writers assume in their treatises on rhetoric, that the personal goodness revealed by the speaker contributes nothing to his power of persuasion; on the contrary, his character may almost be called the most effective means of persuasion he possesses" (153–54). While Isocratean tradition demands that the speaker *be* good, Aristotelian tradition requires simply that the speaker *appear* to be a man "of good sense," "good will," and "good moral character" (Kinneavy and Warshauer 182–88).

5   Granted, the first level of criticism observes the contradictions inherent in its skeptical mode of argument. (It takes a living author to pronounce an author's "death," does it not?) And a theory that claims all texts to be ultimately unreadable must proceed by exempting itself, ironically, from its own linguistic skepticism; in other words, an author like Paul de Man pronounces the failure of interpretation within a discourse that can succeed only by *exempting itself from mis-reading*. Deconstruction has been accused of being anti-aesthetic in confusing "literature" with "philosophy" (Ellis) and elevating its own critical acts to a mode of creative writing; anti-historical in turning its back on fascism and the atrocities of Auschwitz (Hirsch); anti-political in denying texts their force as action-in-the-world (Eagleton, *Literary Theory*); and—most important for this essay—anti-humanist in reducing individual human agency and personality to a "mere" effect of language (Ellis, Lehman, Steiner). Others have come to the defense of deconstruction, affirming that its textual practices are liberatory and, ultimately, ethical in aim: see Baker, Felperin, Miller, Norris, Parker.

6   Citing Luc Ferry and Alain Renault, who argue that "in Derrida's writing 'subjectivity stubbornly resists its own disappearance'" (13), David Parker makes the point succinctly: "there is no mistaking the turning of Derrida against Derrida, or the implication that deconstruction focused reflexively on itself yields suppressed humanist assumptions" (13–14). Of course "any terminology," as Burke tells us, "is suspect to the extent that it does not allow for the progressive criticism of itself" (*Religion* 303); deconstruction is no different from Marxism or humanism in this regard.

7   A survey of composition textbooks reveals their typically simplistic view of *ad hominem*—in contrast with textbooks of logic, which acknowledge its occasional validity. Logician Stephen F. Barker writes, "not all *ad hominem* arguments are fallacious. The abusive form of *ad hominem* argument says that, because a man has some weakness or defect, his views are incorrect. This is often but not always a worthless line of reasoning; sometimes it can be quite a good argument and not a fallacy at all. For instance, the fact that Dr. Smith

is a stupid, maladjusted man of paranoid tendencies increases the probability that his views on economic theory are unsound, for we know from past experience that economic theory is a difficult subject and that intelligent men of balanced judgment are likely to have sound views about it" (200–01).

Composition theorists rarely cede this point. Serving merely to "divert attention from the issue under debate" (Seyler 32), the *ad hominem*, as Dorothy U. Seyler describes it, is "one of the most frequent of all appeals to emotion masquerading as argument" (33; see also Horner 44 and Spurgin 207). Edward P. J. Corbett presents a more balanced view: "a man's character can have some relevance to an argument—when, for instance, we are attempting to assess the reliability of his testimony or the likelihood of his having done something—but a discussion of a man's character becomes an irrelevancy—and thereby a form of fallacy—when such a discussion is used merely to distract attention from the issue at hand" (92; see also Barnet and Bedau 203).

8   In *A Grammar of Motives*, Burke offers an image to describe the transformative processes of dialectic: "Distinctions, we might say, arise out of a great central moltenness, where all is merged. They have been thrown from a liquid center to the surface, where they have congealed. Let one of these crusted distinctions return to its source, and in this alchemic center it may be remade, again becoming molten liquid, and may enter into new combinations, whereat it may again be thrown forth as a new crust, a different distinction. So that A may become non-A. . . . we must take A back into the ground of its existence, the logical substance that is its causal ancestor, and on to a point where it is consubstantial with non-A; then we may return, this time emerging with non-A instead" (994).

9   In a court of law—or, for that matter, of public opinion—would we ever allow such a claim as, "I did not say (or write) this, *one of my personae did*"?

10 Note that we do not deny the utility of textualized theories of *ethos*; our point, simply, is that readers and writers alike *reject* textualized theories, whenever they wish to make claims regarding the ethical implications of discourse. In this regard, Jim W. Corder recounts his own ambivalent response to a review of his personal essays: "One of the newspaper reviewers said some moderately nice things about what he was pleased to call my voice and character in the book. I was tickled and danced a little jig. And I was startled when I realized what else was in my mind, startled when I realized that I was already talking back to the reviewer. 'Listen, you out there,' I was saying, 'don't think I'm so easy to catch. There's more to me than meets the eye, and less. You'll not catch me so quickly'" (349). Corder comments on the contradiction: "At the moment that I want *ethos* in the text, I deny it. I am not there, but elsewhere" (349).

11 In the late 1980s it was discovered that de Man had composed wartime articles for *Le Soir*, a Belgian newspaper sympathetic to Nazism. As John Brenkman argues, the articles "furnish the evidence, beyond a reasonable doubt, that he was at that time a fascist and an anti-Semite as well as an

active collaborator with the Nazi occupation of Belgium" (23). For the complete text of de Man's wartime journalism and a collection of initial responses—including Derrida's essay, "Like the Sound of the Sea"—see Hamacher, Hertz, and Keenan. In subsequent paragraphs, we shall turn in earnest to the de Man controversy.

12 In "Derrida's Negative Autobiography" (a chapter in his *Ethical Turn*), Peter Baker analyzes Derrida's "How to Avoid Speaking: Denials," which meditates on the problematic relations among writing, authorship, and autobiography. For a discussion of "the signature" as a Derridean concept, see Clark.

13 Alexander Gelley, for example, offers to excuse him: "Perhaps . . . the young de Man was very clever in both satisfying the demands of the Nazi-controlled organ for which he was writing and, at the same time, maintaining a certain distance to its slant, a distance that possibly a few astute contemporary readers might catch" (224).

14 In "De Man and Guilt," Allan Stoekl makes this argument explicit: the later texts can now be read as "extremely elaborate devices whose net effect is to defuse the very question of de Man's responsibility or guilt" (378). Norris disagrees, observing that "such arguments, for all their patent absurdity, have . . . convinced many people that there must after all be something deeply suspect about the whole deconstructionist enterprise" (179). Regardless, our knowledge of the wartime journalism necessarily affects the way we read de Man's later work. Introducing the second edition of *Blindness and Insight*, de Man writes, "I am not given to retrospective self-examination and mercifully forget what I have written with the same alacrity I forget bad movies—although, as with bad movies, certain scenes or phrases return at times to embarrass and haunt me like a guilty conscience" (quoted in Stoekl, 375). How do we read this *now*?

15 And what if the thinker is mad or evil? Are we then so willing to place our own psyches at the disposal of another's thought? "Nothing," James A. Herrick writes, "is more clearly definitive of who we are than how we think, so we may feel defensive when we realize that someone is trying to influence the way we think. Some people even see argumentation as a kind of aggression when it aims at persuasion. . . . Thus, ethical questions come up the moment argumentation begins" (45). Indeed, the need to resist ideas will always proceed from ethical (and psychological) rather than logical grounds.

And, we should note, Heidegger's point can be turned against his own philosophy, as David Hirsch suggests: "It is now clear that Heidegger's attraction to National Socialism and his extended membership in the Nazi party were consistent with, rather than aberrant to, his thinking. By the same token, it is possible to contemplate connections between National Socialism and the post-Auschwitz perpetuation of Heidegger-inspired antihumanist theories in the guise of what has come to be called postmodernism" (255–56).

16 In *The Rhetoric of Romanticism*, de Man rejects autobiography as a mode of self-knowledge: "The interest of autobiography, then, is not that it reveals

reliable self-knowledge—it does not—but that it demonstrates in a striking way the impossibility of closure and of totalization (that is, the impossibility of coming into being) of all textual systems made up of tropological substitutions" (71).

17 And why not? In fine Burkean manner, Stern asks, "Did de Man believe that to 'confess' his past error would lead to his death—figuratively at least, the death of his reputation?" (34).

18 Describing their "autobiographical resonance" (26), Brenkman argues that "a self-portrait of the radical young intellectual emerges" (25) from specific articles. "Fascism," he concludes, "provided de Man with the means of interpreting his private experience . . . and of connecting that experience to values that would orient his active participation in a public world. He placed himself within, and measured himself against, the intellectual and political culture of French fascism" (34). Doubtless, their journalistic mode implies an historicism and referentiality that allows, even invites, autobiographical readings. Far from fictionalized or ironic, de Man's *Le Soir* pieces remain so many expressions of their author's personal convictions. How can we think otherwise?

A fallacy, as defined by Eisenberg and Ilardo, is a "deceptive and misleading tactic used intentionally or accidentally by an advocate, which may have the effect of deluding an opponent or onlooker. . . . It creates an illusion based on deception. Unless fallacies are exposed, the arguments in which they occur assume a false air of legitimacy. Once the inner workings of a fallacy are revealed, the illusion of proof and the false air of legitimacy vanish" (83).

20 Re-evaluating traditionally logocentric views, contemporary argumentation theory in fact affirms this aspect of our argument, observing that "the broad view of fallacies encompasses moral and procedural (rather than logical) failings" (Willard 225); indeed "some fallacies," Willard suggests, "are rooted in Ethics and Political Science. The reasons for condemning loaded terms, ambiguity, vagueness, popularity . . . are more ethical than logical" (224).

21 If "words do their work by making the world more fully present to us" (Spellmeyer 910), so the converse is true: our words should make ourselves more fully present as well. And yet "academic literacy," Spellmeyer argues, remains "deeply complicit with the same culture of disembodiment that makes possible Elvis look-alikes and the stalking of the stars by their admirers, who cannot break free from obsession except by murdering their idealized alteregos" (909). That is, we often write so as "to *become* Derrida, to *become* a second Foucault or a little Lacan," much as "Madonna's fans dress . . . walk and talk like her" (Spellmeyer 909). He concludes: "for all our celebrations of resistance to revolt, no alternative is more revolutionary than our resistance to disembodiment and the pursuit of wholeness" (910).

22 In this respect, the *argumentum ad hominem* serves as a useful and often valid sanction against rhetoric that claims not to be, on some fundamental

level, a personal narrative. It is a reminder that all discourse is about and for ourselves as both individual and social beings.

We should observe, though, that the opposite has been argued. For Wittgenstein, "it is the continuity of bodily existence, the resemblance of one's body to itself over time, that gives an individual a false sense of identity and thus masks the lack of identity in the elocutionary instance" (Baker 14). The "I" of "I speak" remains a function and effect of grammar.

23 "Arguments based on emotional appeal (including *ad hominem*) can be good in a critical discussion because they can link an argument to an arguer's so-called dark-side commitments to an issue." So notes the communication theorist Douglas Walton, who adds that such personal commitments "are not known to the arguer in any explicit form; they could be described as 'veiled' or 'deeper' commitments that the arguer is only aware of as 'gut feelings.' A critical discussion reveals these implicit commitments to an arguer" (27). Acknowledging the extent to which motives are "not known" to the speaker, Walton amazes us, nonetheless, by his avoidance of the term *unconscious*. As if nodding to Freud might unsettle the sociological basis of argument, Walton seems forced into euphemism.

Burke again, by the way, anticipates our argument: "the rhetorician and the moralist become one at that point where the attempt is made to reveal the undetected presence of . . . an identification" (*Rhetoric* 1023).

24 As de Man writes, "we do not 'possess' language in the same way that we can be said to possess natural properties. It would be just as proper or improper to say that 'we' are a property of language as the reverse" (*Allegories* 160).

25 Felperin writes, "the reaction to deconstruction is analogous to an early and still persistent reaction to psychoanalysis: an irrational fear that, if this sort of analytical activity is pursued, the subject of it . . . will eventually disappear, be analyzed, as it were, out of existence." This "fear of self-annihilation," he suggests, results from "a superstitious or magical, or sacramental view of language, within which the relation between signifier and signified is a sacred and inviolate given: words mean exactly what they say" (185). Yet Felperin misunderstands the "magical" or sophistic view (such as Gorgias claimed to practice), which emphasizes the powers of language *to change* its relationship with external, silent reality (and, thereby, to change our perceptions of reality itself); implicitly, too, he rejects the Burkean notion of consubstantiation, which invokes a "sacramental view of language." Felperin describes, rather, a form of positivism which is itself a "superstition" *when measured against* the "language scepticism that deconstruction cultivates, indeed, flaunts" (184). For a counter to Felperin's demystification of language, see Steiner.

26 Gorgias claims, "All who . . . persuade people of things do so by molding a false argument" (41). An assertion of possibility rather than a manipulation of appearances (Poulakos), *apate* recognizes the fact that human reality is verbally constructed and subject, therefore, to change. Gorgianic theory, we must note, differs from contemporary theories of deconstruction in asserting language's demiurgic power (Untersteiner). "Speech is a powerful lord," Gorgias

declares, "which by means of the finest and most invisible body effects the divinest works: it can stop fear and banish grief and create joy and nurture pity" (41).

In the final analysis, what deconstruction lacks is a commitment to the possibility of consubstantiation—to the possibility, in short, of *persuasion*. As we have described it, humanism teaches strategies of resistance and critique as a counterweight to persuasion, by this means balancing the ethical against the political, the individual against the collective; deconstruction, in contrast, renders persuasion impossible by denying texts their referentiality and human subjectivity. (Without a world or a human subject to address, where is persuasion?)

27 Hence the sophist articulates Western culture's first rhetoric of social-construction: if the world is as we speak it, then—parodying our old friend Quintilian—our search for an ethical rhetoric might end with a "good world skillfully spoken."

28 On the contemporary theoretical front, several projects have special relevance to the formulation of ethics. Martha Nussbaum's *Fragility of Goodness* is part of her ongoing exploration of the notion of virtue in human narratives.

Rudolf Arnheim's theory of "Beauty as Suitability" addresses the function of form. While agreeing with Kant that beauty is comprised of perfection, harmony, and good proportion, Arnheim points out the need to know what purpose an object serves, for nothing in the organic world exists without purpose. The function of humans, Arnheim postulates, is the fullest experience and understanding of the physical and psychological conditions of existence in this world (Arnheim 252).

29 Ironically, it is the deterministic doctrine that has the most to teach us about character. The Stoics, the most famous being the slave Epictetus and Roman emperor Marcus Aurelius, were paradigms of responsible citizenry in the best ethical sense; yet they believed that their fate was fixed. They did not entertain philosophy as a way to undermine the forces of fortune.

Instead, the philosophy of Epictetus privileged the analogy of theater to ethical behavior. Stoic belief stresses that the script of life's drama is not written by humans, nor is each individual role within the play. The only freedom that people can cultivate lies in how each person interprets and performs the part assigned. Yet at the same time that one is but an actor on the stage, one is in the audience as well. For reason gives humans the power to observe themselves in action (a process that Epictetus called *apatheia*, translated as "disinterestedness") to regard and direct their movements from a privileged balcony (objectivity), and the humor to parody themselves when their improvisation verges upon the ridiculous.

30 Early forms of the word *aesthetic* reveal its original connection with ethics. It was formerly spelled with the Old English *f* in place of *ae*. *F* is derived from the Gothic or Sanskrit *ewa*, meaning "the way" or "moral truth." The word *f* was also used to translate the Hebrew word for *Torah* in its original sense as "direction" or "law."

31 See J. Derrida, *Speech and Phenomena* trans. by D. B. Allison (Evanston: Northwestern UP, 1973) for the critique of the Husserlian *Bedeutung* and the demonstration that the sign-expression (meaning) cannot be separated from the sign-index (signification).

32 See J. Derrida, *Positions* trans. by A. Bass (Chicago: The U of Chicago P, 1981).

33 See J. L. Austin, *How to Do Things with Words* (London: Oxford UP, 1977).

34 For the critique of Searle's theory of speech act and of Austin's presuppositions as well, see J. Derrida *Limited, Inc.* (Baltimore: The Johns Hopkins UP, 1977).

Works Cited

Aristotle. *Rhetoric*. Bizzell and Herzberg, 144-94.

Baker, Peter. *Deconstruction and the Ethical Turn*. Gainsville: UP of Florida, 1995.

Bakhtin, Mikhail M. *Art and Answerability: Early Philosophical Essays*. Ed. Michael Holquist and Vadim Liapunov. Trans. Vadim Liapunov. Austin: U of Texas P, 1990.

Barker, Stephen F. *The Elements of Logic*. 2nd ed. New York: McGraw-Hill, 1974.

Barnet, Sylvan, and Hugo Bedau. *Critical Thinking, Reading, and Writing: A Brief Guide to Argument*. Boston: Bedford, 1993.

Barthes, Roland. *Image, Music, Text*. Trans. Stephen Heath. New York: Hill and Wang, 1977.

Baumlin, James S., and Tita French Baumlin, ed. *Ethos: New Essays in Rhetorical and Critical Theory*. Dallas: Southern Methodist UP, 1994.

Bennington, Geoffrey, and Jacques Derrida. *Jacques Derrida*. Trans. Geoffrey Bennington. Chicago: U of Chicago P, 1991.

Bernasconi, Boston: Beacon, 1961.Robert. "Humanism." *Encyclopedia of Ethics*. 2 vols. Ed. Lawrence C. Becker and Charlotte B. Becker. New York: Garland, 1992. 1.558-61.

Bizzell, Patricia, and Bruce Herzberg, ed. *The Rhetorical Tradition: Readings from Classical Times to the Present*. Boston: St. Martin's, 1990.

Bloom, Harold. *Omens of Milennium: The Gnosis of Angels, Dreams, and Resurrection*. New York: Riverhead, 1996.

Booth, Wayne C. *The Company We Keep: An Ethics of Fiction*. Berkely: U of California P, 1988.

Brenkman, John. "Fascist Commitments." Hamacher, Hertz, and Keenan, 23-35.

Burke, Kenneth. *A Grammar of Motives*. Bizzell and Herzberg, 992-1018.

———. *A Rhetoric of Motives*. Bizzell and Herzberg, 1018-43.

———. *The Rhetoric of Religion*. Boston: Beacon, 1961.

Capaldi, Nicholas. *The Art of Deception*. New York: Donald W. Brown, 1971.

Clark, Timothy. "The Event of Signature: A 'Science' of the Signature?" *Derrida, Heidegger, Blanchot: Sources of Derrida's Notion and Practice of Literature*. Cambridge UP, 1992. 150-80.

Colish, Marcia. *The Mirror of Language: A Study in the Medieval Theory of Knowledge*. Lincoln: U of Nebraska P, 1983.

Corbett, Edward P. J. *Classical Rhetoric for the Modern Student.* 2nd ed. New York: Oxford UP, 1971.

Corder, Jim W. "Hunting Lieutenant Chadbourne: A Search for *Ethos* Whether Real or Pretended." Baumlin and Baumlin, 343-65.

De Man, Paul. *Allegories of Reading.* New Haven: Yale UP, 1979.

———. *Paul de Man's Wartime Journalism, 1939-1943.* Ed. Werner Hamacher, Neil Hertz, and Thomas Keenan. Lincoln: U of Nebraska P, 1989.

———. *The Resistance to Theory.* Ed. Wlad Godzich. Minneapolis: U of Minnesota P, 1983.

———. *The Rhetoric of Romanticism.* New York: Columbia UP, 1984.

Derrida, Jacques. "Circumfession: Fifty-nine periods and periphrases *written in a sort of internal margin, between Geoffrey Bennington's book and work in preparation (January 1989-April 1990).*" Bennington and Derrida, 3-315.

———. "How to Avoid Speaking: Denials." *Derrida and Negative Theology.* Ed. Harold Coward and Toby Foshay. Albany: State U of New York P, 1992. 73-142.

———. "Interpreting Signatures (Nietzsche/Heidegger): Two Questions." *Dialogue and Deconstruction: The Gadamer-Derrida Encounter.* Ed. Diane P. Michelfelder and Richard E. Palmer. Albany: State U of New York P, 1989. 58-71.

———. "Like the Sound of the Sea Deep within a Shell: Paul de Man's War." Hamacher, Hertz, and Keenan, 127-64.

———. *Memoires for Paul de Man.* Trans. Cecile Linday, Jonathan Culler, and Eduardo Cadava. New York: Columbia UP, 1986.

———. *Specters of Marx.*

Eagleton, Terry. *Literary Theory: An Introduction.* Minneapolis: U of Minnesota P, 1983.

———. *The Significance of Theory.* Oxford: Blackwell, 1989.

Eisenberg, Abne M., and Joseph A. Ilardo. *Argument: A Guide to Formal and Informal Debate.* 2nd ed. Englewood Cliffs, NJ: Prentice-Hall, 1980.

Ellis, John M. *Against Deconstruction.* Princeton: Princeton UP, 1989.

Felperin, Howard. "The Anxiety of American Deconstruction." *Deconstruction: A Critique.* Ed. Rajnath. Hong Kong: MacMillan, 1989. 180-96.

Foucault, Michel. *The Birth of the Clinic: An Archaeology of Medical Perception.* Trans. A. M. Sheridan. New York: Vintage, 1995.

———. "What Is an Author?" *Textual Strategies: Perspectives in Post-Structuralist Criticism.* Ed. Josue V. Harari. Ithaca: Cornell UP, 1979. 141-60.

Gelley, Alexander. "Regarding the Signatory." Hamacher, Hertz, and Keenan, 221–25.

Gorgias. "Encomium of Helen." Bizzell and Herzberg, 38–42.

Gregory, Marshall. "The Many-Headed Hydra of Theory vs. The Unifying Mission of Teaching." *College English* 59 (1997): 41–58.

Halloran, S. Michael. "The End of Rhetoric, Classical and Modern." *College English* 35 (1975): 621–31.

Hamacher, Werner, Neil Hertz, and Thomas Keenan, ed. *Responses on Paul de Man's Wartime Journalism*. Lincoln: U of Nebraska P, 1989.

Herrick, James A. *Argumentation: Understanding and Shaping Arguments*. Scotsdale: Gorsuch Scarisbrick, 1995.

Hirsch, David H. *The Deconstruction of Literature: Criticism After Auschwitz*. Hanover, NH: UP of New England, 1991.

Horner, Winifred Bryan. *Rhetoric in the Classical Tradition*. New York: St. Martin's, 1988.

Iser, Wolfgang. *The Implied Reader: Patterns of Communication in Prose Fiction from Bunyan to Beckett*. Baltimore: Johns Hopkins UP, 1974.

Isocrates. *Antidosis*. Bizzell and Herzberg, 50–54.

Kinneavy, James L. and Susan C. Warshauer. "From Aristotle to Madison Avenue: *Ethos and* the Ethics of Argument." Baumlin and Baumlin, 171–190.

Krueger, Heidi S. "Opting to Know: On the Wartime Journalism of Paul de Man." Hamacher, Hertz, and Keenan, 298–313.

Lanham, Richard. *Style: An Anti-Textbook*. New Haven: Yale UP, 1974.

Lehman, David. *Signs of the Times: Deconstruction and the Fall of Paul de Man*. New York: Poseidon, 1991.

Luckhurst, Roger. "Petition, Repetition, and 'Autobiography': J. G. Ballard's *Empire of the Sun* and *The Kindness of Women*." *Contemporary Literature* 35 (1994): 688–707.

Mauss, Marcel. "A Category of the Human Mind: The Notion of the Person; The Notion of the Self." *The Category of the Person*. Ed. Michael Carrithers, Steven Collins, and Steven Lukes. Cambridge: Cambridge UP, 1985. 1–25.

Miller, J. Hillis. *The Ethics of Reading: Kant, de Man, Eliot, Trollope, James, and Benjamin*. New York: Columbia UP, 1987.

Nealon, Jeffrey. "The Ethics of Dialogue: Bakhtin and Levinas." *College English* 59 (1997): 129–48.

Norris, Christopher. *Paul de Man: Deconstruction and the Critique of Aesthetic Ideology*. New York: Routledge, 1988.

Parker, David. *Ethics, Theory, and the Novel.* Cambridge: Cambridge UP, 1994.

Peckham, Morse. "Personality and the Mask of Knowledge." *Victorian Revolutionaries.* New York: George Braziller, 1970. 84–129.

Pirie, Madsen. *The Book of the Fallacy: An Intellectual Training Manual for Intellectual Subversives.* London: Routledge, 1985.

Poulakos, John. "Rhetoric, Sophists, and the Possible." *Communication Monographs* 51 (1984): 215–26.

Quintilian. *The Institutes of Oratory.* Bizzell and Herzberg, 297–363.

Richards, I. A. *The Philosophy of Rhetoric.* Bizzell and Herzberg, 975–988.

Rinaldi, Jacqueline. "Rhetoric and Healing." *College English* 58 (1996): 820–834.

Seyler, Dorothy U. *Understanding Argument: A Text with Readings.* New York: McGraw-Hill, 1994.

Spellmeyer, Kurt. "After Theory: From Textuality to Attunement with the World." *College English* 58 (1996): 893–913.

Spurgin, Sally De Witt. *The Power to Persuade: A Rhetoric and Reader for Argumentative Writing.* 3rd ed. Englewood Cliffs, NJ: Prentice-Hall, 1994.

Steiner, George. *Real Presences.* Chicago: U of Chicago P, 1989.

Stern, Frederick C. "Derrida, de Man, Despair: Reading Derrida on De Man's 1940s Essays." *Textual Practice* 4 (1990): 22–37.

Stoekl, Allan. "De Man and Guilt." Hamacher, Hertz, and Keenan, 375–84.

Untersteiner, Mario. *The Sophists.* Trans. Kathleen Freeman. New York: Philosophical Library, 1954.

Vogel, Arthur A. *Body Theology: God's Presence in Man's World.* New York: Harper, 1973.

Walton, Douglas. *The Place of Emotion in Argument.* University Park: Penn State UP, 1992.

Willard, Charles A. *A Theory of Argumentation.* Tuscaloosa: U of Alabama P, 1986.

Chapter 11

A Rhizomatic Ethics of Interpretation

David L. Erben and Kelli Erben

Ethics, the sense of purpose formed by a moral agent, is the rational order that prevents appetitive chaos. Otherwise, "all of us . . . are like vessels full of holes, vainly pouring into ourselves, again and again, a satisfaction that as promptly deserts us" (Plato, "Gorgias" 493A). The question of a rhizomatic ethics of interpretation is yoked to the question of reading because reading is, first of all, hearing the text affirmatively. A rhizomatic ethics is an ethic of encounter, without judgment, an ethics of affirmation. Reading is passive to the extent that the text interpolates the reader; however, at the same time, it is the reader who gives voice to the text. Ethics moves from passivity. The problem of a rhizomatic ethics of interpretation is in finding an affirmative response (Deleuze *Spinoza* 123). The meaning of the text exists only in, and because of, the hermeneutic operation. The text summons up the interpreter and has no meaning in itself outside the interpretation. But the text is not given over to the arbitrariness of the interpreter. The text is not delivered but only at the moment that it delivers. Thus, hermeneutics is guided by an ethics of reading: one must trust the message in order to interpret it, for interpretation is not the mastery of meaning. Rather, interpretation is an activity and the reader is part of the event of comprehension. To appropriate is to be victorious against alienation; it is to make the *a-topon* familiar, to assimilate, to give oneself to *Erinnerung* (Ricoeur 89).

Modern hermeneutics insists that the ethical characterization of the self present in the "I interpret" presupposes the distinction between self-consciousness and self understanding, as well as the elucidation of the latter. For it is not the mastery of subjectivity which constitutes the driving force, but rather its dispossession. Everything revolves around the Hegelian concept of the Spirit. For Hegel, the perfection of consciousness is its capacity to recognize itself in its other. The recognition of alterity is not an operation of the subject, nor is it a mediation of the self by the self; it is rather found in the experience of the self which occurs in the interpretive process.

Gilles Deleuze's rhizomatic thinking recognizes in the dominant model of hermeneutics a rhizomatic ethics of interpretation if it were to sever its alliance with the traditional conception of thought. From the grammatolgical perspective, the issue of the production of the text is critical to this ethics. Production—the text as production—appears as soon as the hermeneutic ethics of meaning is foregrounded. Thus, the question of the difference between effaced textuality—that of the hermeneutic text with its virtual sense and its power of truth—and the foregrounded textuality of grammatology cannot be avoided. From the grammatological point of view, the text is a stage, and writing a *mise en scene*. Everything is performance, role and disguise; every act embraces the intensity of forces. Epictetus privileged the analogy of theater to ethical behavior. Stoic belief stresses that the script of life's drama is not written by humans, nor is each individual role within the play. The only freedom that people can cultivate lies in how each person interprets and performs the part assigned. Yet at the same time that one is but an actor on the stage, one is in the audience as well. For reason gives humans the power to observe themselves in action (a process that Epictetus called *apatheia*, "disinterestedness") to regard and direct their movements from a privileged balcony (objectivity), and the humor to parody themselves when their improvisation verges upon the ridiculous. Yet, it is not just a question of the theatricality of representation, but rather of a kind of theatricality which erases the theme of presence and goes against the hermeneutic moment: according to the latter, the text is representation and textual presence of meaning, conceived against the background of textual mimesis. From the grammatological perspective, textuality is marked by the irreducible excess of the syntactic over the semantic. Instead of polysemy, symbol and metaphor which are hermeneutic concepts thematizing a certain solidarity with the metaphysics of identity, grammatological choice gives prominence to the syncategorematic aspects. Nor is it a question of opposing sense to non-sense, or the presence of a plain sense in hermeneutics to the absence of sense in grammatology. The question instead is about a quasi-empty signifying spacing and about the interval and the articulations which are produced. Dissemination, therefore, is not polysemy.

For hermeneutics, we belong to the texts which are in front of us, as soon as we allow them to interpellate us. For grammatology, we are inside the texts. It is a question of a textual labyrinth, along two interdictions: the interdiction against the author, but also the interdiction against reference. Grammatology keeps the author at arm's length, for it sees in the author the proprietor and despot. But the elimination of the author is not carried out for the sake of the hermeneutic simultaneity; it is carried out for the sake of the temporality which is specific to the text. Regressive readings based on psychobiographic concerns are avoided, because from this perspective the author is also a text.

Grammatology issued a *sui generis* interdict against reference. From the hermeneutic point of view, "ideality of meaning" meant that the text foregrounds the message, which is always an ethical message of truth. Language speaks about things and the question of the referential modalities is not seriously raised: ". . . language exists only through the distinction and the complementarity of a subject of enunciation, who is in connection with sense, and a subject of the statement, who is in connection, directly or metaphorically, with the designated thing" (Deleuze and Guattari *Kafka* 20).

But, for grammatology, the question of reference, which disseminates itself *ad infinitum*, loses its meaning, because it loses its pertinence. We can always find a referent, but the referent is going to be another text. Yet, in the absence of *the* referent, we can still talk about the structure of reference provided that what we mean is deferred reference. Whereas for hermeneutics the text is designated by a present meaning and the structure of reference is essentially representative and representable, for grammatology, reference is at best an illustration and a temporary location for the play of difference.

Hermeneutics and grammatology confront us, therefore, with two different experiences of reading. Hermeneutics discovers that we are always already within the hermeneutic circle. Grammatology discovers that we do not yet know how to read. In fact, grammatology charges hermeneutics with poor faith, as it challenges the privacy of listening which constitutes the hermeneutic instance. For the former, the guiding spool of interpretation is the dissimulation of the texture of the text itself. Interpretation is critical to the extent in that it aims at the production of the significant structure of the text. Hermeneutics alleges to open itself up to meaning, but grammatology wants to survey the cracks and fissures of the texts which resist the immanence of meaning. Since the issue for grammatology is not the question of *Offenheit*—openness of a world—but rather a question of *Oeffnung*—

the gap of a space, grammatology refuses all transgressive readings towards the openness-of-a-world; it chooses rather to become an aggressive reading, not of an *hors-texte*, but rather of the literary symptom which points at the inextricable link between the signifier and the signified.

Deleuze discusses hermeneutics in the context of his hopes for a new model of thought, which is called rhizomatic thinking. Rhizomatic thinking is a task which confronts literature and ethics alike. Majorities presuppose a constant which is taken for granted, and they depend upon it for their definition; they imply an ideal standard which makes evaluations possible:

> The unity of language is fundamentally political. There is no mother tongue, only a power takeover by a dominant language that at times advances along a broad front, and at times swoops down on diverse centers simultaneously. . . . The scientific enterprise of extracting constants and constant relations is always coupled with the political enterprise of imposing them on speakers. . . . (Deleuze and Guattari *Plateaus* 101)

To the extent that the majority is analytically derived from the dominant, ideal standard, this majority is literally no-one, while the minority is all the "becoming" that is available. This phenomenon is the reason why the problem is never how to become the majority for the majority has no becoming. The problem is rather that of the minority—how to become Rhizomatic.

The dominant, majoritarian paradigm of thought has also strongly entrenched postulates affecting writing and the result of writing—the text. To the extent that these postulates block the lines of escape and ritualize the book, rhizomatic thinking has to search them out and displace them in favor of writing and texts which would give a voice to those who do not yet have one. The classical text is a "text-root" or a "text-tree" (*Plateaus* 3-25). Organic, signifying, and subjective, writing is supposed to imitate and reflect the world. Difference and multiplicity are sacrificed for the sake of the center, and the hierarchically organized parts. Modernity is fascinated with a different kind of text, the "system-radicle," where the radicles are fasciculated (12). Here, the identity and linear progression of the elements are replaced by a cyclical unity:

> The book as assemblage with the outside with the outside, against the book as image of the world. A rhizome-book, not a dichotomous, pivotal, or fascicular book. (23)

Nietzsche's notion of culture as training and selection echoes the classical determination of culture as *paideia*. Distanciation and reappropriation of "sedimented" traditions—the foundational categories of the dominant hermeneutics—acquire a different significance when *paideia* is seen as the mnemotechnic dressage of forces for the sake of rendering them autonomous, active, and legislating.

Culture is a human activity and the training and selection it imposes aims at the creation of the ethical individual. But this Kantian ring in this assessment of culture is eliminated through the application of the genealogical critique. The means of culture should not be confused with its ends. The ethical individual, being the end of culture, is not culture's own product. It is the product of a selection which is more fundamental and decisive than the selection that culture can by itself work out. It selects and trains cultures as much as it selects and trains individuals. This now has a Hegelian and a Marxian ring to it, but the similarities—at least according to Gilles Deleuze—are only superficial. If similarities are sought for, one should rather look in the direction of Spinoza. A fascinating aspect of the human experience is revealed in Spinoza's deterministic model of the universal order which makes ethics—order in human behavior—necessary for the prosperity of both individuals and the society in which they live. Writing in general lives on in the anticipation of the decoding of its codes which represents its external limit.

For Nietzsche, the selection and the training of individuals involves an ultimate, ontological moment, and the creation of a plane of consistency: it is the moment of the repetition in the eternal return. Humans as the product of culture must be overcome for the sake of a supramoral human—the human of a new sensibility and a new image of thought. From the vantage point of this overcoming, Kant's ideal of the kingdom of ends appears to Nietzsche to be still "human, all too human." Culture, as training and selection, is the pre-historic element of man, whereas the supermoral individual is the post-historic element. Between pre-history and post-history, history witnesses the becoming-reactive of all forces and the progressive devaluation of all values. The subversion of culture by reactive forces, and the ultimate taking over of culture by them for their own purposes, is not a mere accident, but rather the meaning of universal history.

Culture aims at the production of the autonomous and self-legislating individual. The realization of this end presupposes the training of consciousness and its endowment with memory. But in order for this memory to not obliterate the active force of forgetting and to not reinforce the setting in of traces and the increase of reactiveness, it must no longer be a function of the past, but rather a function of the future, "commitment to the future," and "memory of the future itself." In other words, culture aims at the awakening in consciousness of repetition and the memory of the eternal return. This kind of memory, though, is precisely the memory that the reactive forces which affirm their difference as self-identity are incapable of producing, because it presupposes a simultaneous affirmation of difference and self-overcoming. Culture as *paideia* misfires and culture as sedimentation and passivity begins.

Deleuze's elaboration of Nietzschean exteriority rediscovers a Spinozian proposition: "Will to power is manifested as a power to be affected" (*Difference* 62). This notion allows Deleuze to pose inner experience as a mode of corporeal exteriority. The receptivity of a body is closely tied to its active external expression. Affectivity is an attribute of the body's power. In Nietzsche, as in Spinoza, *pathos* does not involve a body "suffering" passions; on the contrary, *pathos* involves the effects that mark the activity of the body, the creation of joy. The experience of joy follows fluidly from what is necessary to sustain minds, bodies, and spirits. This is the argument that Socrates made in the *Meno* and the *Protagoras*, as well as in the *Republic*. Joy motivates thought. Joy disguises and displaces itself through conduct that it selects. It joins expression and content and becomes an aesthetic form, a home in which one dwells, a mode of relationship and interpretation (Deleuze *Philosophy* 177–97).

Affirmation, however, is not enough for an ethics of interpretation. Ethical reading cannot remain on the plane of speculation, but must first find an avenue to enter the field of practice. Spinoza's conception of joy gives Deleuze the key to this new terrain: "The sense of joy appears as the properly ethical sense; it is to practice what affirmation itself is to speculation. . . A philosophy of pure affirmation, the *Ethics* is also a philosophy of the joy corresponding to such affirmation" (*Expressionism* 272). The affirmation of speculation, then, must be complemented by the joy of practice. This is how ethics realizes its full constructive force, as a practical constitution of being. In effect, affirmative speculation needs a corresponding joyful practice to make good on its claims to creativity and activity. Affirmation by itself, in other words, risks appearing as simply that which grasps and selects the being that is; joy is properly the moment that creates the being to come. This is an ethic without judgment, a reduction of ethics to a condition of affirmation.

Difference today casts its suspicion on metaphysics and on the examination of the Other. Philosophers of difference agree that this structure is language: *tò on légetai*. Admittedly, concerning the translation of this statement, they are not in agreement. Should it be "to be is to be said," or, rather, "Being happens in language"? Whichever perspective one chooses, whether Being happens in language or whether it thinks itself through language, what could the being of language be? Could it be the sign? Could it be the sign-value, or rather the sign-expression? Saussure or Husserl? Which one describes the being of language better? Derrida has demonstrated, in the sign-value, the difference which is built into the concept of "value" and into the arbitrariness which makes this value possible recedes finally and submits itself to identity, presence and Being. Conversely, the plenitude and the evidence which are pursued in Husserl's sign-expression do not, in the end, succeed in dissimulating the play of difference: the very moment that structural linguistics exnominates identity is also the moment which unveils and re-establishes it. But the play of difference does not end up here. The very moment the phenomenologist exnominates difference is also the moment which unveils and re-establishes it.

Deleuze illustrates repetition inside the traditional image of thought in three examples: lawful repetition of natural phenomena (science), habitual repetition of moral laws (ethics), and unconscious repetition of the repressed (psychoanalysis) (*Difference* 9–12, 13–15, 26–30). In nature, law like sequences seem to guarantee the generality of repetition; but even if one chooses to disregard the fact that these sequences are established experimentally, inside closed environments and on the basis of selected facts, the fact remains that law-like sequences and correlations are established between two generalities.

On the other hand, the same capacity of repetition is visible within the ethical repetition of the Kantian system. It is not our effort to repeat according to nature which gives the measure of our duties; whenever we repeat as beings of nature, our effort is condemned in advance. Only repetition according to the law of duty sets us free, since it brings about the spirituality of the repetition whose legislators and subjects we are (14–16). The ethical repetition is therefore specified in terms of a categorical imperative which has generality and universality as its props. It is realized through the generality of (good) habits. But, surely, it is not the mere generality of habits, that is, the indefinite multiplication of lawful acts, which constitutes the ethical instance. It is the other way around: the repetition of lawful acts depends on its lawfulness and generality upon the constitutive instant of the ethical difference. "If repetition is possible," concludes Deleuze, "it is against the moral law, as much as it is against the law of nature . . . it belongs to humor and irony . . . it is transgression and exception" (9). Kant's Copernican revolution does not consist only in the fact that it makes the objects revolve around the subject; it is much more visible in the fact that the good is made to revolve around the Law. It follows that the Law must authenticate and ground itself.

Evaluation and interpretation—both understood as the weighing of forces—are complementary genealogical operations. To the extent that the meaning of an utterance is the result of the forces which take hold of it, genealogy is symptomatology. It deals with utterances as symptoms to be analyzed until these "assemblages" are exposed: "expressions and statements intervene directly in productivity, in the form of a production of meaning or sign-value (*Plateaus* 89).

Only ethics, as the science of liberation and the practical constitution of the world, can map the interpretative process of reading. This process which manifests itself as force, must be organized by means of ethical action. But the ethical action cannot be organized in the way that an object is organized by a subject.

The text, for hermeneutics, has been the inscription of discourse and thereby a moment of alienation; but it is this alienation which gives hermeneutics its chance (Ricoeur 43–44). In fact, from the hermeneutic point of view, the theory of the text is a subordinate theory: it is subordinated to a general theory of discourse. The text is discourse at a certain state, and since ethics and comprehension are present everywhere that there is discourse, the comprehension of texts is a species of the ethics and comprehension of discourse. The privilege of writing consists in the fact that the text acquires its autonomy from the author, the situation of its composition, and the initial addressee. But, for hermeneutics, the transition from discourse to text does not leave us with a pure sign or with a "grapheme" without meaning; on the contrary, it gives us the full ideality of meaning. It does not leave us with a residue, a trace or an index of an irretrievable absence, but rather with a plain sense. The text is intriguing because it can speak, even if the initial speaker and addressee no longer speak (31–32). This is how the text becomes, for hermeneutics, its object *par excellence*. In it, tradition (delivery) is visibly at work. The autonomy of meaning, which is manifested in the written text, establishes the continuity of speaking and writing, since the ideality of meaning which begins in speech prolongs itself in the text (11-12). The text compels us to face meaning as an ideal "*vouloir dire*" (12-22), freed from all psychologizing intentionality.

On the other hand, the inscription of the text brings about a kind of alienation: the text has lost the voice. Hermeneutics, therefore, recognizes itself as a discourse of assistance and ethics. It aims at giving the voice back to the text (43-44). It is true that from the point of view of the old Romantic hermeneutics, the genesis of the text had to be recapitulated by means of a congenial interpretation: the text was still an expression, and the author and the original addressee were, for it, indispensable (75). However, modern hermeneutics, as for example Ricoeur conceives it today, opposes the idea of the text as expression—or, at least, it opposes it in the first instance. The "*hors-texte*"—the perennial preoccupation of historicists and psychologism—is now replaced by what the text says—its message, for it is the message which is present and able to interpolate the reader (26-37). Language gives orders:

> A rule of grammar is a power marker before it is a syntactical marker. The order does not refer to prior signification or to a prior organization of distinctive units. Quite the opposite. Information is only the strict minimum necessary for the emission, transmission, and observation of orders as commands. (Deleuze and Guattari *Plateaus* 76)

We cannot assign an *arche* to language, for language sends us constantly to more language; it is not from the lived or the sensed that one goes to that which is said, but rather always from one saying to another. But the fact that language is anarchic, in this sense, is not due to the indeterminable proliferation of the signifier; it is rather due to the presence of order words (*mots d'ordre*) in it whose function is co-extensive with the function of language:

We call *order-words*, not a particular category of explicit statements (for example, in the imperative), but the relation of every word or every statement to implicit presuppositions, in other words, to speech acts that are, and can only be, accomplished in the statement. Order-words do not concern commands only, but every act that is linked to statements by a "social obligation." Every statement displays this link, directly or indirectly. (*Plateaus* 79)

Deleuze does not forget the work of Austin and the demonstration of the intrinsic relations between speech and actions which one performs as one speaks. These relations are implicit and non-discursive presuppositions of speech and actions and are distinct from the presuppositions which become explicit, as utterances are elucidated through other utterances, and distinct from actions which are extrinsic to them. To be sure, Deleuze appropriates Austin's conclusions only after the deconstructive efforts of Derrida.

Language, according to Deleuze, is a form of indirect discourse. In opposition to the dominant model, which makes direct discourse the presupposition for the indirect, Deleuze asserts the primacy of indirect discourse and the dependence of the former upon the latter. More accurately, he sees in direct discourse the trace of the "free indirect discourse" which enables speakers to speak:

> the first determination of language is not the trope or metaphor but *indirect discourse*. The importance of some have accorded metaphor and metonymy proves disastrous for the study of language. Metaphors and metonymies are merely effects; they are a part of language only when they presuppose indirect discourse. (77)

Every linguistic arrangement plays on two axes simultaneously, one horizontal and one vertical, and each axis is again broken up into two segments. On its horizontal axis, a speech act organizes content as much as it organizes expression. It connects therefore bodies, actions and passions, as much as interactions among them, no less than it connects utterances, acts and statements, distributing meanings and attributing them to bodies. But on its vertical axis, the same speech act is organized along territories and re-territorializations which endow it with stability, and along lines of deterritorialization which destabilize it and make it run away. It was an error, therefore, for semiology to think that linguistic arrangements refer to and presuppose a certain productivity-center of language; they rather refer to and presuppose a veritable expression-machine—the abstract machine—the variables of which determine the use of the elements of language.

These elements are not sufficient by themselves. The primacy of the collective arrangement of utterances is imposed over *langue* and discourse, just as the primacy of the collective arrangements of bodies is imposed over tools and products, and the primacy of collective arrangements is not independent from the movements of deterritorialization which prohibit the determination of language as an homeostatic system. To believe, as semiology believed, that the form of the expression suffices to account for the linguistic system makes no sense. Indeed, whether the system is thought of as a phonological structure of the order of the signifier, or, as Chomsky wants, as a deep syntactic structure, the mistake is the same: it is in the effort to generate in this way the semantic level, to fill the expression once and for all, and to consequently bracket all content as "mere referent," relegating pragmatics to the order of considerations which remain extrinsic to linguistics. The mistake in all these efforts is in the attempt to build an "abstract machine" for language out of synchronically constant elements functioning in perfect linearity.

The scientific model, which postulates that minoritarian languages can only be understood against the background of standard languages, is of one piece with the political model which attempts to impose the homogenization, centralization, and standardization of a language of power, which would be majoritarian and dominant. Paul Feyerabend exposes the irony in the consequences of this model. While the intention behind the accumulation of a body of knowledge may be the enlightenment of humanity, it seems that often, just the opposite has occurred in Western culture (102). Behind every "mother-tongue" there is the rise to power of dominant order words and grammatically correct sentences are the preamble to the submission to the laws: "When the schoolmistress instructs her students on a rule of grammar or arithmetic, she is not informing them, any more than she is informing herself when she questions a student. She does not so much instruct as 'insign,' give orders or commands" (Deleuze and Guattari *Plateaus* 75). The development of ethics responds to the human quest for power, an assertion of free will, a type of self-sufficiency that denies the forces of destiny (Nussbaum 91).

The reigning paradigm does not merely postulate the eternal referral of one sign to another together with the circular motion of this reference; it postulates also the multiplicity of circles: the sign refers to other signs as it moves from one circle to another and from one spiral to another (*Plateaus* 146–7). It is as if the signifying system of signs anticipates its own death in entropy, and tries to postpone it indefinitely, through the creation of more circles and spirals and through the offerings of more signifiers to its despotic center. These offerings are not made haphazardly, because the paradigmatic proliferation of circles, the jumps from the one circle to the other, and the displacement of the stage, require a secondary mechanism—the mechanism of interpretation:

> the syntagmatic axis of the sign referring to other signs is added a paradigmatic axis on which the sign, thus formalized, fashions for itself a suitable

signified . . . The interpretative priest, the seer, is one of the despot-god's bureaucrats . . . interpretation is carried to infinity and never encounters anything to interpret that is not already itself an interpretation. (114)

Deleuze makes it clear that the signifying regime of signs outlines a certain function of language, because it outlines first of all the imperial, despotic systems, and all the centered and hierarchical groups, whether they are political parties or whether they are literary schools (163). The most fatal mistake of the dominant paradigm of thought and language is to have taken the signifying sign regime as the only regime of signs available. Semiology and hermeneutics have identified themselves with the signifying regime, and, therefore, semiology and hermeneutics are only one sign regime among others. Deleuze stresses the importance of pragmatics in challenging the monopoly of this one system. For, in fact, there are other semiotic systems, not in the sense that they exist in isolation from each other, but rather in the sense that they all criss-cross one another in order to weave collective arrangements.

For Deleuze, to write has nothing to do with signifying, and everything to do with surveying and mapping out. Not only the writer, but the reader as well must be a stylist and make the book better, teasing out of it new threads. A book has no object; it is rather an arrangement, and as such, the book is always in connection with other arrangements. Reading and writing are desiring processes, and they should therefore be evaluated on the basis of the qualities that all fluxes have: activity/re-activity, affirmation/negation, slowness/speed. To ask what a book means—whether the question is raised in terms of the signifier or whether it is raised in terms of the signified—is a non starter. The right questions are rather here: how does a book function? In connection with what else does it generate intensities? In which multiplicities does it introduce change, and how is it being changed in return? Which bodies does it befriend, and which abstract machine empowers it? When one writes, one has to ask only one ethical question: into which other machine must writing be plugged in order to function?

Altogether different from the traditional image of the book is the "book-rhizome": "In a book, as in all things, there are lines of articulation or segmentarity, strata and territories; but also lines of flight, movements of deterritorializaiton and destratification" (*Plateaus* 3).

Any part of the book can be connected with any other part. Instead of fixing points, origins and ends, the book-rhizome is made of collective arrangements, mixed sign-regimes, semiotic chains tied to biological, political, economic and other chains, so that the distinction between sign-regimes present in it and its object cannot radically be made: "A rhizome has no beginning or end; it is always in the middle, between things, interbeing *intermezzo*. The tree is filiation, but the rhizome is alliance, uniquely alliance. The tree imposes the verb 'to be,' but the fabric of the rhizome is the conjunction, 'and . . . and . . . and . . .'" (*Plateaus* 25).

Since there is no referential text or neutral code or degree zero of writing or originary literality, any text can be read and written intensively, that is, projected and hurled into its own death. A text is a combination of powers, conflicts, dominations and resistances which always contain the conditions for the text's destruction of the text and its rhizomatic re-production:

> a book has no sequel nor the world as its object nor one or several authors as its subject. In short, we think that one cannot write sufficiently in the name of an outside. The outside has no image, no signification, no subjectivity. The book is assemblage. . . . (23)

A book has neither subject nor object; it is made out of formed materials on the basis of dates and speeds very different from one another. There is no language in itself, but only a criss-crossing of dialects, idiolects, and slangs. A language can never close upon itself without becoming impotent. A language, just like any other social formation, is less defined by inner conflicts and contradictions, and more by its lines of escape. A collective of arrangements does not have an infrastructure and several superstructures, or a deep structure and a surface structure. All these dimensions are spread upon one and the same plane of consistency of the same surface.

Writing is an ethical project, and hermeneutics must become productive, instead of being merely reproductive, re-appropriating and re-cognitive. To talk about the ethical project of writing means that the functions of textuality and ethics do not stand in a relation external to each other. Deleuze argues:

> Write, create rhizomes, increase your territory through deterritorialization, stretch the line of escape until it covers the entire plane of consistency with an abstract machine . . . Search for the plant which, in this direction, is furthest away from your plant. All those which grow in between these two are yours. (19)

As opposed to centered systems, their hierarchical communications and their pre-established connections, the rhizome is non-centered, non-hierarchical and a-signifying. The book-rhizome takes the multiple as a substantive: but then multiplicity is liberated from the grips of the One—whether subject or object. In this case, the identity imputed to the author is an illusion, for the author is made out of multiple fibers. The ethics of interpretation needed for the book-rhizome is an ethic of encounter, without judgment, an ethics of affirmation. Such a rhizomatic ethics of interpretation seeks relations rather than representations. Affirmation—a Nietzschean and Stoic perspective—does not complete this ethics of interpretation; it renders the ethics possible. There are only local, provisional, and questionable ethics; ethical interpretation begins when we reach the limit of our power and face the problem of finding responses to specific readings. Ethical interpretation begins when we accept the fact that we are not yet capable of ethical interpretation.

Works Cited

Deleuze, Gilles. *Difference and Repetition*. Trans. Paul Patton. New York: Columbia UP, 1994.

———. *Expressionism in Philosophy: Spinoza*. Trans. Martin Joughin. New York: Zone Books, 1990.

———. *Nietzsche and Philosophy*. Trans. Hugh Tomlinson. New York: Columbia UP, 1983.

Deleuze, Gilles, and Feliz Guattari. *A Thousand Plateaus: Capitalism and Schizophrenia*. Trans. Brian Massumi. Minneapolis: U of Minnesota P, 1987.

———. *Kafka, Toward a Minor Literature*. Trans. Terry Cochran. Minneapolis: U of Minnesota P, 1986.

———. *Spinoza: Practical Philosophy*. Trans. Robert Hurley. San Francisco: City Lights, 1988.

Feyerabend, Paul. *Science in a Free Society*. London: NLB, 1978.

Gadamer, Hans Georg. *Kleine Schriften, I, Philosophie-Hermeneutik*. Tubingen: Mohr, 1967.

Laruelle, F. *Au-Delà du Principe de Pouvoir*. Paris: Aubier, 1981.

Nussbaum, Martha. *The Fragility of Goodness*. New York: Cambridge, 1986.

Plato. *The Dialogues of Plato*. Trans. W.C. Hembold. Toronto: Bantam, 1986. 287–340.

Ricoeur, Paul. *Interpretation Theory: Discourse and the Surplus of Meaning*. Fort Worth: Texas Christian UP, 1976.

Notes on Contributors

James S. Baumlin is Professor of English at Southwest Missouri State University. A co-editor (with Tita French Baumlin) of *Ethos: New Essays in Rhetorical and Critical Theory* (Dallas: SMUP, 1994), his research interests include critical theory, the history of rhetoric, and seventeenth-century English poetry.

David Bleich teaches writing to graduate and undergraduate students at the University of Rochester. His forthcoming book *is Know and Tell: Disclosure, Genre, And Membership In The Teaching Of Writing And Language Use* from Heinemann-Boynton/Cook.

James Comas has taught the history of rhetoric and the history of literary criticism at the University of Oklahoma and at Syracuse University. In addition to publishing articles on the philosophy of rhetoric, the postcolonial aspects of contemporary literary theory, and the ethics of academic publishing, he is the author of *Theoretical Communities: Studies in the Rhetoric and Ethics of American Literary Criticism, 1921–1994*. (NCTE Press, forthcoming).

David L. Erben is Assistant Professor of English at the University of Toledo, Ohio, where he teaches Native American literature and World Film and Literature. He is the editor of the electronic journal *Seulemonde* and the author of articles on transformation and marginality in Native American literature and the specialty of "cyberspace."

Kelli Erben has a M.A. in philosophy from the University of South Florida. Her thesis explored the aesthetic aspects of ethics. She has research interests in fine arts, identity and persona, and the role of desire in ethics, particularly as they pertain to aesthetics.

Rosalind J. Gabin is Associate Professor of English and Rhetoric at Binghampton University (SUNY) and author of numerous articles on rhetoric, writing, and critical theory. She is also the editor of the recent *Discourse Studies in Honor of James L. Kinneavy* (Scripta Humanistica).

Fredric G. Gale is Associate Professor of English and Writing at Syracuse University. His most recent book is *Political Literacy: Rhetoric, Ideology, and The Possibility of Justice*. He is editor of *Composition Forum*, a national journal of writing pedagogy.

George H. Jensen is Professor of English at Southwest Missouri State University. His books include *Personality and the Teaching of Composition* (Norwood, NJ: Ablex, 1989) with John DiTiberio, and *The Philosophy of Discourse* (Boynton-Cook, 1992). He is currently working on a rhetorical analysis of storytelling in Alcoholics Anonymous.

James L. Kinneavy is the Jane and Roland Blumberg Professor of English at the University of Texas at Austin, where he has directed the graduate program in rhetoric and the freshman composition program. He has published widely in rhetorical theory, literary theory, and the history of rhetoric. His books include *A Study of Three Contemporary Theories of Lyric Poetry*, *A Theory of Discourse*, and *Greek Rhetorical Origins of Christian Faith*. He is currently working on a book proposing a code of ethics that can be taught in the public schools.

Lance Massey is a doctoral candidate in English at the University of Illinois, Urbana. His recent publications in Romantic poetry and historical rhetoric have appeared in *PMPA: Publications of the Missouri Philological Association* and *SMSU: Journal of Public Affairs*.

Gary A. Olson is Professor of English and Coordinator of the Graduate Program in Rhetoric and Composition at the University of South Florida. His most recent book is *Publishing in Rhetoric and Composition* (SUNY Press), with Todd W. Taylor. In 1993, The Council of Editors of Learned Journals presented Olson with the International Award for Distinguished Retiring Editor for his decade of work as editor of the *Journal of Advanced Composition*.

Notes on Contributors

Phillip Sipiora is Associate Professor of English at the University of South Florida, where he teaches in the graduate program and directs the freshman English program. He has published articles on rhetorical theory in Greek Antiquity, rhetorical strategies in the work of Charles Darwin, and rhetorical approaches in the interpretation of twentieth-century literature.

C. Jan Swearingen served as the 1994–95 Visiting Radford Chair of Rhetoric and Composition at Texas Christian University. Her book, *Rhetoric and Irony, Western Literacy and Western Lies*, shared the 1991 W. Ross Winterowd Award for the best book in Composition Theory. Her teaching and research fields include feminist criticism and theory within rhetoric and composition, cross-cultural approaches to rhetoric and literacy, the rhetoric of religion, and the history of rhetoric. She is currently working on a book on multiculturalism in the ancient world, under contract with Boynton-Cook/Heinemann.

Kathleen Ethel Welch, Professor of English at the University of Oklahoma, is author *of The Contemporary Reception of Classical Rhetoric: Appropriations of Ancient Discourse* and *Electric Rhetoric: Classical Rhetoric, Oralism, and a New Literacy*. She has published numerous essays on historicized rhetoric and composition. She was founding president of the Coalition of Women Scholars in the History of Rhetoric and Composition and president of the Rhetoric Society of America. She currently is writing a book on technology, gender, and composition.

W. Ross Winterowd is Bruce R. McElderry Professor of English at the University of Southern California. He is the author of numerous books on composition theory and other subjects, including *Contemporary Rhetoric: A Conceptual Background with Readings*, and *The Culture and Politics of Literacy*.

Index

Aarons, Victoria, 121, 133
Ad hominum, 183–184, 186–187, 190, 198–200, 202–205, 209–210, 212–213
Aesthetics, 44, 57
Affectus, 131
Alcorn, Marshall, 121–122, 133
Alterite, 51
American Jurisprudence, 26,35
American Psychological Association Style Manual, 148
Anderson, Virginia, 56, 59
Apate, 205–213
Apatheia, 222
Arendt, Hannah, 114, 132, 133
Arete, 40, 117
Aristotle, 22, 40–41, 49, 56, 85, 107–110, 116–120, 123–129, 131, 138–139, 141–142, 149, 150, 199, 202–203, 209
    Nichomachean Ethics, 40, 56, 59, 117, 124
    Rhetoric, 88, 107, 117–119, 124, 129, 131, 138, 202, 216
Arnheim, Rudolf, 214
Ars gratia artis, 66
Artes liberales, 145
Ashton-Jones, Evelyn, 102, 104
A-topon, 221
Auden, W. H., "*Kairos* and *Logos*," 56–57

Augustine, St. Thomas, 111–112, 170, 197
Aurelius, Marcus, 214
Austin, J. L., 215, 229–230

Baker, Peter, 58, 59, 209, 211, 213, 216
Bakhtin, Mikhail M., 43, 51, 54, 59, 120, 184, 189–190, 216
Barker, Stephen F., 209–210, 216
Barnet, Sylvan, 210, 216
Barthes, Roland, 43, 58, 59, 185, 190, 216
Bateson, Gregory, 174
Bauman, Zygmunt, 91, 92, 104
Baumlin, James S., xvi, 112, 116, 120–122, 133, 183, 216, 237
Baumlin, Tita French, 112, 120–122, 133, 216
Bazerman, Charles, 131, 133
Bedau, Hugo, 210, 216
Belenky, Mary Field, 158, 160, 179
Belief, 156
    as an interpersonal posture, xi, 157–161
    as related to ethics, xii, xvii, 171–178
    hermeneutics of, 162–163, 169–171
Bell, Daniel, 4
Bellah, Robert, 4, 9, 13–14, 20
Belles lettres, 67–70

Benedict, Ruth, 13
Bennington, Geoffrey, 197, 216
Berlin, James A., 77, 89, 115-116, 133, 147, 151, 153
Bernal, Martin, 56, 59
Bernasconi, Robert, 57, 59, 216
Berube, Michael, 151, 153
Bhabha, Homi K., 96-97, 99, 104
Bible, 109, 161
Bildungsroman, 160
Bill of Rights, 16
Bizzell, Patricia, 102, 104, 140, 142, 144, 153, 216
Blair, Hugh, 115-116
Blake, William, 166
Blanchot, Maurice, 51-52, 59
Bleich, David, ix, 237
Bloom, Harold, xvi, 185, 216
Bolter, Jay, 59
Booth, Wayne C., 43, 50, 59, 78-79, 83, 89, 208, 216
Bourdieu, Pierre, 87
Brandeis, Louis, 29
Brenkman, John, 198, 210-212, 216
Brindel, June Kachuy, 162, 179
Brown, Stephen, 93, 104
Brown, Stuart, 89
Bruffee, Kenneth, 131, 133
Bruner, Jerome, 157, 161, 179
Buddhism, 8
Burke, Kenneth, ix-x, xvi, 79-84, 86, 87, 111-112, 119-120, 122-123, 141, 186-188, 190, 205, 209-210, 213
   A Grammar of Motives, 122-123, 133, 151, 153, 210, 216
   Permanence and Change: An Anatomy of Purpose, 79-82, 83, 84, 87
   A Rhetoric of Motives, 79, 82-83, 89, 111-112, 119, 133, 153, 187-188, 216

Callicles, 75, 86
Camargo, Martin, 151
Campbell, George, 115-116
Camus, 5

Capaldi, Nicholas, 216
Capella, Martianus, 111-112
Carter, Stephen L., 156, 158, 178, 179
Cartesian subject, 76
Cassandra, xi, 162-168
Cassirer, 58
Chamberlin, Charles, 132, 133
Charney, Davida, 59
Chase, Geoffrey, 58, 59
Chernin, Kim, 162, 179
Cherry, Roger, 132, 133
Chomsky, Noam, 231
Christian, Barbara, xv
Christianity, 3, 5, 8-9, 12, 16-17
Cicero, 5, 15, 108-113, 123-125, 131, 155, 208
   De Oratore, 109-110, 112, 131
Cixous, Helene, 166, 179
Clark, Gregory, 114-115, 133
Clark, Timothy, 211, 216
Clifford, John, 59
Clinchy, Blythe McVicker, 158, 160, 179
Cmiel, Kenneth, 114, 133
Coleridge, Samuel Taylor, 158
Colish, Marcia, 201, 216
College Composition and Communication, 133
Collier, Susan A., 27, 36
Comas, James, ix-x, xii, 75, 237
Commission on Professional Service, 67, 74
Communitarians, 4-5, 9, 15
Conference for College Composition and Communication, 1, 57
Confucianism, 5
Conners, Robert J., 133
Contact zone, 92-95, 98-100, 102
   contact language, 93-94
Contemporary Reception of Classical Rhetoric, 151
Corbett, Edward P. J., 113, 134, 210, 217
Corder, Jim W., 183, 210, 217
Cowen, Zelman, 29-30, 36
Craft, 69-70
Credo ut intelligam, 166

Critchley, Simon, 51-52, 59
Crowley, Sharon, 153
Crusius, Timothy W., 56, 59, 123, 126, 134

D'Amato, Anthony, 35, 36
D'Souza, Dinesh, 145, 149
de Beauvoir, Simone, 184
de Certeau, Michel, 52, 59
de Man, Paul, 43, 46, 57, 60, 183, 186-187, 193, 195-196, 198-200, 204, 206, 209-213, 217
Deconstruction, 156, 186-187, 199-202, 208-209, 214
    Deconstruction of *ethos*, 190-195
Defamation, 31, 35
Delectare, 57, 131
Deleuze, Gilles, xv, 221-234, 235
Denham, Robert, 73
Deontological system, 15-16, 48, 56
Derrida, Jacques, 46-47, 53-54, 60, 153, 186-187, 189-200, 204, 209, 211, 215, 216, 217, 227, 230
    "Interpreting Signatures," 191-195, 197-198, 217
Descartes, 157
Dewey, John, 80
Dialectic, 145, 155
Dianoetikas, 40
Differance, 53
Dikaion, 23
Dike, 23
Diligentia, 131
Dionysius, 40
Docere, 131
Doxa, 46, 119, 142
DuBois, W. E. B., 65
Ducrot, Oswald, 45, 60
Dunamis, 129
Dworkin, 5

Eades, Ronald, 33, 36
Eagleton, Terry, 4, 43, 60, 79, 185, 208-209, 217
Ede, Lisa S., 133
Edel, Abraham, 13

Educational Research Analysts, 33
Eichmann, Adolf, 114, 132
Eighteenth Amendment, 21
Eiseley, Loren, 65
Eisenberg, Abne M., 212, 217
Elbow, Peter, 158, 169, 179
Ellis, John M., 200-201, 209, 217
Elocutio, 113, 131
Engberg-Petersen, Troels, 129, 134
English Department, The, 63, 70
English Law Commission, 31
Enos, Richard Leo, 131, 134
Enos, Theresa, 89, 150, 153
Epictetus, 179, 214, 222
Episteme, 84, 119, 142
Erben, David, xv, 221, 237
Erben, Kelli, xv, 221, 237
Erga, 140
Erinnerung, 221
Ethics, 75, 92, 108, 116, 184, 186, 207-208
    applied ethics, 47-55
    and human agency, 201-203
    as habit, 227-228
    component of *ad hominem* argument, xvi, 186, 203-205
    in the 20th Century, 120-123
    individual ethics, 14-17
    social ethics, 3-5, 9
    meta-ethics, 10-13
    language dimension, 1-2, 6, 12-16, 83, 140
    part of the writing classroom, xv, 41
    political project, 78-79
    relation to *ethos*, 117-120
    Rhizomatic ethics of interpretation, 221-222, 224, 226, 231-232, 234
Ethikos, 40, 84
Ethopoeia, 204
Ethos, 56, 76-78, 84-85, 88, 107, 110, 116, 131, 141, 143, 185, 202-203, 205, 207, 209-210
    abode, dwelling, or habitation, 85-86, 117

as a component of *ad hominem*
    argument, 198-200
as authority in the classroom, xiii-
    xiv, 108
character, 39-40, 55, 84-85
deconstruction of, 190-195
history of, 108-117
in the 20th Century, 120-123
part of writing classroom, 123-
    130
political, 77-78
relation to ethics, 117-120
scientistic, 76-78
Ethos anthropoi daimon, 85
Etzioni, Amitai, 4, 9, 13-15
Exodus, Book of, 164, 167

Faigley, Lester, 52, 57, 60, 126-129,
    134, 142, 153
Fascism, 212
Faust, 168
Felperin, Howard, 184, 186, 209,
    213, 217
Ferry, Luc, 209
Feyerabend, Paul, 231, 235
Fiorenza, Elizabeth Schussler, 164,
    179
First Amendment, 30
Fish, Stanley, 145
Flower, Linda, 131, 134
Formalism, 200
Foucault, Michel, 122, 139, 153,
    185-186, 188-189, 204,
    217
Frank, Manfred, 120, 134
Freeman, Kathleen, 85, 89
Freeman, Samuel, 27, 36
Freire, Paulo, 99-100, 102, 103,
    104, 184
Freud, Sigmund, 151, 157, 169, 184,
    213
Frye, Northrop, ix, 67, 74, 76-78,
    86, 87, 89, 166-168, 179
Frymer-Kensky, Tikva, 161, 164, 179
Fukuyama, Francis, 204

Gabin, Rosalind J., xiii, 107, 134,
    237

Gabler, Mel and Norma, 33
Gadamer, Hans Georg, 235
Gale, Frederic, xii-xiii, xviii, 21, 35,
    36, 238
Gale, Xin Liu, 103, 104
Galston, William, 4
Gates, Henry Louis, Jr., 43, 60, 145,
    151, 157, 153, 158, 167,
    171-173, 177, 179
Gauman Poma de Ayala, Felipe, 93,
    103
Geertz, Clifford, 42, 60, 159, 179
Geist, 177
Gelassenheit, 84
Gelley, Alexander, 211, 218
Gillespie, Sheena, 60
Gilligan, Carol, 160, 168, 179
Giroux, Henry A., 102, 104146-
    147, 151
Glendon, Mary Ann, 4
Gless, Daryl J., 146, 153
Godzich, Wlad, 52, 60
Goffman, Erving, 114, 134
Goldberger, Nancy Rule, 158, 160,
    179
Good Samaritan Rule, 26-29, 31
Gorgias, 109, 139, 205-206, 213-
    214, 218
Gorgias, 75, 119, 221
Graff, Gerald, 77, 89, 156, 172,
    174, 179
Gram, 53
Grammar, 40, 82-83, 145, 155, 213
Grammatology, 222-224
Grassi, Ernesto, 113, 134
Greenblatt, Stephen, 74
Gregory, Marshall, 184-185, 218
Grimaldi, William M. A., 107, 109-
    110, 118-119, 134
Guattari, Feliz, 223-224, 229, 231-
    233, 235
Gunn, Giles, 74

Hall, Stuart, 58
Halloran, S. Michael, 114-115, 133,
    205, 218
Hamacher, Werner, 211, 218
Hamlet, 17-18

Hampshire, Stuart, 60
Haraway, Donna, 60
Harris, Joseph, 94–95, 104
Harrison, Jane Ellen, 165–168, 179
Hartman, Geoffrey H., 159, 174, 180
Hassett, Michael, 125–126, 134
Hebrew Scriptures, 161, 164, 167
Hegel, 176, 222
Heidegger, Martin, 5, 46, 48, 56, 57, 84–85, 88, 89, 191–195, 199, 211
Heilbroner, 4
Heim, Michael, 60, 120, 134
Hennard, George Jo, 5–6
Heraclitus, 85
Herkovits, Melville J., 13
Hermeneutics
  of ethics, 221–224, 228–229, 233–234
  of suspicion, xii, 46, 156
Herrick, James A., 186, 211, 218
Hertz, Neil, 210, 218
Hesiod, 85
Hilligross, Susan S., 60
Hinduism, 9
Hirsch, David H., 200, 209, 211, 218
Hirsch, Fred, 4
Hirsh, Elizabeth, 102, 104
Hobbs, Catherine, 151, 153
Holmes, Stephen, 172–173, 178, 180
Homer, 18–19, 40, 85
Horner, Winifred Bryan, 146–151, 153, 210, 218
Hors-texte, 224, 229
Hulliung, Mark L., 45, 61
Humanism, 75, 76184–186, 202–203, 208, 209
Husserl, 58, 227
Hutcheon, Linda, 100, 104

Ideology, 42–55, 57, 102
  definition, 42–44
Ideology of the human, 185–186, 190, 208
Ilardo, Joseph A., 212, 217

Iliad, 18–19, 85, 88
Imagination, 64–65, 67–69
Imhoff, Tom, 125, 136
Ingenium, 131
Invention (as reason), 64–65, 67–68
Irigaray, Luce, 102
Irwin, T. H., 134
Iser, Wolfgang, 218
Islam, 3, 5, 12, 17
Isocrates, 40, 132, 137–145, 147–149, 150, 153, 183, 208, 218
  Antidosis, 142, 151, 183

Jaeger, Werner, 39–40, 60
Jameson, Frederic, 46, 79, 143
Jamieson, Kathleen Hall, 145–146
JanMohamed, Abdul J., 98–99, 104
Jarratt, Susan, 134
Jenkinson, Edward, 32–33, 36
Jensen, George, xvi, 183, 238
Johnson, Nan, 114–115, 134, 150, 153
Johnson, Randall, 87, 89
Johnson, Samuel, 65
Joues, Reverend Henry Stuart, 88, 150, 154
Journal of Advanced Composition, 103
Judaism, 3, 5, 8–9, 12, 16–17
Jung, 188

Kairos, 41–42, 55, 57, 140, 142–144
  Kairos Program, 145–149
Kant, 214, 225, 228
Kantianism, 5, 82, 227
Kearney, Mary Kate, 27–28, 36
Keenan, Thomas, 211, 218
Kelber, Werner H., 180
Kennedy, George A., 131–132, 135, 138, 146, 150, 154
Kierkegaard, Søren, 155, 157, 174–177, 180
Kimmel, Lawrence D., 121, 135
Kincaid, James, 71
Kinneavy, James L., xiv–xv, 1, 56, 58, 116–117, 123–124,

135, 137–144, 147, 149, 154, 160, 165, 177, 180, 202–204, 209, 218, 238
Kirk, G. S., 87, 89
Kleine, Michael, 102, 105
Kluckhohn, Clyde, 13
Knoblauch, C. H., 102, 104
Kristeva, Julia, 166, 169–171, 180, 184
Kromsch, Claire, 73
Krueger, Heidi S., 208, 218

Landow, George, 60
Langue, 230
Lanham, Richard, 60, 108–109, 121, 124–125, 135, 206–207, 218
Lankford, Scott, 24–26, 36
Laruelle, F., 235
Law Cases, Table, 37
Law Commission, 36
Le Clerc, 24–25
Lehman, David, 209, 218
Lentricchia, Frank, 67, 74
Letteraturizzazione, 132
Leverenz, Carrie Shively, 125, 135
Levinas, Emmanuel, 49, 51, 57, 58, 61, 84, 85–86, 89, 102
Levi-Strauss, Claude, 13
Lewis, David, 65
Libertarianism, 3–4, 14–17
Liddell, George, 88, 150, 154
Logocentrism, 186, 199–200, 212
Logos, 41–42, 55, 57, 97 112, 139, 140–141, 186, 199–200
Lu, Min-Zhan, 100–101, 104
Luckhurst, Roger, 199, 218
Lunsford, Andrea A., 133, 154
Lycophron, 23
Lyotard, Jean-François, 4, 49, 57, 61, 78, 126, 128–129

Macaulay, Lord, 35, 36
Macbeth, 17–18
MacIntyre, Alasdair, 2–5, 9–10, 13–14, 17, 20, 123, 128, 135
Mackey, Louis, 176, 180

Mackie, J. L., 13, 20
Macridis, Roy C., 45, 61
Maranhão, Tullio, 158–159, 177, 180
Marino, Godon D., 158, 172, 175, 180
Market logic, 76–77
Marrou, H. I., 151
Martin, Biddy, 66, 74
Marx, 174–175
Marxism, 5, 80, 102, 151, 156–157, 169, 185–186, 209
Massey, Lance, xvi, 183, 238
Mauss, Marcel, 191, 218
May, James M., 110, 123–124, 131, 135
McLellan, David, 43, 61
Mead, Margaret, 184
Melville, Herman, xv
Meno, The, 221
Merleau-Ponty, Maurice, 51, 58, 61
Metalogicon, 155
Meyers, Carol, 161, 164, 180
Middlebrook, Dianne, 64–65
Miller, J. Hillis, 49–50, 61, 63–64, 67, 74, 78–79, 89, 209, 218
Miller, Richard E., 24–25, 34, 36, 95, 105
Miller, Thomas P., 146, 154
Mimesis, 118, 120, 222
Mise en scene, 222
Mitchell, W. J. T., 61
Modern Language Association (MLA), 44, 63, 65–68
Mohanty, S. P., 100, 105
Moore, Michael S., 36
Moore, Sandy, 102, 105
Mores, 107, 117
Morrison, Toni, xv
Moss, Jean Dietz, 154
Motivorum, 79, 82
Mots d'ordre, 229
Movere, 131
Murphy, Cullen, 180
Murphy, James J., 135
Murphy, Michael, 164, 167, 180

Myers, Greg, 53, 58, 61

Natura, 131
Natural law theory, 22–23
Nazism, 193, 198, 210–211
Nealon, Jeffrey, 208, 218
Neel, Jasper, 66, 117, 135, 151, 154
Negligence, 24–27
Neoliberal Arts, 145–149
New Criticism, 63, 68
New Rhetoric, 120
New Testament, 161, 167
Newman, John Henry Cardinal, 172–173
Nietzsche, 4, 5, 122, 166, 169, 191–195, 199, 225–226, 234
Nomos / nomoi, 22–23
Norris, Christopher, 157, 159, 166, 180, 198, 209, 211, 218
Norton, Robert, 132, 135
Nosce te ipsum, 184
Nussbaum, Martha, 214, 231, 235

Occupational psychoses, 80–81
Odyssey, 88
Oedipus, 19
Oeffnung, 223
Offenheit, 223
Olson, Gary A., xiv–xv, 91, 102, 104, 105, 238
Ong, Walter J., 151, 158, 160, 178, 180
Other, The, 50–55, 58, 69, 86, 91–101, 148–149, 170, 195, 227
Outreach, 70–72
Oxford English Dictionary, 21, 53

Paideia, 39, 75, 139–140, 142, 225–226
Parker, David, 209, 219
Parry, Benita, 97, 105
Pathos, 107, 110–115, 131, 141, 143, 168, 226
Peaden, Catherine Hobbs, 178, 180
Peckham, Morse, 191, 219

Perelman, Chaim, 120
Persona, 114
Phaedrus, 144
Phelps, Louise Wetherbee, 73, 125, 135, 167, 180
Phenomenology, 58
Philosophia, 75, 145
Philosophical hermeneutics, 157–158
Phronesis, 123, 128–129, 131–132
Physis, 22, 84, 165
Pirie, Madsen, 219
Pisteis, 140–142
Plato, 22, 40, 75, 84, 109, 119, 139–142, 144–145, 149, 155, , 166, 174, 177, 235
Poetics, 83–84
Poiesis, 138
Polis, 123, 128–129
Politics of Liberal Education, The, 146
Politikon zöon, 128
Porter, James E., 87, 102, 105
Postcolonial theory, 95–98, 100–101
Poster, Mark, 61, 126, 128
Post-modernism, 76, 91–92, 100–120, 146, 156, 184
Post-structuralism, 63, 184–186, 204, 208
Poulakos, John, 213, 219
Pratt, Mary Louise, 93–95, 102, 103, 105
Praxis, 138
Pringle, David L., 61
Profession 1996, 63–64, 67
Prosopopoeia, 207
Protagoras, 22–23
Protagoras, The, 221
Prudentia, 131
Psyche, 177

Quadrivium, 146–148
Quintilian, 107, 110–111, 131, 208, 214, 219

Ramus, 132, 138, 140, 151
Ransom, John Crowe, 63, 74
Rassias, John, 73

Raven, J. E., 87, 89
Rawls, 5
Renault, Alain, 219
Republic, The, 221
Responsive Community, The, 4
Reynolds, John Frederick, 151, 154
Rhetoric, 75, 82-84, 108-109, 111, 113, 121, 139-140, 145, 147, 155, 187, 201, 206, 212, 214
Rhetorica Ad Herennium, 111
Rhizome, xv, 221-234
    Book-Rhizome, 224-225, 232-234
Richards, I. A., 120, 201, 219
Ricoeur, Paul, 46, 221, 228-229, 235
Right to privacy, 29-33
    rights of writing students, 30-32
Rinaldi, Jacqueline, 206, 219
Rorty, Amelie Oksenberg, 135
Rorty, Richard, 43, 61, 146
Rose, Mike, 127, 129

Said, Edward W., 53, 61, 99, 105, 158, 171, 173, 180
Salisbury, John of, 155, 180
Sallis, John, 61
Salomon, Willis A., 121, 133
Sartre, Jean-Paul, 5, 184
Saussure, 227
Schilb, John, 42, 59, 61
Schnakenberg, Karen Rossi, 131, 134
Scholes, Robert, 47, 65, 74, 145, 151, 154
Scientism, 75
Scott, Robert, 88, 150, 154
Searle, 215
Seibers, Tobin, 120, 135
Selfe, Cynthia L., 60
Seven Liberal Arts in the Middle Ages, 151
Sexton, Anne, 65
Seyler, Dorothy U., 210, 219
Shedd, William, 115-116
Shelley, Percy Bysshe, 64, 74

Singleton, Robert, 60
Sipiora, Phillip, xvii, 39, 132, 135, 238
Slevin, James F., 65, 73
Smith, Barbara Herrnstein, 39, 61, 146
Socrates, 23, 75, 175-177, 226
Sophocles, 19, 85
Spellmeyer, Kurt, 58, 61, 208, 212, 219
Spinoza, 225-226
Spivak, Gayatri Chakravorty, 44, 49-50, 52, 61, 96-97, 99, 105
Spurgin, Sally De Witt, 210, 219
Steiner, George, 209, 213, 219
Steneck, Nicholas H., 20
Stern, Frederick C., 183, 198, 200-201, 212, 219
Stoekl, Allan, 198, 211, 219
Stoics, 214, 222, 234
Stroup, Timothy, 20
Subaltern, 96-97
Sulleri, Sara, 99, 105
Sullivan, William M., 4-5, 9, 13-14, 20
Swaffar, Janet, 73
Swearingen, C. Jan, x-xiii, xv, xvii, 20, 119, 135, 155, 158, 180, 239
Symbolic, the, 82-84

Tarule, Jill Mattuck, 158, 160, 179
Teleological system, 3, 15-16, 48, 56
Telos, 3
Ten Commandments, 8-9, 15-16, 56
Thebaud, Jean-Loup, 61
Themis, 165-167
Theology, 187, 201-203
Theoria, 138
Theremin, Franz, 115-116
Thomas, Terry, 30, 36
Thompson, John B., 43, 62
Thurow, Sarah Baumgartner, 173, 180
Tillich, Paul, 41-42, 56-57
Tò on légetai, 227
Tompkin, Jane, 68

Topos, 80
Torgovnik, Marianna, 159, 174, 180
Toulmin, Stephen, 5, 13, 20, 120
Trible, Phyllis, 161, 164, 180
Trivium, 145–147
Tuman, Myron C., 62

Ulmer, Gregory, 62
Untersteiner, Mario, 213, 219
Utilitarianism, 5, 81, 82

Valesio, Paolo, 111, 117–118, 135
Vernant, Jean-Pierre, 151, 154
Vickers, Brian, 112–113, 131–132, 135, 136
Vico, Giambattista, 75, 89, 113
Villanueva, Victor, Jr., 58, 62
Vir bonus dicendi peritus, 208
Vitanza, Victor J., 62, 122, 136
Vogel, Arthur A., 201–202, 219
Vouloir dire, 229
Vox populi, 163

Wacks, R., 30, 36
Wagner, David L., 151
Wallace, Michele, 151
Walters, Frank D., 58, 62
Walton, Douglas, 213, 219

Warshauer, Susan, 116–117, 123–124, 135, 202–204, 209, 218
Welch, Kathleen E., xiv–xv, 102, 105, 131, 136, 137, 151, 152, 154, 239
Westermarck, Edward, 10–13, 16, 20
Whatley, Richard, 115–116
White, Edward M., 174, 180
White, James Boyd, 108–109, 114, 125, 130, 132, 136
Wild, John, 51, 62
Willard, Charles A., 199–200, 212, 219
Wills, Gary, 178, 180
Wilson, Thomas, 112
Winterowd, W. Ross, xvii–xviii, 63, 74, 239
Wittgenstein, 213
Wolf, Christa, xi, 162–168, 180
Wolf, Thia, 125, 136
World Parliament of Religions, 9
Wright, Lauren, 125, 136
Writing Program, 69–70

Yeats, William Butler, 156, 180
Young, Iris, 128

Zizek, Slavoj, 45, 62

Studies in Composition and Rhetoric

Edited by Leonard A. Podis

This series welcomes both single-author and essay collections. Titles may refer to case studies but should consistently deal with larger theoretical issues. At the moment, we are especially interested in books that might be used for graduate courses in one or more of the following subjects: cultural studies and the teaching of writing; feminist perspectives on composition and rhetoric; values and ideologies in the teaching or writing; postmodernism and composition/rhetoric; and the composition as a site of knowledge production and research. At the same time, we also seek proposals in the following areas: the influence of social context on composing; the relationship of composition and rhetoric to various disciplines and schools of thought; new ways of conceiving discourse analysis, the composition classroom and the writing process, or the history of rhetoric; analyses of research methods, such as ethnography and textual hermeneutics; the relationship of theory and practice; and current and potential roles for composition and rhetoric in the academy.

For additional information about this series or for the submission of manuscripts, please contact:
>Peter Lang Publishing, Inc.
>Acquisitions Department
>275 7th Avenue 28th Floor
>New York, NY 10001

To order other books in this series, please contact our Customer Service Department at:
>(800) 770-LANG (within the U.S.)
>(212) 647-7706 (outside the U.S.)
>(212) 647-7707 FAX

or browse online by series at:
>WWW.PETERLANG.COM